FORTY WEEKS

An Ignatian Path to Christ
With Sacred Story Prayer

Classical Art Edition Workbook

William M. Watson, SJ

Other Books by William Watson, SJ

Sacred Story:
An Ignatian Examen for the Third Millennium

Inviting God into Your Life:
A Practical Guide for Prayer

Reflections and Homilies:
The Gonzaga Collection

Sacred Story Press
1401 E Jefferson St, STE 405
Seattle, WA 981222

Dedicated to Our Lady of the Way

IMPRIMI POTEST
Patrick J. Lee, SJ

IMPRIMATUR
J. Peter Sartain
Archbishop of Seattle

Unless otherwise indicated, Scripture quotations are from the Holy Bible, *New American Bible, revised edition* © 2010, 1991, 1986, 1970 Confraternity of Christian Doctrine, Washington, D.C.

Photography by William Watson, SJ –Sacred Heart - Arrupe Jesuit Chapel - Seattle
Jacket and Book Design: William Watson, SJ

Manufactured in the United States of America
ISBN-13: 978-1484849033
ISBN-10: 1484849035

Acknowledgements

The opening lines of *Sacrosanctum Concilium*, the first of Vatican II's documents, proclaim the Council's high ideals:

This sacred Council has several aims in view: it desires to impart an ever increasing vigor to the Christian life of the faithful; to adapt more suitably to the needs of our own times those institutions which are subject to change; to foster whatever can promote union among all who believe in Christ; to strengthen whatever can help to call the whole of mankind into the household of the Church.

Sacred Story Institute is profoundly grateful to be advancing the goals of the Council: especially in this Year of Faith, 2013, the Council's fiftieth birthday. We wish to express our gratitude to Archbishop Sartain for linking us with the pastors and hundreds of lay faithful in six parishes of the Seattle Archdiocese who, like St. Ignatius, became pilgrims for Christ:

St. Cecilia Parish, Bainbridge Island

Holy Rosary Parish, West Seattle

Our Lady of the Lake Parish, Seattle

St. Mary Magdalen Parish, Everett

Holy Family Parish, Kirkland

Holy Rosary Parish, Edmonds

Their fidelity to the Council's vision of increasing the vigor of the faithful has helped shape the lessons of *Forty Weeks* into a dynamic prayer resource for their brothers and sisters throughout the world. Their labor will produce fruit that endures to eternity. May the Divine Physician, whose healing and redeeming love anchors the universe, draw all of us into His SACRED STORY.

Thank you, and God bless you!

Contents

FORTY WEEKS

Author's Preface

Twenty years after entering the Society of Jesus, I was fortunate to spend the final period of Jesuit spiritual formation, called *Tertianship*, in Northern Ireland. The year-long spiritual renewal program, which included a thirty-day retreat, helped me regain a spiritual focus I had not known since my novitiate days. It was a good thing the program had this effect. That was Ignatius' aim.

In my final months in Ireland, I became quite anxious. How would I keep my compass in the hectic university world I would soon rejoin? By God's grace, I was led to the *Examen* prayer of St. Ignatius. Although Ignatius mandates Jesuits pray this very strategic prayer twice-daily (as the *Spiritual Exercises* in miniature), I had let its practice slip. Now, twenty years into my religious vocation, I was finally ready to follow my founder's "rule."

By the time I returned to my apostolate as Director of Retreats at Georgetown University, a twice-daily practice of the *Examen* was a fixed discipline in my life. The prayer fulfilled the role Ignatius intended. Yes, I still sometimes became distracted and unfocused. But praying this prayer twice a day always brought me back to the center of my heart, and back to Christ. It brought great structure and clarity to a monthly practice of spiritual direction combined with Reconciliation that had been my custom before Ireland.

The *Examen* helped me see patterns of both grace and dysfunction in my life I had not before noticed. This is not surprising for a prayer that is geared to awakening one's *conscience* and *consciousness*. But the prayer also brought balance to my life. In the first six years of its practice, I did not suffer from any physical illness. This was a marked change from my pre-*Examen* days of contracting nearly every bug incubated by the college students I worked with. The *Examen*, I discovered, was therapeutic both spiritually and physically.

So important was the *Examen* in my newly reborn spiritual life that I wanted to be its evangelist. I had built many retreat programs based on the *Spiritual Exercises* in my previous fifteen years of ministry. But I was aware that many people who had good retreat experiences did not know how to bring spirituality into daily life. It was time to build a retreat specifically for teaching this daily

1

spiritual discipline that was proving so therapeutic in my own life.

Georgetown's "Weekend Ignatian Retreat" was the new program designed for this purpose. It was constructed around five meditations that corresponded to the five elements in Ignatius' *Examen*. The retreat weekend taught a daily prayer discipline, just what I was hearing that students, faculty, alumni and board members wanted.

I continued to refine this program after I left Georgetown. I created an updated version for Gonzaga University when I became the Vice President for Mission in 1999. I developed yet another version for the Magis Institute in California (now run by Fr. Robert Spitzer, SJ), geared toward business executives and their spouses.

CȜ

In 2004, I was privileged to start a doctoral program at The Catholic University of America while acting as Provincial Assistant for International Ministries for the Oregon Jesuits. My doctoral work at CUA focused on the Ignatian *Examen*.

The doctorate afforded me time to research Ignatius' prayer discipline, revitalize it for contemporary audiences, and measure its effectiveness with dozens of practitioners. Those who volunteered for my doctoral research prayed daily for ten weeks using a refined version of the *Examen* I had developed. They filled out weekly online surveys to let me know both what they were doing, and what they were experiencing. Two thousand pages of feedback data helped me to further refine the prayer discipline into the ten-week program detailed in the book; *Sacred Story: An Ignatian Examen for the Third Millennium.*

What I learned anew from the doctoral project is that the Ignatian *Examen* is a spiritual tool of *profound impact*. You could simply say: "It works!" I discovered from the data that the prayer made people sensitive to their interior life, but it did not foster scrupulosity; one of the charges leveled against it. The prayer also helped individuals source sinful patters in both the spiritual and psychological dimensions of their lives, aiding a more integrated conversion process and on-going spiritual growth. It made people more sensitive to evils in the world—social sin—and did not foster an interior, privatized spirituality as some critics of the prayer claimed. It opened people to the transcendent and helped them see their lives linked to God in a future Kingdom of Peace, while at the same time anchoring them more firmly in the present moment so their lives "produce fruit that endures."

And most importantly, the prayer discipline, when practiced with regular Sacramental Reconciliation—the powerful combined practice taught by the early Jesuits—deepened individuals' sense of gratitude, their willingness to forgive others while at the same time fostering a more profound humility. When people have the on-going experience of clearly seeing their "sinfulness" and personally encountering the Lord of Mercy who forgives us our sins, you have the basis for that fundamental evangelization that has always enlivened and renewed the Church in every age.

ᥴᴈ

Fast-forward to January of 2012. "The Sacred Story Institute" (SSI) was founded to promote third millennium evangelization using this vital prayer discipline. We research different groups' engagement with the *Sacred Story Examen* method. The data from our research creates prayer resources for people from all walks of life to nurture their faith.

The goal for SSI's first research project was to expand the ten-week version of *Sacred Story* into a more intuitive and self-guided prayer journey for the average adult Catholic. The book in your hands is yet a further refinement of the *Sacred Story Examen* method based on this forty-week research project with hundreds of lay volunteers from six Catholic parishes in the Seattle Archdiocese

Participants engaged *Sacred Story* daily for a forty-week period and provided weekly feedback via survey questions at our research website. They studied their lessons, prayed daily, journaled and confessed. After 12 weeks of sifting through the different narrative strains of their life histories, over 180 adults across the six participating parishes made a "life confession". Almost to a person, they described it as transformative. Hundreds of volunteer hours were contributed by many participants. They offered suggestions on how prayer lessons could be simplified and re-structured. Their input has made the book as intuitive as possible for every new pilgrim seeking to open their own heart to Christ.

All in all, about twenty years' worth of reflection, study, testing, feedback, and refinement have gone into this updated version of St. Ignatius' powerful *Examen* prayer; *Forty Weeks: An Ignatian Path to Christ with Sacred Story Prayer*. Its publication date was March 19, 2013 the Solemnity of St. Joseph, patron of the universal Church. That date was also the consecration of Pope Francis, the 266th successor to St. Peter; our first "Jesuit" pope.

Also on this very same day, I received a letter from Fr. Adolfo Nicolás, the Father General of the Society of Jesus, thanking me for *Sacred Story: An Ignatian Examen for the Third Millennium*, on which *Forty Weeks* is based. He says: "The book is a good reminder of the significance of the *Examen* in our daily life and of its profound impact in the lives of people of all times." Needless to say, it was a spiritually potent day!

Those who know me would confirm that I have a pious side that sees God's finger in holy synergies like those detailed above. I believe this holy synergy is a positive sign of future blessing and of the "profound impact" *Forty Weeks* will have for those who walk the narrow path of the Ignatian *Examen*. You and the parish communities who use *Forty Weeks* to find Christ in your daily life can be assured of my prayers. But more importantly, know that you will be carried by the Divine Physician, the Good Shepherd, the Lord of All, the Beginning and the End, our brother, the Lord Jesus.

Continue to invite Christ, the Divine Physician, into your heart. Pray for everyone seeking to live life as a *Sacred Story*. Thank God that you have been invited to participate with Christ in His Great Work of Reconciliation.
Commit to daily prayer in *Sacred Story* to realize integrated spiritual growth and holiness. Help others draw close to Christ.
Activate your faith daily in all your thoughts, words and deeds.
In this, we all work for that New Evangelization first mentioned
by Pope John Paul II early in his papacy,
continued by Pope Benedict XVI,
and now strongly proclaimed by Holy Father Francis:
Be not afraid!

ॐ

Fr. Bill Watson, SJ
March 19, 2013
Solemnity of St. Joseph

సొ

There are very few who realize what God would make of them if they abandoned themselves entirely to His hands, and let themselves be formed by His grace. A thick and shapeless tree trunk would never believe that it could become a statue, admired as a miracle of sculpture…and would never consent to submit itself to the chisel of the sculptor who, as St. Augustine says, sees by his genius what he can make of it. Many people who, we see, now scarcely live as Christians, do not understand that they could become saints, if they would let themselves be formed by the grace of God, if they did not ruin His plans by resisting the work which He wants to do.[1]

St. Ignatius Loyola

ઉ

Introduction

How To Engage *Forty Weeks*

St. Ignatius became a great spiritual guide by surrendering his heart to Christ under the guidance of the Church. He passed his wisdom along in his *Spiritual Exercises* and the methods of *Examen* (on which *Forty Weeks* is based), and in his letters and instructions. His spiritual disciplines invite a deep, personal relationship with Christ. It is Christ's forgiving and healing love that burns away the selfishness and hardheartedness of sin's legacy in one's history, transforming it into a *Sacred Story*: fruit that endures to eternity.

Following Ignatius's wisdom, all you need to engage this spiritual journey is a generous heart and a willingness to be transformed by Christ's purifying forgiveness and mercy. It is the narrow path to holiness held out by the Church for millennia and the one followed by every saint in our history. The weekly lessons are not complicated. Pray for a generous heart and ask Christ for His help every step of the way. Trust the wisdom of the structure presented here, and resist the temptation to rush or "pray the weeks" out of their natural order. Simple enough!

ℰↄ

What Do We Mean by "Weeks?"

You may be engaging this prayer journey as an individual or as part of a group. If you are doing this by yourself, you may find it beneficial to discipline yourself to stick to a seven-day week for each chapter of *Forty Weeks*. St. Ignatius' spiritual wisdom for the 4 weeks of the *Spiritual Exercises*, was to allow one to move forward based on the fruit being experienced. In this framework, a "week" was measured by the spiritual profit being received, and not on hours and days. Use the time frame of spiritual fruit to measure your weeks if you so desire. Sometimes it may helpful to repeat a week several times to fully internalize the lesson! Trust your heart

If you are part of a group doing these spiritual disciplines, my best advice is to discipline yourself to stay together as a group. That is, keep a 7-day week structure for the whole forty weeks. You can mark places and weeks that you may want to revisit for additional reflection and spiritual profit. Great spiritual fruit is also gained by tracking your "weeks" with the community you belong to.

No matter which way you are doing *Forty Weeks*—solo or with a group— realize that the exercises are incremental, building on each other. Doing them slowly and in order will help you stay better focused and live in the present moment. Trust the structure, and do not read or practice the disciplines out of their natural order.

Listen to your heart, at all times, in the present moment. God is *in* the present moment. This way, the *Sacred Story* prayer will, by God's grace and your free submission, lead you to the deepest desires of your heart.

&

The 15-Minute Rule of St. Ignatius

St. Ignatius proposed 15-minutes as the optimal time for his Examen prayer discipline. Twice-daily was the recommendation for Jesuits. The laity who practiced the prayer were encouraged to do it at least once daily. As you begin this prayer journey, make a decision whether you want to pray once or twice daily. You can always adjust your commitment to either of the options, but setting a goal for your practice is important.

Our extensive experience has shown that those who have practiced the *Sacred Story Examen* method in *Forty Weeks* have found praying in the morning, at mid-day or mid-afternoon to be the most sustainable over time. Those who set evening hours for their prayer were less faithful to the discipline. Use your judgment. Ignatius advised it be done at mid-day and after the evening meal. Everyone has different schedules and life rhythms.

You will receive further guidance on the structure and use of these 15-minute times of quiet as the lessons progress. For now, it is sufficient to choose the time(s) you intend to pray daily. You would do well also to select a primary location for your 15-minute prayer times. Let it be a place apart: a technology-free zone. Ask God to strengthen your resolve and desire for entering these times of reflection. Your fidelity to *Sacred Story* depends *less on you*, and more on your decision to *continually ask God to* be faithful.

&

Additional Resources for Your Spiritual Journey

There are other resources besides this book to help you along. Those participating in the research for the *Forty Weeks* project also helped shape a weekly series of supplemental resources we call *Encouragements & Wisdom* or "E&W." The E&W are very important aids for deepening your understanding of the prayer materials. We are keeping them online so that the size and cost of this *Forty Weeks* book remains affordable.

Once you begin the *Forty Weeks* prayer, you are not given prompts to consult the E&W. Please make a mental note to do this weekly. You will be greatly blessed! Many of the additional questions you are likely to have as you move forward are contained in this very helpful supplemental prayer resource. How to access these lessons is explained below.

A simple journal exercise is a discipline linked to the *Forty Weeks Sacred Story* prayer. Purchase a small spiral notebook for this purpose and have it with you when you do your structured 15-minute prayer periods. We have also left a blank page at the end of each chapter and eight more at the back of the book for Notes. Feel free to use this as your notebook if you so desire.

Many of the instructions are written in the personal "I." For example: "I am invited; I will now…". The reason for this is for you to affirm your role in opening to Christ. It also helps emphasize the relational dimension of faith and prayer.

৪১

What To Do If You Hit A Wall

If you reach a point in the forty week prayer process where you think you can't continue, here is my advice. Jump to the last chapter, *Abide in Me*, and read it. I placed this chapter at the end to encourage people to commit to a life-long process of *Sacred Story* prayer. But sometimes, that encouragement is necessary to simply complete the process that will carry you for life. Just keep trying and Be Not Afraid!

৪১

Help Us Make *Forty Weeks* a Better Prayer Resource

We will continue to refine this prayer discipline with your feedback. Parishes and individuals using *Forty Weeks* are strongly encouraged to give us feedback on the weekly lessons and the E&W. Please do so by signing up to be a Member at our website: **sacredstory.net** and click on the navigation link titled

"**Members**." Once you register, the "**Members**" section will be available to you.

Each of the "weekly" areas of the website provides an option for you to send us your feedback on the prayer lessons and the E&W. We count on hearing about your experiences with *Sacred Story* prayer. We strongly encourage you to comment on any (or all!) of the weeks; the lessons and the E&W.

Tell us what helped you and what you found transformative. Tell us what you did not understand and propose suggestions to help clarify ideas or concepts. Share stories of faith and transformation in your life. What you share will become part of the living community of *Sacred Story* prayer. Your own "encouragement and wisdom" will be a source of blessing for countless more pilgrims in need of deepening their connection to Christ, in their walk of faith as Catholics and Christians. And remember, Be Not Afraid!

St. Ignatius, pray for us!

അ

Part One
Listening to Your Story

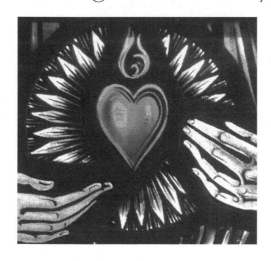

"Come to me, all you who labor and are burdened, and I will
give you rest. Take my yoke upon you and learn from me, for I
am meek and humble of heart;
and you will find rest for your selves.
For my yoke is easy, and my burden light."
Mt 11:28-30

Entering Your Sacred Story

Rules of Engagement

   Sacred Story prayer, modeled on St. Ignatius' classic examination of conscience, is a proven path to spiritual growth. It is the narrow road, but the one taken by many saints and ordinary laity in the Church's history. If you are ready to make Christ the center of your life, you will find no better daily spiritual prayer discipline. Divine love is an abiding relationship that God invites you to share daily. Listen to the wisdom below to help prepare you to enter this relationship with God before you begin Week 1.

✦   If you are looking for quick fixes to spiritual or psychological problems, you will soon lose heart. The full healing of your wounds, and the path to complete peace, only begins on this earth. You will achieve no final victory for what ails you this side of eternity. However you will find the *path* to that final victory and it is here that you will find peace.

✦   If you seek only external confirmation of religious or political biases, you will be frustrated. Surrendering fixed ideologies and a judgmental heart is required fare on your *Sacred Story* journey.

✦   If you live principally by rules and laws, or if you avoid all rules and laws, you will be surprised. Those who live by laws alone will encounter the fierce Love that exceeds all laws. And those who reject laws will discover that Love has unambiguous boundaries of right and wrong.

✦   If you are being asked to do these spiritual exercises to fulfill someone else's plan, or for any sort of program requirement, kindly tell your sponsor, "no thank you." Unless you engage them in complete freedom of heart, you will fail in their practice, and undermine their purpose.

So how should you engage this prayer journey? St. Ignatius wanted people with generous hearts who were aware that they needed God's help.

✠　Jesus proclaimed that the sick needed a Physician, not the well (Mk 2:17). We are all sick and only those willing to see their spiritual ills will submit to the Divine Physician's healing embrace in these exercises. If you know you are ill, and believe you *cannot* get better without God's help, welcome.

✠　Jesus calmed the storm that terrified His disciples (Mk 5:35-41). Engage *Sacred Story* prayer if you are distressed about the chaos in your life and believe God is calling you to a secure shore.

✠　Jesus can heal chronic illness, but He has come to forgive us our sins, and open to us eternal life (Lk 5:17-26). Engage in these exercises if you want to experience Jesus' power to forgive your sins.

✠　Jesus encouraged John the Baptist and his followers not to take offense at Him when their faith in Christ brought them suffering and threats (Mt 5:2-6). Engage these exercise if the practice of your faith is causing you to suffer persecution for Christ's sake. Hold fast to belief in Him as the Son of God and take no offense.

✠　Jesus invited the weary and the overburdened to find rest in Him (Mt 11:25-30). Engage these exercises if you are weary with your life and find yourself overburdened.

✠　Jesus invited the rich young man to surrender his possessions and follow Him (Mk 10:17-25). Engage these exercises if you are ready to let go of what is holding you down, and are willing to follow a new path.

✠　Jesus invited Zacchaeus to come down from his tree and follow Him home (Lk 19:1-10). Engage these exercises if your privilege, position and places of honor have not brought you the peace, security and hope they promised.

✠　Jesus invited the woman of Samaria to drink the living water that wells up to eternal life (Jn 4:4-42). Engage these exercises if you are ready to surrender the cynicism of failed love and relationships, are ready to forgive, and ready to move forward with your life.

✠　Jesus chided the work-anxious Martha to allow Mary to sit at His feet (Lk 10:38-42). Engage with these exercises if you are ready to sit still awhile, each day, and listen to the Kingdom within.

✠   Jesus invited Peter to join Him in His work (Lk 5:10-11). Engage these exercises if you trust that your sins, addictions and failures do not limit Jesus' desire to take your hand in discipleship as He writes your *Sacred Story*.

✠   Jesus demanded to know the names of the Gerasene's demons (Mk 5:1-20). Engage these exercises if you are weary of your spiritual, psychological, and material demons. Welcome these exercises if you are willing to name them, with Jesus by your side, and allow Him to exorcise and heal the spiritual and psychic darkness—the habits, sins, and addictions—that rob you of freedom and peace.

✠   God invited the Blessed Virgin Mary not to fear but to say *yes* and participate in the eternal plan of salvation (Lk 1:26-38). Engage these exercises if you are ready to let your heart be Christ's home and so labor with Him for universal reconciliation.

✠   Jesus invited His disciples to dine with Him (Jn 15:1-17). Enter *Sacred Story* if you desire unbounded love, joy, peace and a share in Jesus' glory — and His sufferings — that endure to eternity.

✠   Jesus invited anyone wishing to follow Him to deny themselves, pick up their cross daily, and follow Him (Lk 9:23). Engage these exercises if you can *willingly* allow Christ to reveal your narcissism and by His grace, transform your life into *Sacred Story*.

✠   Jesus invited His disciples to keep a vigilant heart, to reject carousing and drunkenness, and to avoid getting trapped in the anxieties of life, lest they be surprised on the day of the Son of Man (Lk 21:34-36). Engage these exercise if today is your day to hearken to the Son of Man, and to return to God with all your heart.

ℰↄ

Before advancing to Week 1, we will take the time necessary to prayerfully and reflectively read one of the four Gospels. Many of us have never taken the time to listen to Jesus' story by reading, prayerfully, one of the four accounts left for us by the early followers. Only read one of the Gospels, but read it reflectively and prayerfully in a place of restful solitude. This place can be at home or some other favorite place you love to be alone in peace and quiet. Perhaps it will be your place of prayer for these next 40 weeks to allow Jesus to reveal your *Sacred Story*.

Which Gospel should you read? Matthew writes to convince the Jews that Jesus is indeed the promised Messiah, the Davidic King, foretold by the prophets. Mark's focus is to reveal Jesus as the true Son of God who suffered and died to achieve complete victory over sickness, sin and death. Luke, the physician, writes to reveal Jesus as the promise and hope of the poor and the weak. And John reveals Jesus as the Logos, the Word of God, who pre-existed creation with the Father, the One who will save us. Read the Gospel that immediately speaks to your heart at this time in your life. Don't rush your reading of the Gospel. There is no hurry. Relish The Story of the One who holds you and all creation in being.

Jesus is real and wants to become part of your daily life. He wants a relationship with you. He waits to be your hope, your forgiveness and your peace. Open your heart to Him as you read His SACRED STORY.

‍ଔ

Week 1

FIRST

I will choose one or two times each day to set aside for a 15-minute space of contemplative rest and reflection. This should be a place of quiet, free of technology—a place apart.

SECOND

I will be specific about the time of day, and the place (or places) where I can find these moments of reflective quiet. I will take a moment to ponder where these will be and see them in my imagination.

THIRD

I will take my 15-minute quiet moments this week to read through the lesson that follows: "Sacred Story Affirmations."

Set your heart to the path you are to take. Trust it. The path leading to Christ in the *Sacred Story* practice has some simple Rules that will help you immensely.

I will not read ahead.
I will awaken to the present moment.
I will take each day and each exercise as it comes.
I cannot do *Sacred Story* better by going faster.

೮൦

Read this at the beginning of the week

You will have a new prayer exercise for every week of this journey. The exercises for this first week offer discernment principles that will help you on your journey. Listen to the exercise and pay attention to your feelings. Engage the prayers and exercises of *Sacred Story* with your whole being--with *your mind in your heart.* Be a thinking, reflective "feeler" and believer. Awaken!

Remember, you are a pilgrim (journeying alongside Ignatius himself) in this prayer journey. The Lord Jesus will reward you for your courage and your resolve. Christ promises to be faithful to you! He will help you every possible step of the way because He came, lived and died so you might have abundant life and bear fruit that endures to eternity. Thank Him in advance for the great blessings and insights you will receive. Live a life of gratitude to God for all life's blessings and gifts.

Sacred Story Affirmations

The *Affirmations* sketch most of the realities you will encounter in your spiritual journey with *Sacred Story* prayer. As your first spiritual disciplines of this process, take some days to reflectively contemplate these *Affirmations* for your *Sacred Story* practice. Use your 15-minute *Sacred Story* prayer times for this purpose. Take as many days as you desire and listen attentively to them. Do not limit the number of days or sessions you spend with them. Your heart, by its peacefulness, will lead you forward to the next exercises at the right time. Trust God's grace working in your heart to lead you.

As you listen to *Sacred Story Affirmations*, be attentive to all the persons, events and issues in your life. Be especially attentive to the things that cause fear, stress, anxiety, anger or grief. When these feelings/emotions surface, notice *how* and *if* they connect with the *Affirmations* that you are contemplating. Always listen with your mind in your heart to the events, issues and persons in your life story. Be curious. Listen to how or why these events, issues, and persons may be linked to the spiritual, emotional and moral dimension of your experiences. Again, pay particular attention to those that might stimulate grief, anxiety, stress, anger and fear.

Sacred Story focuses attention on things that are both delightful and difficult to experience. But as St. Ignatius learned, focusing attention on the difficult things is very fruitful. These aspects of your life history have the potential to rob you of hope, joy, love, and freedom. You can experience deeper, lasting peace by letting difficulties arise and allowing the Divine Physician to heal you. We have nothing to fear with Christ by our side. Take as long as you desire to reflect on the *Affirmations* of your *Sacred Story*.

Sacred Story Affirmations

My *Sacred Story* takes a lifetime to write.

Be Not Afraid:
Fear comes from the enemy of my human nature.

The pathway to God's peace and healing runs through my heart's brokenness, sin, fear, anger and grief.

God resolves all my problems with time and patience.

☙

I will have difficulties in this life.

There are just two ways to cope with my difficulties.
One leads to life, one to death. I will choose life.

☙

"Impossible" is not a word in God's vocabulary.

Sacred Story leads to my freedom and authenticity,
but does not always make me feel happy.

☙

My life's greatest tragedies can be transformed
into my life's major blessings.

Times of peace and hope always give way to times of difficulty and stress.

Times of difficulty and stress always give way to times of peace and hope.

☙

I will not tire of asking God for help
since God delights in my asking.

18

The urge to stop *Sacred Story* practice
always comes before my greatest breakthroughs.

℘

God gives me insights, not because I am better than others,
but because I am loved.

The insights and graces I need to move forward in life's journey
unfold at the right time.

℘

My personal engagement with *Sacred Story* accomplishes, through Christ, a work of
eternal significance.

Inspirations can have a divine or a demonic source. I pray for the grace to remember
how to discern one from the other.

℘

Christ, who has walked before me, shares my every burden.

Christ, who has walked before me, will help me resolve every crisis.

Christ, who has walked before me, knows my every hope.

Christ, who has walked before me, knows everything I suffer.

Christ, who walks before me, will always lead me home to safety.

℘

I will strive to curb temptations to react to people and events.

I will ask myself what causes my anger and irritation at people and events.
I will seek to identify the source of my anger and irritation.
I will give thanks for what angers and upsets me;
for identifying their source will help to set me free.

I will strive to listen, watch and pray; listen, watch and pray.
I will listen, watch and pray!

ℰℐ

Everyone has been mortally wounded spiritually, psychologically, and physically by
Original Sin and the loss of paradise.

Journeying with Christ to the roots of my sins and addictions
will help break their grip.

I will not waste time worrying about my sins and failures.
I will use my time wisely and ask God to help me
understand the source of my sins and failings .

I will trust that Christ came to heal all my wounds.

ℰℐ

I alone control Christ's ability to transform my life into a *Sacred Story.*
The process begins when I ask for the grace to
honestly name my sins and addictions.

The process continues when I invite Christ to illuminate my narcissism.

Only God's grace and mercy can write my *Sacred Story.*

ℰℐ

I will strive daily to pick up the cross, for it leads to my life.

The closer I get to holiness, the more I will see and feel sin's disorder in my life.

The more I experience sin's disorder, the more tempted I will
be to disbelieve my life as *Sacred Story.*

The way through the temptation is to surrender my powerlessness to God.

ℰℐ

It is never too late to open my heart to Christ
and live my life as *Sacred Story*.

Christ, who is close to the brokenhearted, restores my lost innocence.

The path to my *Sacred Story* is
Creation, Presence, Memory, Mercy, and Eternity.

℘

Your heart is prepared and you have awakened to the path you are to take.
Trust it. Remember: Do not read ahead. Do not exercise ahead. Awaken to the
present moment. Take each day, and each exercise as it comes.

☙

I am starting a Relationship that will carry me
for the rest of my life.

I will learn the fundamentals and strive to
open my heart to God.

I trust that God will lead me.

I believe that my *Sacred Story* will unfold in truth,
in powerlessness and with my patience.

I believe that Jesus awaits me with His grace, mercy and forgiving love.

What do I need for this journey?
a generous heart;
the willingness to take 15-minutes to pray daily
and the humility to always ask God for help.

℘

Week 2

FIRST

I will choose a place of contemplative rest and reflection. It will be a place apart—a technology-free zone!

SECOND

I will make a decision on whether to take one 15-minute or two 15-minute prayer breaks a day. Regularity is key to sustainable disciplines of any kind, and is especially true of this prayer relationship with Christ.

THIRD

During my 15-minute quiet moments this week I will slowly and thoughtfully read Part One of St. Ignatius' conversion story. I will commit to read reflectively and take my time. I will ask the Spirit to inspire me to fully see and hear Ignatius' story, especially as it relates to my life. I will pray for an open mind and heart.

I will not read ahead.

I will awaken to the present moment.

I will take each day and each exercise as it comes.

I cannot do *Sacred Story* better by going faster.

ଔ

Read this at the beginning of the week

The exercises for this second week are related to the conversion story of St. Ignatius. Your prayer exercise for this week is to read and ponder the beginning of St. Ignatius' *Sacred Story*. Pay careful attention to what in Ignatius' experience touches your own unique history. Thank Christ in advance for the blessings and insights you will receive.

Read and ponder. You may be inspired to reflect on the *Affirmations* from last week. Be attentive to any memories that might arise and the feelings that stir as you pray this week. St. Ignatius was very clear in his teachings that careful attention to your internal spiritual movements marks the beginning of discernment. This heart-focused attention attunes your radar to the voices of the spiritual world.

⁊

Part One: St. Ignatius and His Legacy

A Fallen Soldier

Until his thirtieth year Ignatius Loyola was unconscious of the sacredness of his life. Instead, he was sincerely devoted to life's pleasures and vanities. He was a gambling addict, sexually self-indulgent, arrogant, hotheaded and insecure. Ignatius' mother died when he was an infant and his father died when he was sixteen.

By our contemporary measures, Ignatius' family was dysfunctional. Was this person a possible candidate for sainthood? It did not look promising. But God does not judge by human standards. It is God's nature to pursue all who have fallen asleep through sin, addiction and selfishness. God judges the heart; with unbounded grace and patient mercy God reaches into the ruins that sin makes of our lives and transforms them into *Sacred Stories*.

Ignatius, with all his narcissism, psychological problems and sinful vices, was awakened by God's great love. A failed military campaign and a shattered leg forced him into a lengthy convalescence back at Loyola castle, his family home. Ignatius' time of recuperation provided an opportunity for Love to shine a light on much more serious and life-threatening wounds that were spiritual, emotional and psychological in nature.

These wounds were supported by the evolution of a destructive, sinful narcissism. For thirty years Ignatius' narcissism had rendered him unconscious to his true human nature and oblivious to his life as *Sacred Story*. The pleasures he indulged in and the power he wielded functioned like a narcotic to numb the pain of his hidden spiritual and psychological wounds. His sinful vices and self-indulgent pleasures blinded him to his authentic human nature and a fruitful life guided by a well-formed conscience.

God's grace reached into the reality of Ignatius' life and awakened in him a desire for innocence. His long-buried aspirations for living authentically suddenly became his prime motivation. He noticed it first while convalescing at Loyola. He became aware of new desires and a different energy while he daydreamed in reading stories of Christ and the saints. Pondering the saints' lives he imagined himself living a different, selfless life.

He compared these new daydreams to his usual vain, narcissistic daydreams. The old daydreams drew energy from a life of sin, addiction and vice while the daydreams of selfless generosity produced their own energy. Ignatius noticed a significant difference between the two sets of daydreams and the feelings they produced. The vain fantasies entertained him when he was thinking about them. But he noticed that when he set them aside, he felt empty and unsatisfied.

The new holy daydreams also entertained him when he was thinking about them. Yet when he set these aside, he remained content and felt an enduring calm and quiet joy. By paying close attention to the ultimate affective results of these two sets of daydreams and discerning their difference, Ignatius made a discovery that transformed his life and the history of Christian spirituality.

A graced experience of God's love opened Ignatius to: → ↓	**GIVE THANKS FOR FAVORS RECEIVED** ↓
A dissatisfaction with vain fantasies which led to surrendering to holy daydreams, characterized by consolation, which in turn: → ↓	**PRAY FOR GRACE TO SEE CLEARLY** ↓
Caused him to review his life and actions leading to: → ↓	**GIVE A DETAILED ACCOUNT OF CONSCIENCE: GENERAL AND PARTICULAR** ↓
Grief with yearning for penance and repentance for his past sins, culminating in: → ↓	**ASK PARDON FOR ONE'S FAULTS** ↓
Ignatius' passion to amend his life and a desire to love God wholeheartedly. →	**RESOLVE AND AMEND TO SERVE GOD**

The Voice of Conscience

Ignatius discovered that the new, selfless aspirations were influenced by Divine inspirations. He further discovered that these inspirations reflected his true human nature and that the vain fantasies deadened his conscience. His narcissistic daydreams led him away from enduring peace because they masked his authentic human nature. The old daydreams were powerful, ego affirming, and familiar. He knew in his heart that living their fantasy was the path to self-destruction. On the one hand he would be judged successful by the standards of the world, a world that measured success in terms of riches, honors, and pride. On the other hand, he would be judged a failure by the standards of the Gospel, standards that advocated a life of spiritual poverty, humility and consequential service—a *Sacred Story* that endures to eternal life.

Ignatius was awakened to the emotional wisdom and spiritual truth of his new daydreams. He became aware of the significant damage that his old lifestyle had done to both himself and others. What had been awakened in him was the divine gift of conscience, and with it, Ignatius experienced profound regret and sorrow for having wasted so much of his life on self-indulgent pleasures and fantasies, seductions that could never bring him lasting peace and satisfaction. He began to understand that living in pleasure and fantasy destroyed his authentic human nature and silenced his deepest desires.

Divine inspiration inspired Ignatius to seek forgiveness for wasting his life and abusing his innocence. Grace enabled Ignatius to take responsibility for his sins against God and his authentic human nature. Divine inspiration provided Ignatius with the desire, energy, and courage to renounce the thoughts, words, and deeds of his sinful habits. Grace, received through the Sacrament of Reconciliation, heightened Ignatius' consciousness and enabled him to imagine a new path for his life, and new ways to express his gifts and talents.

As usually happens when people respond to the grace of conversion, Ignatius' new aspirations confused and disconcerted many of his closest family members and friends. Nonetheless he acted on these aspirations. Ignatius was now able to understand a path to God, a *pattern of conversion* that countless thousands would imitate.

A Menacing Fear Unmasked

After some months of living in the light of these new positive virtues, habits, and Divine inspirations, Ignatius was suddenly gripped by terror and panic. How could he manage to live the rest of his life without the pleasures of the past? It was easy to live virtuously for some months, but for the rest of his life? This was a real crisis because Ignatius began to wonder if this was an impossible goal.

Ignatius had two vital insights about this menacing fear. First, he realized it was a counter-inspiration prompted by the *enemy of his true human nature*. The panicky fear led him to think that it would be impossible to live virtuously for such a long time. Second, the counter-inspiration tempted him to return to his old narcissistic vices and habits. Seduced by their powerful influence, Ignatius would abandon all hope for a life of virtue. In essence, Ignatius was tempted to surrender living the authentic life that had finally brought him peace. He sensed an evil source inspiring this menacing fear and he challenged it head-on: "You pitiful thing! Can you even promise me one hour of life?"

A Decisive and Enduring Commitment to Remain Awake

Not knowing how he would endure, Ignatius dismissed the counter-inspiration and its evil author by re-committing to this new wakefulness for the remainder of his life. This was Ignatius' second insight: NEVER trust the messages prompted by menacing fears. Counter them with a firm commitment to stay the course, to awaken and remain conscious. This decisive, enduring commitment to persevere restored tranquility, and his fear abated. Ignatius had discovered, unmasked and confronted the deceiver. In this Ignatius learned another lesson about speaking truth to power that would guide his new life and help shape his first set of foundational discernment principles.

A enemy voice evokes Ignatius' fear of a lifelong struggle with his sinful habits. → ↓	**CONSCIOUS FEAR AND ANXIETY OVER SURRENDERING SINFUL AND ADDICTIVE HABITS** ↓
Ignatius rejects the "enemy of human nature" and confronts his false promises. → ↓	**CONFRONTING THE THREATENING "VOICE" OF SIN AND ADDICTION WITH THE "TRUTH" THAT THEY BRING DEATH, NOT LIFE** ↓
Peace is restored after truthfully naming sin and addiction as death dealing. →	**PEACE RETURNS AND ANXIETY DISSOLVES**

Ignatius had to face these same fears many, many more times. Eventually he knew they were false fears, *inspirations* of the enemy of his human nature. Most importantly, he gradually learned how to diffuse them, and to defend against them. It is vital that we understand this lesson from Ignatius: anyone who changes his or her lifestyle through a Divine awakening and who, by grace, consciously and consistently enters his or her *Sacred Story*, will encounter the same menacing fears. You can be strongly tempted to fall asleep and slip back into old habits and vices. When you are faced with these menacing fears—*when*, not *if*—confidently recommit to the path of life, and to the Author of life. The fears, in time, will subside. The enemy of human nature will always be disarmed.

Our spirit, body and God's grace at work in us compose a holy trinity. God made us this way. All three parts working cooperatively are necessary for holiness and human growth. In the paradise depicted in Genesis, the perfect cooperation of this trinity of human nature rendered us immortal. By turning from the fullness of God's grace, our immortality was lost: the perfect balance of the Divinely crafted trinity of human nature—body, spirit and God's grace—shattered. Christ's incarnation and death opened the way to immortality once again.

Our Christian life is a labor of love. In order for God's love to heal us we must do our part to open ourselves to God's graces. This requires conscious and ongoing effort to abstain from sinful, addictive habits in thoughts, words and deeds. There is a need to pray for God's grace. First we must awaken to that grace. With that same grace, we have the strength to resist and abstain from sinful, addictive attitudes and behaviors, both spiritual and material. God's grace infuses our spiritual disciplines, activating the trinity of our human nature. Grace helps us climb out of the spiritual, mental physical and emotional ruts of our bound self. In doing so, God graces us with a future of increased hope holiness and balance.

ಚಿ

I am starting a Relationship that will carry me
for the rest of my life.

All relationships require time and patience.
I will strive for patience and ask for God's help
when I don't understand a lesson.

I will learn the fundamentals and open my heart to God.

I trust that God will lead me.

I believe that my *Sacred Story* will unfold in truth,
in powerlessness and with my patience.

I believe that Jesus awaits me with His
grace, mercy and forgiving love.

ಎ

Week 3

FIRST

I will find a place each day where I can pull aside for a 15-minute space of contemplative rest and reflection free from technology's distractions.

SECOND

I will review my decision on whether I will take one 15-minute prayer break or two 15-minute prayer breaks a day.

THIRD

During my 15-minute quiet prayer periods this week, I will gradually read through Part Two of St. Ignatius' conversion story. Reading reflectively, I will take my time. I am reading for spiritual insights about Ignatius' *Sacred Story* and my own. Prayerful reading, known in the Catholic Tradition as *lectio divina* (holy reading) is done slowly. Resisting the *efficiency pressures* of the modern age, I realize *Sacred Story* is not about going faster, but deeper.

I will not read ahead.
I will awaken to the present moment.
I will take each day and each exercise as it comes.
I cannot do *Sacred Story* better by going faster.

℘

Read this at the beginning of the week

Welcome to the third week of our pilgrimage. The exercises for this week continue with the conversion story of St. Ignatius. As you listen to St. Ignatius' history, reflect on your own. As you read, recall that Ignatius woke up to the fact that there were two plots in his daydreams: Plot "A" entailed the goals and fantasies rooted in his wounded heart and following narcissistic dreams. Plot "B" entailed fantasies of a heart rooted in Christ and discovering healing and peace by following holy dreams. You are invited to search your own daydreams and fantasies for signs of these two plots. Consider your life as you listen to Ignatius' story. God used him to guide us. Each person has the same challenge of finding the narrow path that leads to our true human nature.

You have two options for how to pray with this week's text. Some like to read during the 15-minute periods, while others prefer to read the whole text on Sunday and then focus on smaller sections during the 15-minute prayer periods for the rest of the week. Do whatever is best for you. Your goal is to listen to Ignatius' story and be attentive to any issues that seem important to you. *Listen to Ignatius' story and pay attention to whatever stirs in you, be it hope and peace or anxiety and fear.* Doing this sharpens your spiritual radar for things that make your heart say: "Pay Attention!" Thank Christ in advance for the blessings and insights you will receive.

Part Two: A Journey to the Heart

Ignatius in Control

Ignatius' decisive and enduring commitment to his conversion launched him directly into the center of his heart's brokenness and the pride masking those wounds. After leaving home Ignatius traveled to Montserrat and spent three days reviewing his life. It was at this time that he made a general confession of all his past sinful deeds. This first life confession initiated an enduring habit of weekly confession and communion. In this written confession Ignatius consciously detailed his sinful attitudes, behaviors and passions: gambling addiction, sexual self-indulgence, arrogance, and violent outbursts of temper. It took all three days to write the story of his past life.

Yet he discovered that simply detailing and confessing his sinful habits and addictions did not disarm them. That would require going deeper, to their source in his heart and history. Only in these deepest recesses could he confront the pattern of spiritual and psychological dysfunction that was most responsible for eroding his freedom and distorting his authentic human nature.

It is this inward journey that fully awakened his conscience. It was only at this depth that he discovered his authentic human nature and regained the creativity of childlike innocence. We do well to understand the tipping point of Ignatius' life from his root vices and narcissism to his new life of wakefulness, light, peace and hope. This is how his story unfolded.

Ignatius' new, pious habit of regular confession evolved into a destructive obsessive and compulsive torture. He confessed and re-confessed past sins multiple times, never feeling he had gotten to the bottom of his immoral deeds.

This excruciating spiritual and psychological torment lasted for months. He was so anguished by his obsessive guilt that numerous times he wanted to commit suicide by throwing himself off the cliff where he prayed.

Well aware of the emotional damage caused by this obsessive confession habit, he still could not let it go. Instead he initiated new, harsher physical disciplines and spiritual regimens. His goal was to gain complete control and self-mastery over his immoral and dissolute past. He wanted to remember every detail of his past sins so he could be perfectly cleansed. But nothing worked!

Finally, exhausted and disgusted with his efforts, he realized he intensely despised the spiritual life he was living. Ignatius had an urgent and compelling desire to "stop it!" This thought alarmed Ignatius, and his spiritual radar went on high alert. Ignatius discerned the inspiration came from another source but what could it be? He discovered the inspiration's origin and author only by understanding where the inspiration was taking him. It occurred to him that the inspiration was leading him in the same direction as the menacing fear he had previously experienced. Inspired to abandon his newly awakened life, Ignatius was being tempted to abandon the peace, the service to others, and the virtuous life of his *Sacred Story*. But *how* did this counter-inspiration succeed in gaining control? Ignatius' decision to stop re-confessing his past sins reveals the enemy's strategy.

Surrendering Control to Embrace Powerlessness & Innocence

Ignatius' decision to stop his damaging confession habit appears inconsequential. But the choice was the most significant spiritual decision in his entire life. It was also the most difficult, because that one choice meant fully surrendering his life to God. It meant admitting his powerlessness over his sins and in humility allowing God, not himself, to be the source of his holiness.

Reflecting on the temptation to walk away from his new Christian life, Ignatius received an insight that the burdensome, destructive habit of re-confessing past sins was rooted in a pride to try and save himself. This pride forced him to his knees. On seeing this he "awoke as if from a dream," and was given the grace to stop the habit.

Looking at his life spiritually and psychologically, it appears that behind the sexual misdeeds, addictive gambling, and violent temper, there was a controlling, narcissistic pride and a broken heart. Our narcissistic control is solidified by the searing spiritual and psychological pain of lost innocence: the pattern of sins we inherit from the Original Sin, along with those sins committed against us early in life, and later those sins committed by us.

Our narcissism, if you will, *godifies* us, severely restricting our ability to respond to the true God. We fill the void of our wounded, broken hearts with self-centered strivings for attention, power and control. It is a false identity, an anti-story. Our narcissism blinds us to our authentic human nature and the deepest desires of our heart. It blinds us to our *Sacred Story*.

Ignatius' first life confession at Montserrat documented the *visible* manifestations of this deep distortion in his human nature. The Divine Physician next led Ignatius to the source of those visible sins. It was his wounded human nature that fueled the controlling, narcissistic personality. The pattern of *visible* sins, vices and addictions was only the tip of the iceberg. It is vital to remember that Ignatius' weaning from the narcotics of aggression, addictions, and dissoluteness opened a portal to his broken heart—his wounded human nature—where he could fully confront his powerlessness and brokenness. It is here that he finally meets Christ face to face. It is here, in accepting Christ's forgiveness, that healing love begins. It is here that Ignatius admits his powerlessness to save himself and surrenders control of his life to God. This is the spiritual paradigm of powerlessness.

Ignatius' struggle with the obsessive habit of re-confessing past sins was the *symbol* of his *hidden* root sin of pride. Christ labored hard to meet Ignatius right where he was, in this harrowing place. Ignatius' frenzied, damaging re-confessing of past sins was only the latest manifestation of the same hidden narcissism that distorted his first thirty years of life.

The same sin was in full view on the battlefield at Pamplona when Ignatius forced his will on the commander and all the other knights, to engage a suicide mission against a far more numerous and well-armed militia. Ignatius' pride earned him a shattering defeat and a shattered leg. Fortunately his defensive pride was shattered by God's grace awakening him "as if from a dream."

From that moment of surrender at Manresa, Ignatius acknowledged his powerlessness and surrendered control of his life to God. Since Ignatius was very young, God had waited to transform his deepest desires into a *Sacred Story* whose legacy would endure to eternity. This *surrender* defines Ignatius' second set of foundation discernment principles:

Ignatius' struggle with scruples hiding his vainglory ↓ →	The initial confrontation with one's root sin ↓
Ignatius' constant re-confessing to seek salvation by willpower alone → ↓	The effort to control one's root sin ONLY by personal effort or force of will ↓
Ignatius' suicidal impulses, disgust and the desire to walk away from his new found faith ↓ →	Despair and desire to give up faith when human effort alone fails ↓
Ignatius' tracing the spirit of disgust to a demonic source → ↓	Insight that desire to reject the spiritual journey is a temptation ↓
Ignatius abandoning his compulsive confessing of past sins →	Admitting powerlessness to save oneself and surrendering prideful actions

An outpouring of mystical grace flooded Ignatius at this point. More importantly a humble and obedient spirit was beginning to emerge which enabled him to respond to the slightest movements of God's grace in his thoughts, words and deeds. In this humility and docility he discovered a life of service that changed the Church and the world. Later in life he reflected:

There are very few who realize what God would make of them if they abandoned themselves entirely to His hands, and let themselves be formed by His grace. A thick and shapeless tree trunk would never believe that it could become a statue, admired as a miracle of sculpture...and would never consent to submit itself to the chisel of the sculptor who, as St. Augustine says, sees by his genius what he can make of it. Many people who, we see, now scarcely live as Christians, do not understand that they could become saints, if they would let themselves be formed by the grace of God, if they did not ruin His plans by resisting the work which He wants to do.

The proud narcissist, the man who was master of his own universe, became a humble and obedient servant of the universe's true Master and Creator. To arrive at this point, Ignatius had to admit his powerlessness. He had to surrender control over his life and the distorted aspects of his human nature that had evolved over the years. He had to learn how to live out of his newly emerging authentic self, his *true* and free human nature, a true nature that was hidden behind his wounded heart. Because of this, Ignatius had to also learn how to dismantle the narcissism that had evolved over the first thirty years of his life. The counter-inspirer, the enemy of his human nature, had cleverly concealed his true human nature and Ignatius had to begin life over again, this time allowing God to reveal his authentic self. This was why, after the resolution of this greatest of his life's crises, Ignatius experienced himself being taught by God. It was, he said, exactly like "a child is taught by a schoolmaster."

The Divine-Inspirer and the counter-inspirer

This harrowing crisis taught Ignatius a most vital lesson about counter-inspirations. The willpower and resolute commitment to live virtuously for the rest of his life could be manipulated and turned against him by means of subtle *inspirations*. What seemed like a holy, pious, and noble practice—a serious approach to confession—devolved into a damaging habit that made him loathe his spiritual life, and in frustration, *inspired* him to abandon it. He learned that the counter-inspirations of the enemy of his human nature could act like "an angel of light." These inspirations appear holy but when followed, they end in disaster, distancing one from God and from one's authentic self.

Ignatius gained clearer knowledge of the two spiritual forces that inspire and seek to guide the evolution of one's *story*. Ignatius gathered what he had learned from "speaking truth to power" to the enemy of human nature, and what he had learned from surrendering control of his life to God, into guidelines for discerning these different inspirations. For now it is sufficient to say that the Divine-Inspirer is the author of one's *original innocence*, that is, one's authentic and free human nature. The Divine-Inspirer works gently in and through every situation, especially the misfortunes associated with the damaging spiritual and psychological ordeals of life.

It is the nature of the Holy Spirit to offer forgiveness and provide shelter from the enemy of human nature whose sole purpose is to destroy innocence. The Divine-Inspirer forgives sins, restores lost innocence, mends broken and wounded hearts, releases captives, sets the oppressed free, and illumines one's *Sacred Story* and true human nature (Lk 4:18).

The counter-inspirer works through all the events of one's life and relationships. His work is evident in the distortions of spirit and mind, the deep wounding caused by the evolution of sin from the Original Sin and also sin inherited from one's family and culture. The counter-inspirer works to corrupt innocence and deform one's spiritual, emotional, physical and psychological nature—one's *true* human nature. Jesus condemned the violation of the innocent and the child-like. No human being can escape the machinations this evil breeds in one's body, mind and spirit. Since the Original Sin, this evolutionary force has infected every person and consequently all of human history.

The counter-inspirer conceals our original wounds, counseling and guiding our steps to build a false identity, an anti-story, characteristically identified by a distorted ego and defended by narcissism. Our narcissistic pride rationalizes the habits, vices, addictions and lifestyles that form our anti-story. The counter-inspirer renders us unconscious to our *Sacred Story* and to our true Divinely shaped human nature.

God led Ignatius through this distorted evolution back to the lost innocence of his true human nature. To get there Ignatius had to confront his pattern of spiritual and psychological distortions signified by his narcissistic pride. It was a mighty castle that he had built on the shifting sands of a child's wounded innocence, on a child's lonely, broken heart. God provided Ignatius the inspiration and grace to allow that castle to crumble. The shattering of his powerful defenses and the unmasking of his prideful, narcissistic pattern proved to be the tipping point of Ignatius' entire conversion process.

Wakefulness, Holiness and Heightened Consciousness

Ignatius' conversion from his anti-story and his full awakening to his *Sacred Story* was not a single event but rather a gradual process. His full evolution from a vain egomaniac to a saint took the rest of his life. This is evident in his *Autobiography*. In three linked narratives recounting personal near-death experiences, Ignatius reveals his growth in holiness, a process that evolved over a long, twenty-eight-year period.

In the first account he is filled with fear of judgment because he understands that pride is still a strong temptation for him. In the second account he is no longer afraid of death but instead, he is filled with sorrow for his delayed response to God. In the third account, grace floods his heart and he is filled with an intense devotion and desire for eternal union with God. These three episodes mirror the three classical stages of mystical growth: purgation, illumination and union. The three episodes also convey the reality of Ignatius' patience with the process of his spiritual growth:

Ignatius, justifying himself, anxiously recoils and focuses on his sinfulness → ↓	Panic over one's salvation due to weakness and sinfulness →	**PURGATION** ↓
Ignatius, no longer fearful, regrets not having responded sooner to God's graces → ↓	Sadness at slowness of one's response to God's love and invitation to intimacy →	**ILLUMINATION** ↓
Ignatius' intense joy at the thought of dying and being with God →	An ardent, all-embracing love of God and desire for complete union with the Trinity →	**UNION**

A Life-Long Commitment to Christ in the Church

It took Ignatius the remainder of his life to develop into the saint we know today. His was a gradual, steady evolution from a sinful narcissist in control of his own life to an innocent, obedient servant of God. He discovered and embraced the power and energy of living in the holy trinity of his authentic human nature—spirit, body and God's grace working in unison. Growth in holiness requires desire, patience and daily effort to awaken to our authentic human nature. It takes time for grace to penetrate the influence of our anti-story so that our *Sacred Story* can more fully emerge. There are no short cuts to holiness, not even for saints.

If you desire to surrender your anti-story and open to your *Sacred Story*, grace will awaken you, like Ignatius, to places in your heart's memories you might not wish to visit. The awakening will begin like Ignatius'. It starts with an honest identification of the *visible* manifestations of those spiritual and psychological distortions in the particulars of your human nature. These distortions disclose your lost innocence and a heart broken by the Original Fall and the cumulative sins of your family, clan and culture. Ignatius started this process with his life confession. He truthfully identified the habits, addictions, sins and compulsions characteristic of his lost innocence and broken heart.

Open yourself to the graces of God that will illumine the distinctive narcissistic elements fueling your sinful, compulsive behaviors. Ignatius needed much grace to overcome his defenses and unlock this hidden truth about his life. Everyone who embraces this invitation to walk this path can confidently rely on the same grace to navigate this vital part of the process.

Finally awakening to your *Sacred Story* will take you to the places in your heart where your innocence is wounded, your true human nature is distorted, and your heart is broken. Awakening to your *Sacred Story* will reveal the outlines of your anti-story. You will need to honestly evaluate the narcissistic pattern in your own life, identifying the pleasures, powers, and habits that act as narcotics, blocking the pain of your broken heart and lost innocence.

This pattern that masks your authentic self and your true human nature is the pattern of your false self. It is the deceit of the anti-story that hides the radiance of your authentic human nature and the sacredness of your life story. This was Ignatius' experience. By divine inspiration he discovered his false-self masquerading as a pious, conscientious penitent.

Once he reached this point, Ignatius awakened, "as if from a dream," to his *Sacred Story*. By so doing, he was graced to unite mind and spirit, action and contemplation, the eternal in the present moment, and so to see the Divine Presence in all people and in all creation. His new consciousness of God so energized him that he could daily enter the stream of his *Sacred Story*, enabling him to reengage life's duties and obligations with a serene heart and with clarity of purpose. He courageously allowed God to write his *Sacred Story* over the remainder of his life—hourly, daily, weekly, monthly, yearly.

The vitality of Ignatius' personal relationship with God, in Father, Son and Spirit, was possible through the grace and gratitude he experienced in the constant encounter with his personal sinfulness and disordered passions. These graced encounters always brought illumination, insight, energy and hope, never discouragement, fear or despair.

A proud, dissolute, insecure narcissist finally found serenity and security in God's full love, acceptance, mercy, and forgiveness. Interestingly enough, this happened in and through Ignatius' powerlessness and weaknesses and perhaps even because of them! That which so marred his early life became the very source of his strength and sanctity. Ignatius discovered, like St. Paul, that in his weaknesses and sin, he was strong in Christ (2 Cor 12:10). It will be the same for you.

⋙

I am starting a Relationship that will carry me
for the rest of my life.

All relationships require time and patience.
I will strive for patience and ask for God's help
when I don't understand a lesson.

I will learn the fundamentals and open my heart to God.

I trust that God will lead me.

I believe that my *Sacred Story* will unfold in truth,
in powerlessness and with my patience.

I believe that Jesus awaits me with His grace, mercy and forgiving love.

∽

Surrendering control of my _entire_ life to God.

I don't feel good about others. I get disgusted at their selfishness.

I am so sad about the drugs. It literally breaks my heart. Why does God allow this — why doesn't he help them? I want my children to be happy but they seem caught up.

Week 4

FIRST

I will review my faithfulness to my daily 15-minute time(s) of contemplative rest and reflection. If my commitment has wavered it may be helpful to write down the specific location and the time(s) of day. I ask God for the grace to recommit to this practice, which is the <u>most</u> important dimension of *Sacred Story* prayer. I will resist the temptation to judge myself harshly when I fail to live up to the ideal. Each day, I will do my best to be faithful to the commitment I have made.

SECOND

I will purchase a small spiral notebook (if I have not already done so). It will be needed later.

THIRD

During my 15-minute quiet moments this week, I will read through Part Three of St. Ignatius' conversion story. It is spiritual reading. I will read and re-read reflectively and take my time. I will invite God to be my companion as I read. I will ask the Lord to help me listen with my heart and be attentive to what moves me spiritually. I will use the process that works best for me. If I can better reflect on the materials during my 15-minute prayer periods by reading it all first on Sunday, then I use that method. It may be helpful to highlight the sections of the readings that created hope and/or anxiety, and bring those sections to reflection and prayer.

I will not read ahead.
I will awaken to the present moment.
I will take each day and each exercise as it comes.
I cannot do *Sacred Story* better by going faster.

౭

Read this at the beginning of the week

Welcome to the fourth week of our pilgrimage together. The exercises for the fourth week move from the conversion story of St. Ignatius to your own story. You are invited to make a commitment to join with St. Ignatius and all the holy women and men in the Church, to give your life to Christ for this great work of reconciliation.

Listen to the call and pay attention to whatever stirs in you, be it hope and peace or anxiety and fear. Doing this sharpens your spiritual radar for things that prompt your heart to say: "Pay Attention!" Thank Christ in advance for the blessings and insights you will receive.

Part Three: The Call to Universal Reconciliation

Your Sacred Story

As with Ignatius, God extends an invitation to awaken to the pattern of spiritual, emotional and psychological dysfunction that has formed our anti-story. God invites us to awaken to our lives as *Sacred Story* and to produce fruit that endures to eternity. The awakening and growth will reveal where our freedom is compromised and how we close our hearts to our authentic human nature. Christ compassionately shows us how our selfishness and pride have corrupted our creativity, robbing us of the joy of innocence. God's invitation is gentle. God's awakening is merciful. Rest assured that God's passion is to pursue us, rescue us, heal us and bring us back to our original innocence. God's passion is Personal. God's passion is Love. God's passion is Christ Jesus.

God's intention is to gradually heal and transform our thoughts, words and deeds. For every thought, word and deed influences my history in the direction of an anti-story or a *Sacred Story*. Every thought, word and deed, for good or ill, touches all people in my life, all the world and all of creation, shaping history's final chapter. The effects of sin and narcissism—as well as the effects of virtue and selflessness—have individual, social, physical, spiritual, and ecological ramifications that reach to the ends of creation. For everything and everyone is one in Love—one in Christ Jesus—through whom and for whom everything was made (Rom 11:36).

Every thought, word, or deed, no matter how discreet, has positive or negative significance in the interconnected web of life that God has fashioned through Christ. It is Christ's being—His *SACRED STORY*—that links each of our individual *Sacred Stories*. It is in Christ that the entire cosmos is joined together. God in Christ has made us responsible for and dependent upon each other and upon the earth that sustains us.

The Christ of the Cosmos—through whom and for whom everything was made—became man, and confronted, absorbed, and diffused all the destructive

43

force of evil's evolutionary anti-history running through human nature and the created cosmos. Christ reconciles in Himself everything in the heavens and on the earth to bring peace to all by the blood of His cross. His *SACRED STORY* redeems and renews every chapter in our history, individual and collective.

Christ Jesus passionately awaits our participation to join His work of universal reconciliation. Our willingness to accept the path of conversion entails truthfully identifying our sins, dysfunction and addictions. It entails experiencing and admitting our powerlessness to save ourselves. It requires the patience of a lifetime while Christ writes our *Sacred Story*.

My participation in Christ's work of reconciliation is the only worthy vocation and the only labor that produces fruit enduring to eternity. My accepting the invitation unlocks the very mystery of life.

When I accept the invitation, Christ promises to share His universal glory. Accepting the invitation to intentionally enter my *Sacred Story* has momentous consequences.

Now is the Time to Wake from Sleep

Our time on this earth is so very brief. Since the time of Christ's birth, life, death and resurrection, our story can only be measured and valued in light of His eternal mission of Reconciliation. Intentionally entering my *Sacred Story* will, over time, enable me to know God more intimately and serve God more generously. Like Ignatius, I am called to awaken from sleep—to awaken to wholeness and holiness. I was created and infused with the gift to awaken to a life that reverences the God, who in Christ and the Holy Spirit, is present in all things: all persons, and all creation.

Awakening to my *Sacred Story*, like Ignatius, calls for courage in the cleansing of the spirit and psyche that it initiates. The process requires discipline in the face of temptation and monotony. It requires consciously asking, even begging if necessary, for God's graces. It requires time and patience; deliberately choosing each day to be faithful to time and space for God. Awakening requires the patience of a lifetime. Embraced and trusted, the journey is rich with blessings beyond our wildest expectations. Encountering Christ daily in *Sacred Story* forever changes life, relationships, the earth, and eternity.

What is needed for the journey will be provided each day. In my journey through the memories and experiences, past and present, I am promised the power and mercy of the LOVE that maintains and guides the entire cosmos. It is this LOVE that waits to transform your sins, addictions, angers, fears, grief, guilt and shame. It is this LOVE that restores your broken heart into a vessel of forgiveness, light and peace. The more embedded and impenetrable the web of darkness, compulsion, sin, and addiction in your life, the more strategic and magnificent is God's grace in breaking its grip, for nothing is impossible with God (Lk 1:37).

On this journey you will gain personal and real knowledge of sin and mercy, creation and eternity. You will come to know, experientially, our gracious God, present in Christ's Body in the Church, in the sacraments, in yourself, in others, and in all creation. Some of your insights will come in a flash; others will unfold over weeks, months, or years. From now on the whole process of your life is about waking from sleep (Eph 5:14; Rom 13:11), bending to the real, to the authentic, to your true human nature, living and working for fruit that endures to eternity.

Your Sacred History

Your life (and each person's life) is inextricably interwoven and integrated to Christ's *SACRED STORY* in ways both mysterious and sublime. It is mysterious because the ways of this world are not the ways of the Kingdom. What is deemed valuable and successful in this present age is in fact foolish and useless in the spiritual life. It is sublime because the most private sufferings offered to God, the faintest cries for mercy and forgiveness, and the simplest acts of care, kindness or generosity done for one's enemy, God's beloved poor, and His magnificent creation, are written in gold in the Book of the Lamb. These are the thoughts, words, and deeds that will endure to eternity.

There are no short cuts to the story's unfolding. Conversion is lifelong but measurable when I intentionally, daily, consistently, and faithfully enter my *Sacred Story*. My story begins where Ignatius' began, in the grace of the call to conversion. My conversion will begin to take shape when I accept that call and follow the pattern of Ignatius' own conversion. I will discover things that disquiet, create shame and confusion, and unlock hidden angers, fears and grief. I will encounter a heart broken, and innocence and paradise lost.

But most important, in all of this, I will be held, sheltered and guided by the only thing necessary, Christ's love. I will be given strength to speak truth to power. I will be given grace to see and honestly name those sins, habits and addictions that bring death—spiritual, physical, psychological—and not life. Then, surrendering to my powerlessness in favor of God's power, the Divine Physician will rewrite my life as *Sacred Story*.

Surrendering control of my life to the care of the Divine Physician by admitting my powerlessness to save myself will enable me to be vulnerable, creative, innocent, and humble. Once my heart is open, the Spirit of God will continue to write my *Sacred Story*. My lifetime of patience will bear fruit that endures to eternity. My pilgrim journey, like Ignatius', follows the proven and time-tested mystical path to wholeness and holiness. There are *no* shortcuts. Recall that Christ Jesus Himself has traveled the path. He will guarantee my journey's safe passage and carry my burdens, failures, shame, broken heart, and confusion.

I will hold in my heart the humble example of Jesus washing my feet. He endured humiliations, torture, and a disgraceful death, so that I can find hope and healing for everything in my life that needs healing, forgiveness, and redemption. From the beginning of time His *SACRED STORY* is mystically imprinted into the souls of His chosen people and the Church. Through the pattern of His *STORY*, I, the Church, and all people can have their history rewritten as *Sacred Story*.

I will intentionally enter my life narrative for 15-minute intervals once or twice each day. My story linked to Christ's *SACRED STORY* and to all people and to all creation, runs from my birth in all the thoughts, words and deeds to shape my destiny here, and in the hereafter. The prayer will help me attune to Creation, Presence, Memory, Mercy, and Eternity. When I encounter the fears, stresses, angers, temptations, failures, addictions and sins in my day, I can briefly attune to Creation, Presence, Memory, Mercy, and Eternity, and ask for the grace to see my whole story. By so doing, the Divine Physician can heal me and awaken my heart to its true human nature.

Christ extends the invitation and His Love, at the Heart of the Universe, awaits my response. I pray for the courage and generosity to enter with Christ into my *Sacred Story*.

ॐ

I am starting a Relationship that will carry me
for the rest of my life.

All relationships require time and patience.
I will strive for patience and ask for God's help
when I don't understand a lesson.

I will learn the fundamentals and open my heart to God.

I trust that God will lead me.

I believe that my *Sacred Story* will unfold in truth,
in powerlessness and with my patience.

I believe that Jesus awaits me with His grace, mercy and forgiving love.

જી

NOTES

Week 5

First

I select my 15-minute quiet time(s) for the week ahead. I visualize where I will go each day and at what time(s). I ask God for the grace to make those appointments throughout the week, in a technology-free zone.

Second

From this point forward, I will bring my notebook to my prayer sessions for the remainder of the forty weeks.

Third

My 15-minute prayer times this week consist of two exercises:

1.   I ask for the inspiration to discover the name of God that speaks directly to my heart. It can take two or more days to discover the name that unlocks my heart to God's love and mercy. If God does not inspire me in the first two days, I will set this exercise aside and move to the second exercise.

But I will continue to ask for the inspiration for the rest of the week to find the name. I will thank God in advance, because God will give me the inspiration I need to reveal the name that speaks to my heart. I will thank God in advance for this important grace.

2.   For the remainder of the week, I listen to the three parts of Ignatius' conversion story in light of my own story. A simple spiritual reflection associated with this exercised is described below.

I will not read ahead.
I will awaken to the present moment.
I will take each day and each exercise as it comes.

I cannot do Sacred Story better by going faster.
I will ask God to help me.

ᘓ

Read this at the beginning of the week

Take a moment to ask God for this grace: "Lord, open me to the knowledge of my own heart." For the heart is where the important work of prayer takes place. The mind reveals facts. The heart reveals the truth of my being. The heart is how Scripture describes the most important aspects of the human condition. Here are a few examples:

- ✠ The heart reveals the state of corruption caused by sin (Gen 6:5; Jer 17:9-10; Mt 15:9). [2]
- ✠ The heart is where the process of conversion and forgiveness takes place (Ez 36:26; Mt 18:35; Rom 2:29).
- ✠ The heart is the point of convergence, where self-condemnation comes face-to-face with hope in God's power (1 Jn 3:19-20).
- ✠ The heart's purity enables one to see God (Mt 5:8).
- ✠ The heart is the locus of compassion (Lk 7:13).
- ✠ The heart is the custodian of memory and contemplation (Lk 1:29; 2:19, 51).
- ✠ The heart is the vessel holding the secrets that illuminate the true meaning of life (Mt 6:21; Lk 24:32; Ps 85:9).
- ✠ The heart is defined as the center of human consciousness and action, wherein God discerns the rightness or wrongness of my thoughts, words, and deeds. The heart is the center from which each person will stand before God and render the ultimate account of their thoughts, words, and deeds (Heb 4:12-13).
- ✠ The heart perceives love as the ultimate end, gift, and purpose of being (1 Cor 13).
- ✠ The testimony of Christ in Scripture speaks to the heart's desire for innocence, based on the weariness of life, and the burdens it carries resulting from corruption (Mt 11:28-30.).
- ✠ Christ also promises to respond to the heart searching for Him, and gives the conviction that He can be found by those who seek Him (Lk 11:9-11).

Seek *knowledge of the heart* and ask God for the grace to open a pathway to your heart. Seek also knowledge of God's heart, present in Christ's Sacred

50

Heart. This grace will help to unite your heart to the heart of Christ. "Lord, open me to the knowledge of my heart."

ℭℬ

I will allow two days of my 15-minute prayers periods for this spiritual exercise.

Once you are settled in your place of prayer, ask for God's inspiration for this time. Then ask, in words from your heart, to be inspired to discover or remember the most intimate and/or meaningful name for God the Father, Son and Spirit that you have used in prayer.

The name will resonate deeply in your heart and reflect God's relationship to you and your personal relationship with God. The following may be helpful:

Merciful Father, Loving Father, Almighty Father, Our Father, Father God, Loving Creator, Creator God, God of Love, My God, Holy God, Father of the Poor, God of All Mercy, God of All Compassion, Father of Jesus, Lord Jesus Christ, Lord Jesus, Christ Jesus, Dear Jesus, Adorable Jesus, Adorable Christ, Good Jesus, Jesus, Merciful Savior, Jesus My Savior, Son of God, Dearest Lord, My Lord, My Lord and My God, Sacred Heart of Jesus, Lamb of God, Good Shepherd, Crucified Savior, Holy Spirit, Spirit of Jesus, Spirit of the Lord, Loving Spirit, Holy Spirit of God, Love of God, Divine Spirit, Creator Spirit, Creator God.

Ask for the grace to discover the name for God that touches your heart most intimately. You will know the right name because it has the power to unlock your trust and your love, and to stir your affections.

Write the name for God in your notebook when you discover it. From this point forward, use this name when you address God. God delights when you to speak directly from your heart.[3]

For the remainder of my 15-minute prayer periods this week

Review Ignatius' story and your own: Use this question as the focus for these exercises: "Like Ignatius, have I discovered the one area of my life that convinces me, beyond any doubt, that I cannot save myself, and must rely on God to save me?"

Recall the two parts of St. Ignatius' *Sacred Story* narrative. In your prayer times review the sections of his story that resonate with your own story. In these prayer periods, recall those parts of his story that moved your heart in one of two ways:

1). What spontaneously evoked *anxiety* in me as I listened to Ignatius' story? I will reflect on <u>why</u> my anxiety was provoked. In my notebook, I will record what evoked my anxiety and why.

2). As I listened to Ignatius' conversion story, what *inspired* or gave me *hope* about my life? I will reflect on <u>why</u> I was inspired or hopeful. In my notebook I will record what inspired me and why.

For my last fifteen minute prayer period at week's end

I will use my notebook jottings for my prayer text today. As I sift through the entries I ask for the grace to identify the <u>one</u> issue or idea that caused me the <u>most</u> anxiety. I record this in my notebook. Then I will write down why I felt the anxiety. (I may not know why something causes anxiety so if it is not clear yet, I will not be anxious). I will invite God into this unknown area: "Lord, why did this make me anxious?"

In my notebook I also record what I discovered that caused me the <u>most</u> hope or inspiration and <u>why</u>. If I don't know, I will invite God to reveal this to me by praying: "Lord, why did this cause me hope?"

I will be <u>brief</u>, and <u>specific</u> in my notebook entries. My reflection plus my writing exercises ought not to extend beyond the allotted time of 15-minutes that encompass my prayer period.[4]

CB

I am starting a Relationship that will carry me
for the rest of my life.

All relationships require time and patience.
I will strive for patience and ask for God's help
when I don't understand a lesson.

I will learn the fundamentals and open my heart to God.

I trust that God will lead me.

I believe that my *Sacred Story* will unfold in truth,
in powerlessness and with my patience.

I believe that Jesus awaits me with His grace, mercy and forgiving love.

꙾

NOTES

Week 6

First

I will plan my 15-minute quiet time(s) for the week ahead. I will visualize where I will go each day and at what time(s). I will ask God for the grace to help me keep those appointments throughout the week. I will seek a technology-free zone—a place apart.

Second

I will have my notebook at hand for each prayer period.

Third

The prayer exercise for this week is composed of two parts. I will take half of the week's prayer periods for the first part and the other half of my prayer periods for the second part:

1.   Once settled in prayer I will ask God to reveal to me the most important persons, life events, and/or issues that generate gratitude, hope and love in me.

2.   Then I will ask God to reveal to me the most important persons, life events, and/or issues that evoke anger, fear or grief in me.

I will not read ahead.

I will awaken to the present moment.

I will take each day and each exercise as it comes.

I cannot do *Sacred Story* better by going faster.

I will ask God to help me.

Focus Affirmation for Week Six

I will say this affirmation aloud once daily:

I ask God to reveal to me the most important people, life events and/or issues in my story up to this point.

C03

Read this at the beginning of the week

Each of us has persons, issues and life events that shape our life story, our history. We are conscious of some of these pieces, while others are buried deep in our memory. We seek grace to understand those things that, in negative and positive ways, most strongly shape our thoughts, actions, feelings, and beliefs linked to God, the world and ourselves. These persons, life events and issues are often linked to the spiritual plotlines in our life story, leading towards or away from God.

This week we seek God's grace to awaken to our *affective memories*. That is, we want to recall the persons, life events or issues, and *feel* the emotional weight, and the heart value they have in our history. Because these significant elements often evade our conscious awareness, we need to rely on grace to reveal them.

Naturally, I seek insight into the closest, most intimate circle of people and events in my life story—my parents, family, friends, and important events. I will be attentive to the feeling these memories evoke.

For one life event, I might feel fear (something that has the power to generate the anxiety I know as fear). For another life event, my predominant feeling might be anger (someone or something that hurt me or a loved one). For one person, I might feel mostly love (someone who has cared deeply for me). For another person, I might feel anger (someone who hurt me in some way). For one issue, my predominant feeling might be grief (the loss of a loved one or an opportunity that grieves my heart). For another issue, my experience might be gratitude or hope (an issue that has positively transformed my life for the better).

Pray that God enlighten your mind and heart to know each person, issue or life event and the *single, predominant* feeling (fear, anger, or grief—gratitude, hope or love) each inspires.

For your prayer periods this week, sit apart in your quiet place. Find a comfortable position that permits you to be alert. Breathe deeply for a few minutes, mindful that God's love sustains your very life. Next, using the personal name for God you identified last week, ask God to enlighten your memory and imagination so that the most significant people, issues and life events come into your mind and heart.

As you become aware of each, pause briefly and write down the name of the person, or the issue or life event that comes to memory. Next to each of these, write a single word for the most predominant feeling that arises in your heart. A word of caution here: do not succumb to the temptation to analyze or judge the feelings as they arise.

1). For the first half of the week, use the first chart to ask God to inspire you to remember the elements (person, issue, or life event) that generate gratitude, hope or love. Pray that those elements *most important* to your history come into your mind and heart.

2). For the second half of the week, use the next chart to ask God to inspire you to remember the person, issue, or life event that generate fear, anger or grief. Pray that those elements *most important* to your history come into your mind and heart.

TEN PERSONS/LIFE EVENTS/ISSUES THAT GENERATE GRATITUDE, HOPE OR LOVE

Persons/Life Events/Issues	*Gratitude/Hope/Love*
1.	1.
2.	2.
3.	3.
4.	4.
5.	5.
6.	6.
7.	7.
8.	8.
9.	9.
10.	10.

ℰℭ

TEN PERSONS/LIFE EVENTS/ISSUES THAT GENERATE FEAR, ANGER OR GRIEF

Persons/Life Events/Issues	*Fear/Anger/Grief*
1.	1.
2.	2.
3.	3.
4.	4.
5.	5.
6.	6.
7.	7.
8.	8.
9.	9.
10.	10.

ॐ

I am starting a Relationship that will carry me
for the rest of my life.

All relationships require time and patience.
I will strive for patience and ask for God's help
when I don't understand a lesson.

I will learn the fundamentals and open my heart to God.

I trust that God will lead me.

I believe that my *Sacred Story* will unfold in truth,
in powerlessness and with my patience.

I believe that Jesus awaits me with His grace, mercy and forgiving love.

ℰↄ

8\30
Tues

Week 7

FIRST

I will review my 15-minute quiet time(s) for the week ahead and visualize where I will go each day and at what time(s). I will ask God for the grace to keep those times sacred. I will have my notebook at hand for each prayer period.

SECOND

During my 15-minute quiet prayer this seventh week there are two prayer exercises. I will take the first half of the week's prayer periods for the first exercise, and the second half of my prayer periods for the second exercise.

THIRD

1. . I will ask God for the grace to identify how the Ten Commandments fit into my life as a *gift* to bring awareness, healing, balance and God's peace.
2.   I will ask God for the grace to identify the deepest hope of my heart for my life and my future.

I will not read ahead.

I will awaken to the present moment.

I will take each day and each exercise as it comes.

I cannot do *Sacred Story* better by going faster.

I will ask God to help me.

Focus Affirmation for Week Seven

I will say this affirmation aloud once daily:

The Ten Commandments are a profound gift from God to the Chosen People and to all humankind.

☙

Read 1 & 2 before starting your prayer sessions this week:

1). For the first half of the week, use the Decalogue Examination of Conscience to better understand your life story and the gift of healing and balance that God desires for you. Pray that your imagination be graced so that the *most important* issues in the Commandments, those that illuminate your history (your story),will come into your mind and heart. Pray to "see" what you have *never* seen before. Pray to see your life as God sees your life.

The Commandments were given to the Chosen People in a Covenant that was sealed with a blood sacrifice. The Church reflects that the power of the animal sacrifice sealing the Covenant receives its power from Christ's blood, which it foreshadows. The Commandments, as *gift,* are a foundation for God's work to repair our broken human nature, to forgive us, and reopen the way to eternity: the work of Christ's death and resurrection. It is no wonder then that laws enshrining the Commandments' truths have transformed stories of violence and injustice to stories of civility and justice for countless millions of people in the last three millennia.

For this exercise, we are reflecting on the Commandments to enhance our understanding of their richness and wisdom. The exercise will help to clarify how each Commandment carries its own responsibilities and boundaries. These *Decrees*—a synonym for *Commandments*— will ignite your imagination so you will be able to hear them differently. These decrees—statements by God—serve as a reminder to us when we have forgotten to *remember and know the truth* about God, humanity and oneself. They are a *gift* to guide our way home so our thoughts, words and deeds bring life, not death.

Before concluding your prayer period, use your notebook to record where in your life you have missed the mark in living the Decree you reflected on. Be specific, honest and courageous. Ask for the grace of integrity and openness to embrace the truth of your own experience.

This may be a helpful format to follow as you reflect on the each Decree. Identify the Decree (and the sub-themes in the Decrees) as mild, moderate, or strong depending on the challenge this specific Decree presents to you. For example, you may write "6th—moderate, especially regarding (issue);" "4th—mild regarding (person);" "7th/10th—strong regarding (event)." Use codes if you prefer to safeguard confidentiality and augment honesty.

Note: The purpose of this exercise is to simply identify your challenges with the Commandments. With Christ by your side, watch with curiosity and detachment, without self-blame. God sees beyond any patterns of sin and failure you have, or think you have. God knows *you* for who you are. God loves you. God is the Divine Physician who desires to help you honestly see your life as it is so He can bring forgiveness, healing, freedom and peace.

2). For the second half of the week, pray for the grace to remember the books, stories, songs, events, movies and art, that have the power to bring you to tears. Pray to remember the turn of phrase, the lyric, the dialogue, the word spoken to you, the melody, and the image that has touched your heart so profoundly that your only response is to weep. The shortest phrase in the Scripture is "*Jesus wept*" (Jn 11: 35). What causes us to weep holds significance in our history, and informs our story. Pray to remember and feel what moves you to tears.

The Gospels record that Jesus wept twice. He wept over Jerusalem, for failing to recognize that the time of its deliverance was at hand (Lk 19: 41-44). And He wept for His good friend Lazarus, "see how he loved him" (Jn 11: 33-6). Both instances reveal Jesus' deep longing for humanity's reconciliation and peace. It is Christ's desire to bring freedom from death's grip, that death which resulted from humanity's disobedience. Jesus' weeping expresses the deepest longings of His heart. His tears reveal His mission in life, a mission He received from the Father, for those He loves.

Tears reveal the deepest longings of our heart. They are a window to the heart and soul. Ask God for the grace to remember and understand what brings you to tears, what breaks your heart or expresses your heart's longings for healing and peace.

Use your 15-minute prayers in the second half of the week to recall what causes you to weep, that is, what brings you to tears and expresses the deepest longings of your heart. Do not spend more than 15-minutes for each of your prayer periods. For your prayer, sit apart in a quiet place. Find a comfortable position that permits you to be alert. Breathe deeply for a few minutes, mindful that God's love sustains your very life.

Next, using the personal name for God you identified, ask God to enlighten your memory and imagination so that you can remember and understand what brings you to tears, and why. How is your life mission—your story—revealed in your tears? What stories, movies, books, songs move you to tears and what can God help you understand about your life from them?

Before your prayer period ends, write down what caused your tears. Record why this caused your tears (if it is clear). Reflect further on what this might possibly reveal to you about your story. Do your tears reveal your deepest longings and God's desire to bring you hope and peace?

☙

THE DECALOGUE EXAMINATION OF CONSCIENCE [5]

First Decree: I am the Lord your God, you shall have no strange gods before me.

Is God the center of my life? Have I displaced God with my career, work, concern for wealth and pleasure? Does the worship and honor of God take shape in my weekly religious practices? Do I pray often? Do I turn to God for forgiveness often? Have I resorted to relying on superstition, the occult or astrology in place of asking for God's assistance?

Second Decree: You shall not take the name of the Lord your God in vain.

Do I casually take God's name in vain? Do I have a habit of swearing in jest or in anger? Do I use God's name to damn other people? Do I nurse hatred of God in my heart? Do I harbor anger towards God for the difficult things in my life or in the world? Do I reverence God in my heart?

Third Decree: Remember to keep holy the Sabbath day.

Do I make every effort to prepare myself for the Sunday Liturgy? Do I make every effort to attend the Sunday Liturgy? Do I allow social or sporting events to displace or limit my attendance at the Sunday Liturgy? Do I limit unnecessary servile work on Sunday? Is Sunday a true day of spiritual rest and refreshment?

Fourth Decree: Honor your Father and Mother.

Do I give proper reverence to my mom and dad for the gift of life? Do I thank them? Do I spend time with them? Do I strive to forgive the shortcomings of my parents? Do I hold anger or grudges against them in my heart? Do I try to respond to them with love and charity? Do I attend to them in their sufferings and weaknesses? Am I patient with their infirmity as they age?

Fifth Decree: You shall not kill.

Do I strive to overcome the prejudices I have against individuals or groups? Do I resist acting on my prejudices so as not to harm persons with my words or deeds? Do I act with cruelty towards others? Do I risk my life or the lives of others by using illegal drugs? Do I risk my life or the lives of others by driving recklessly or intoxicated? Do I strive in words and deeds to promote the value of life from conception to natural death? Have I ever helped someone terminate a pregnancy or end his/her own life? Do I strive to do everything I can to uphold the value of each person? Do I harbor satisfaction in my heart at the death of those people whom I consider evil? Do I vote for politicians/civil servants because of their positions to protect and promote abortion, euthanasia, capital punishment or pre-emptive war? Do I mourn the loss of all human life, no matter the cause of death?

Sixth Decree: You shall not commit adultery.
Ninth Decree: You shall not covet your neighbor's spouse.

Do I protect my covenant relationship with my spouse and uphold its sacredness? Do I strive daily to support my spouse? Do I turn to other persons for emotional support to make my spouse envious? Do I denigrate my spouse by comparing her/him to others? Do I speak harshly about my spouse behind his/her back to gain the affections of others? Do I uphold the sacredness of my covenant commitment by never seeking the sexual attention of those to whom I may be attracted? Do I uphold my covenant by never engaging in any sexual activity with someone other than my spouse? Do I use pornography to arouse my sexual appetites, or to avoid intimacy with my spouse? Do I denigrate the spiritual integrity of persons by focusing on their physical beauty or appearance? Do I protect my covenant relationship by not purposely fantasizing about sexual relations with someone other than my spouse? Do I hold sacred the gift of sexuality for marriage? Do I strive to cultivate purity of heart as a sign of God's own single-heartedness? Do I reverence sexual intercourse first and foremost as the gift most akin to God's creative energies, a gift of love to create a human life destined for an eternity with God? Do I casually inhibit God's presence in this divine gift with drugs or medical procedures when there is no legitimate reason?

Seventh Decree: You shall not steal.
Tenth Decree: You shall not covet your neighbor's goods.

Do I cheat on papers and exams to steal a better grade? Do I take things that do not belong to me? Do I keep things I have borrowed? Am I honest in my investments, taxes, and in all my financial dealings? Do I use legal loopholes in tax laws or business practices to harvest financial rewards that ultimately hurt the less fortunate? Am I honest and truthful in my business dealings even if it means I may lose profits or customers? Do I vandalize or harm property or goods that do not belong to me? Do I envy those who have more than I do? Do I let concern for wealth and comfort take center place in my life? Do I live lavishly because I have the resources to do so? Do I spend money on luxury goods I do not need? Do I live with envy of those who have more than I do? Do I respect the limited resources of the earth as a divine inheritance to benefit all people? Do I give a percentage of my earned income to the poor? Do I strive to live so as to minimize waste and protect the environment? Do I examine my investment patterns to discern if companies I own, or in which I have stock, are treating their employees justly and are protecting the environment in their practices? Do I ever put the drive for profits ahead of the welfare of persons or the environment?

Eighth Decree: You shall not bear false witness against your neighbor.
Do I uphold the honor of other people's reputations? Do I avoid spreading gossip and avoid seeking gossip from others? Do I share information about people with third parties, even if it is true, when that information threatens the person's reputation? Do I avoid spreading lies or rumors about other people? Do I challenge people who gossip and spread damaging information about others? Do I avoid and denounce TV, radio, magazines and newspapers that employ the tactics of personality destruction and malicious gossip to sell news and generate profits? Do I tell others what they ought to do instead of getting my own house in order?

☙

I am starting a Relationship that will carry me
for the rest of my life.

All relationships require time and patience.
I will strive for patience and ask for God's help
when I don't understand a lesson.

I will learn the fundamentals and open my heart to God.

I trust that God will lead me.

I believe that my *Sacred Story* will unfold in truth,
in powerlessness and with my patience.

I believe that Jesus awaits me with His grace, mercy and forgiving love.

❧

NOTES

Week 8

FIRST

I will select my 15-minute quiet time(s) for the week ahead and visualize where I will go each day and at what time(s). I will ask God for the grace to keep those times sacred throughout the week in a technology-free zone.

SECOND

I will have my notebook on hand for each prayer period.

THIRD

My 15-minute quiet prayer this week consists of two prayer exercises. I will take the first half of the week's prayer periods for the first exercise and the second half for the second exercise. If I find it more beneficial, I can combine the two with the alternate exercise.

First Spiritual Exercise: I will ask God for the grace to become aware of any habitual vices that obstruct my quest for holiness and interfere with the freedom God desires for me.

Second Spiritual Exercise: I will ask God for the grace to become aware of any addictions I possess that are eroding my quest for holiness and the freedom God desires for me.

Alternate Spiritual Exercise: I will ask God for the grace to see the connections between any habitual vices that erode my freedom and their link with addictive behaviors in my life story.

I will awaken to the present moment.
I will take each day and each exercise as it comes.
I cannot do *Sacred Story* better by going faster.

I will ask God to help me.
I will awaken to my spiritual nature and to the inspirations that
inspire faith, hope and love.
I will awaken to the inspirations that
inspire cynicism, impatience and lusts. I will wake up!

Focus Affirmation for Week Eight
I will say this affirmation aloud once daily:
*I believe that understanding the source of my vices and addictions can
lead to greater joy, authenticity and holiness.*

℞

Read 1, 2 & 3 before starting any prayer sessions this week.

The two powerful spiritual diagnostics for this week's lesson offer you the potential for great enlightenment. Vices and addictions reveal valuable information about our life stories. If we seek medical advice for pain, the doctor asks us where we hurt. Christ, the Divine Physician, sees our vices and addictions as manifestations of where we are hurting, and our unsuccessful attempts to anesthetize our hurt. The Gospel calls them "sin" because they manifest habits that erode our true human nature and our faith, hope and love. The doctor calls them destructive because they ruin our lives and relationships.

If you can honestly identify addictions and vices in your life story, you are on a path to freedom. If you prayed to Christ, the Divine Physician, *to wake up* to the *connections* between them in your life story, you should rejoice. Because your healing, leading to interior freedom, can now begin. Christ came to save sinners, not the righteous, and *Sacred Story* is *about allowing Christ to help us identify* where we need His healing graces. This is the great gift He wants to give to us. Be not afraid. Christ knows you are working with him, *to wake up.*

Pray with words from your heart that will enable you to see what you have not seen before *and* to see connections between aspects of your life story. A word of caution: resist the temptation to be judgmental, anxiously plan corrective therapies, or get lost in fear. If you find yourself slipping into any of these, gently stop the exercise and refocus your heart. These two exercises, like all the others, are to be approached with a compassionate, honest eye. It may be helpful to recall that you are reflecting on these components of your life narrative with the Divine Physician by your side. The goal is simply to wake up! Watch and pray!

1. For the first half of the week pay attention to the vices (Pride, Gluttony, Lust, Sloth, Envy, Avarice, Anger). They are sometimes called capital sins (from *caput*, the Latin word for *head*) because they are root habits or vices that lead to many other problems. All of us are subject to vices which have the ability to hook us mildly, moderately or strongly.

Simply identify your capital sins/vices. Ask Christ, the Divine Physician, to help you understand their *source* and *context* in your life history. Ask for the grace of deeper understanding, and then with Christ, observe your life with compassionate curiosity, and with objectivity. God sees beyond any vices you have, or think you have. God knows you for who you are and loves you. Jesus, the Divine Physician, watches compassionately and carried the burden for all your vices. He desires that you gain greater understanding and freedom. He has great compassion and patience for those seeking His help and healing.

At the end of each prayer period mark down in your notebook all the capital vices that trap you and to which you are susceptible. Be brief in your writing, but specific. List which capital sins/vices ensnare you and how intensely (mildly, moderately or strongly) they ensnare you.

2. For the second part of the week, pay attention to your addictions. Ignatius had addictions to gambling and possibly to sex. Everyone has addictions (whether mild moderate or strong) to one or more things. Our addictions reveal valuable diagnostic information that is worth bringing to the Divine Physician.

Do not exceed your fifteen minute limit for each prayer period. For your prayer, sit apart in a quiet place. Find a comfortable position that permits you to be alert. Breathe deeply for a few minutes, mindful that God's love sustains your very life. Next, using the personal name for God you identified, ask God to enlighten your memory and imagination so that you can see any addictions you have in the context of your life story.

Before completing your prayer period, record any addictions that surfaced. Be brief and specific. Identify each addiction by name and frequency: **S**eldom, **O**ften, or **C**onstantly. For example, you may write:

Television—S; Exercise—O; Gambling—C.

3. Alternatively, you can combine the above spiritual diagnostics into a single prayer exercise. Here is how you might do it. For your first two prayer exercises of the week, pray for the grace to honestly recognize the vices and addictions that erode your freedom and compromise your true self. Write them out in your notebook as indicated above, listing the vices as mild, moderate or strong, and the addictions as seldom, often or constantly.

Begin your prayer sessions in the standard manner. During your prayer

71

session, review what you wrote in your notebook and ask Christ, the Divine Physician, in very personal words, to help you discover the *connections* between the vices and addictions. For example, you may notice that when you are angry, you might move toward one or other addictive behavior. When you are envious, you might be drawn to other addictive behaviors, and so on for the other vices.

Recall that the grace you are asking for is the *inspiration* to *understand* the vices and addictions in and of themselves, and more importantly, to identify the *connections* between them as they manifest in your life story. When, through grace, you begin to wake up to the links between the thoughts, words and deeds of your life story, then growth in holiness and authenticity can occur.

Before the end of each prayer period record any discoveries you make between the vices and addictions that God reveals to you. Thank God for the courage to honestly see yourself as you are. Thank God for the grace to wake up to live in greater freedom.

The Seven Capital Vices

Pride

Pride is an unrestrained and improper appreciation of our own worth. This is listed first because it is widely considered the most serious of the seven sins. Pride—narcissism—was the foundation of Adam and Eve's sin that made them fall for the serpent's temptation "to be like gods." Adam and Eve displaced God, the Creator, as the arbiter of truth and goodness. They, who were creatures, made themselves gods, the final judges of truth and goodness. Their action led to the loss of paradise and to a world of sickness and death. Pride often leads to the committing of other capital sins. Pride is manifest as vanity and narcissism about one's appearance, intelligence, status, wealth, connections, power, successes and all the other things that one uses to stand apart from others and from God.

Greed

Greed is also known as avarice or covetousness. It is the immoderate desire for earthly goods and power. It is a sin of excess. The object of one's greed need not be evil. The problem lies in the way a person regards or desires an object, making it a god and investing it with inappropriate value. Greed can inspire such sinful actions as hoarding, theft, fraud, tax evasion, environmental waste or unethical business practices.

Gluttony

Gluttony comes from the Latin word meaning to gulp down or swallow. It is the sin of over-indulgence and usually refers to over-consumption of food and drink. Gluttony can be eating too soon, too expensively or eating too much. St.

Alphonsus Liguori explained that feeling pleasure in eating is not wrong. Because food tastes good, we are delighted by this gift. It is not right however to eat with pleasure as the only motive and to forget food's function in sustaining vitality and health.

Lust

The sin of lust refers to corrupted desires of a sexual nature. Sexuality is a gift from God and pure in itself. However, lust refers to the impure thoughts and actions that misuse that gift. Lust deviates from God's law and sexuality's sacred purpose of allowing woman and man to participate in God's creative nature. Indulging in the sin of lust can include, but is not limited to, fornication, adultery, bestiality, rape, masturbation, pornography and incest.

Sloth

Sloth is often described simply as the sin of laziness. However, while this is part of sloth's character, its true face is spiritual laziness. The sin of sloth means being lazy and lax about living the Faith and practicing virtue. Paraphrasing The Catholic Encyclopedia, sloth means aversion to labor or exertion. As a capital or deadly vice, St. Thomas calls it sadness in the face of some spiritual good that one has to achieve. In other words, a slothful person is bothered by the effort to sustain one's friendship with God. In this sense sloth is directly opposed to charity.

Envy

The sin of envy or jealousy is more than just someone wanting what others have. Sinful envy leads one to emotions or feelings of upset at another's good fortune or blessings. The law of love naturally leads one to rejoice in the good luck of one's neighbor. Envy opposes such love. Envy is named among the capital sins because of the other sins to which it leads.

Anger

Anger or wrath may be described as excessive and powerful feelings of hatred and resentment. These feelings can manifest as a passionate denial of truths expressed by others. Anger can also manifest in the form of denying truths about one's own life and impatience with the procedure of law. Anger is manifest too, in the desire to seek revenge outside of the workings of the justice system. Anger, in essence is wishing to do evil or harm to others. The transgressions borne of vengeance are among the most serious, including assault, murder, and in extreme cases, genocide and other crimes against humanity. Anger is the only sin not necessarily associated with selfishness or self-interest, although one can be angry for selfish reasons, such as jealousy.

CB

A Short Primer on Addiction

The word *addiction* is used in many contexts. Common usage of the term has evolved to include psychological dependence. In this context, the term goes beyond drug addiction and substance abuse problems. It also refers to behaviors that are not generally recognized by the medical community as addictive problems such as compulsive overeating or hoarding.

When the term *addiction* is applied to compulsions that are not substance-related, such as problem gambling and computer addiction, it describes a recurring <u>compulsion</u> one engages in despite the activity's harmful consequences to one's individual physical, mental, social or spiritual health.[6]

Other forms of addiction could be habitual defrauding or tax evasion, money addictions, work addiction, exercise addiction, habitual overeating, habitual shopping, sex addiction, computer addiction, e-mail addiction, video game addiction, pornography addiction, and television addiction.

Gabor Maté sums up addiction's profile: "Addiction is any repeated behavior, substance-related or not, in which a person feels compelled to persist, regardless of its negative impact on his life and the lives of others. Addiction involves:

a. Compulsive engagement with a behavior, or a preoccupation with it.
b. Impaired control over the behavior.
c. Persistence or relapse despite evidence of harm.
d. Dissatisfaction, irritability, or intense craving when the object—be it a drug, activity, or other goal—is not immediately available."[7]

CB

I am starting a Relationship that will carry me
for the rest of my life.

All relationships require time and patience.
I will strive for patience and ask for God's help
when I don't understand a lesson.

I will learn the fundamentals and open my heart to God.

I trust that God will lead me.

I believe that my *Sacred Story* will unfold in truth,
in powerlessness and with my patience.

I believe that Jesus awaits me with His grace, mercy and forgiving love.

SO

NOTES

Week 9

FIRST

I will select my 15-minute quiet times for the week ahead and visualize where I will go each day and at what times. I will ask God for the grace to keep those times sacred throughout the week. I will have my notebook at hand and spend no more than 15-minutes in each formal prayer session.

SECOND

My 15-minute quiet prayer this ninth week consists of six simple prayer exercises, one each for Monday through Saturday. I can use my Sunday prayer time to read over the prayer exercises to set my heart for the week ahead. If I am doing two prayer sessions a day, I have the option to engage each exercise twice.

THIRD

I will begin each 15-minute prayer period by sitting in a comfortable position. Speaking God's name, and with personal words from my heart, I ask to be open to my own heart and life story as I enter the short time of prayer. If I focus better by breathing deeply and saying God's name with each inhale and exhale, then I will do so. I will pray with personal words from my heart to see what I have not seen before, **and** to see connections between aspects of my life story. I am invited to watch these components of my life narrative with the Divine Physician by my side. Christ invites me to *wake up* in my life.

I will awaken to the present moment.
I will take each day and each exercise as it comes.
I cannot do *Sacred Story* better by going faster.
I will ask God to help me.

I will awaken to my spiritual nature and to the inspirations that inspire faith, hope and love.
I will awaken to the inspirations that inspire cynicism, impatience and lusts.
I will wake up!

Focus Affirmation for Week Nine
I will say this affirmation aloud once daily:
I believe every thought, word and deed of mine carries a force that can change me, others, and history.

ొ

Read this reflection at the beginning of the week

The six spiritual diagnostic exercises for this week's lesson offer you the potential for more enlightenment. Spend your 15-minute sessions this week listening to your heart. Ask God for the grace to discern the key elements in your life story linked to: gratitude; relationships; spiritual, social and financial values; and those you need to forgive, or whose forgiveness you need accept. Take one day for each of the six spiritual diagnostics. Deciphering these can help you see the two plot-lines in your life history more clearly. Be sure to ask for God's assistance to "see" each of these six elements. Use the personal name for God to ask for this grace for each day's prayer.

For your journal exercise, write one short phrase at the end of each day's lesson: one phrase capturing an aspect of what you wrote that increases your faith, hope and love, and one aspect that diminished the same.

First Spiritual Exercise for Monday—GRATITUDE

I ask God for the grace to remember the one experience, event or person for which I am most grateful. It could be a kindness someone showed me. It could be a loving gesture from a parent, friend, husband, wife or child. It could be something that did *not* happen to me—some danger or threat, sickness or accident that was avoided or minimized. It could be some significant event in my life that moved me in a new direction. It could be a spiritual experience that opened me to a deeper hope and joy in my life. What comes to mind? I will pray for the grace to recall the feelings I felt at the time of the event and take note of the reasons why. I pray to see connections in my responses to other prayer exercises as they occur. Before I finish my prayer, I will write my memory in one

sentence below and why it inspires gratitude.
Example: My brother with Down's Syndrome brought our family together and made us realize the true meaning of life and love.

Second Spiritual Exercise for Tuesday—RELATIONAL GOAL

I ask God for the grace to identify the most important relational goal I can imagine for my life story. It could be with God, my spouse, my children, my family or a close friend. This is the one relational goal that if I accomplished it, would cause me to believe my life was fulfilled. I will look for connections in my responses to other prayer exercises as they occur to me. Before I finish my prayer, I will write my relationship goal in one sentence below and why it would define my relational success.
Example: That I can be a faithful father and husband for life.

Third Spiritual Exercise for Wednesday—SPIRITUAL GOAL

I ask God for the grace to understand my most hoped for spiritual goal for my life story. It could be with God, my spouse, my children, my family or a close friend. It is the one spiritual goal that if I accomplished it, would cause me to believe that my life was fulfilled. I will look for connections in my responses to other prayer exercises as they occur to me. Before I finish my prayer, I will write my spiritual goal in one sentence below and why it would define spiritual success for me.
Example: That I do something every day to strengthen my relationship with God and also one thing to serve those most in need.

Fourth Spiritual Exercise for Thursday—SOCIETAL GOAL

I ask God for the grace to understand my most hoped for societal or political goal for my life story. It could be with God, or for my spouse, my children, my family, a close friend or for the Church, the country or the world. It is the one societal goal that if I accomplished it, or helped accomplish it, would cause me to believe my life was fulfilled. I will look for connections in my responses to other prayer exercises as they occur to me. Before I finish my prayer, I will write my societal goal in one sentence below and why it would define social success for me and the world.
Example: That I will not be afraid to take a stand to help promote a culture that respects life from conception till death.

Fifth Spiritual Exercise for Friday—FINANCIAL GOAL

I will ask God the grace to understand my most hoped for financial or economic goal or ambition for my life story. It could be for God, my spouse, my children, my family, a close friend or for the Church, country or the world. It is the one financial goal that if I accomplished it, or helped accomplish it, would cause me to believe my life was fulfilled. I will look for connections in my responses to other prayer exercises as they occur to me. Before I finish my prayer, I will write my financial goal in one sentence below and why it would define financial success for me.

Example: That I work to live and not live to work and that I can teach my children that living simply is the source of joy.

Sixth Spiritual Exercise for Saturday—FORGIVENESS

I ask God for the grace to understand the one person who would be most grateful to receive my forgiveness. I also ask God for the grace to understand the one person whose forgiveness I would be most grateful to receive. Before finishing my prayer, I will write two short sentences below, one for each person, describing why gratitude would be present in each instance of forgiveness.

Example: That I will continue to ask God to help me forgive my parents for getting divorced and breaking our family apart.

I am starting a Relationship that will carry me
for the rest of my life.

All relationships require time and patience.
I will strive for patience and ask for God's help
when I don't understand a lesson.

I will learn the fundamentals and open my heart to God.

I trust that God will lead me.

I believe that my *Sacred Story* will unfold in truth,
in powerlessness and with my patience.

I believe that Jesus awaits me with His grace, mercy and forgiving love.

SO

Week 10

FIRST

I will select my 15-minute quiet times for the week ahead and visualize where I will go each day and at what times. I will continue to ask God for the grace to keep those times sacred. I will have my notebook at hand and I will spend no more than 15-minutes in each formal prayer session.

SECOND

My 15-minute quiet prayer this tenth week is composed of simple prayer exercises for Monday through Saturday to help me find links in my life story. I may use my Sunday prayer time to read over the prayer exercises and diagnostic charts so I can set my heart for the week. If I am doing two prayer sessions a day, I will have more reflection time.

THIRD

I will begin each 15-minute prayer period by sitting in a comfortable position. I will speak God's name, and with personal words from my heart, I ask to be open to my own heart and life story. I will *ask for the grace to see connections between aspects of my life story.* I am invited to watch these components of my life narrative with the Divine Physician by my side. Christ invites me not to be afraid but to *wake up* in my life—my *spiritual* life. I will watch and pray with Christ.

I will awaken to the present moment.
I will take each day and each exercise as it comes.
I cannot do *Sacred Story* better by going faster.
I will ask God to help me.
I will awaken to my spiritual nature and to the inspirations that inspire faith, hope and love.
I will awaken to the inspirations that inspire cynicism, impatience and lusts.
I will wake up!

Focus Affirmation for Week Ten
I will say this affirmation aloud once daily:
I affirm that everything that has happened to me, and everything I have experienced in my entire life,
is present in my memory.

℘

Read 1-5 before starting any prayer sessions this week.

Whether you have or have not done the exercises for weeks six through nine, you can still do this week's exercises. If you wrote notes for the past weeks, refer to them. If not, take this exercise as a stand-alone and sometime later, go back and do the weeks you passed. For week ten, there are five diagnostic charts to contemplate. These charts are designed to help you pray for graced insights from God to better understand your life history. The five diagnostic charts are as follows:

1. A list of the vices and Commandments

2. A diagnostic chart for listing key elements in your life story

3. A diagnostic chart with four elements in your life story where you can pray for insights to see links or connections

4. A diagnostic chart that shows the progressive levels of sin's impact on Ignatius' spiritual and material being, and the way that originating sins and wounds lead to core sin, and finally to the fruit of these sins (those that are most visible or manifest in his story).

5. The same diagnostic chart as above, repeated with blank spaces for you to fill in your own unique experiences.

The data from your life diagnostic charts will be helpful to you throughout the year. You are only in the beginning period of attempting, with God's grace, to see your sin history more clearly. Your goal is to better understand how to listen to your *Sacred Story.* Remember, Christ watches with you with love, patience, compassion and infinite mercy. BE NOT AFRAID! What follows are suggestions for how to best use the 15-minute prayer sessions in this tenth week of *Sacred Story* Prayer:

Sunday—I contemplate briefly all the diagnostic charts and ask God for the grace of openness *to see* both the **trees** (unique elements of my life history) and the **forest** *through the trees* (the unique elements that when combined, form a single life story).

Monday—I fill in the first diagnostic chart (Looking for Links in My Story) *with at least one element* for each of the statements provided.

Tuesday—I fill in the second diagnostic chart with the four elements, with the goal to write at least 3 of the 5 things requested in each category.

Wednesday—I contemplate the diagnostic chart I filled in on Tuesday, praying to see if there are any obvious links between Commandments, vices, addictions, persons and/or events. I draw lines linking those connections that are clear to me.

Thursday—I contemplate the diagnostic chart of how sin impacted the life of St. Ignatius and try to see the links in his original (root), core (trunk), and manifest (fruit) sins.

Friday—I contemplate the elements from the diagnostic charts I filled in earlier in the week and I pray for the grace to see more clearly how sin has impacted me at the roots, trunk and fruit of my life. For each of the blank spaces on the last chart, I will write those elements (at least one each) that I believe are present in my life as Original Sins (root), core sins (trunk) and manifest sins (fruit).

Saturday—I contemplate the charts I filled in this week and ask for God's grace to see any connections that will aid me in my *Sacred Story* journey. I ask for God's grace to be open this entire forty-week journey so I can begin to see my life story in its entirety.

VICES

Pride, Envy, Gluttony, Lust, Sloth, Greed, Anger

COMMANDMENTS

First: I am the Lord your God, you shall have no strange gods before Me.

Second: You shall not take the name of the Lord your God in vain.

Third: Remember to keep holy the Sabbath day.

Fourth: Honor your father and mother.

Fifth: You shall not kill.

Sixth: You shall not commit adultery.
Ninth: You shall not covet your neighbor's spouse.

Seventh: You shall not steal.
Tenth: You shall not covet your neighbor's goods.

Eighth: You shall not bear false witness against your neighbor.

Command — Be in charge

Significance — Do something important

Deliberate — Decision made
    Can see all implications

Close relationships

LOOKING FOR LINKS IN MY STORY

Monday—I fill in the first diagnostic chart (Looking for Links in My Story) *with at least one element* for each of the statements provided.

A COMMANDMENT THAT CHALLENGES ME	
VICES THAT ENSNARE ME	
ADDICTIONS I LIVE WITH	
PERSONS/EVENTS THAT GENERATE FEAR, ANGER OR GRIEF	
PERSONS/EVENTS THAT GENERATE FAITH, HOPE OR LOVE	
STORY LINES IN BOOKS, MOVIES. THAT ALWAYS BRING ME TO TEARS	
WHAT ALWAYS MAKES ME ANGRY	
WHAT ALWAYS MAKES ME GRATEFUL	
WHAT ALWAYS INSPIRES FEAR IN ME	
MY ULTIMATE FAITH GOAL	
THE AREA OF MY LIFE MOST OUT OF CONTROL	

LOOKING FOR LINKS IN MY STORY

Tuesday—I fill in the second diagnostic chart below with the goal to write at least 3 of the 5 things requested in each category.

FIVE COMMANDMENTS I AM MOST CHALLENGED IN LIVING	FIVE VICES THAT ENSNARE ME	FIVE ADDICTIONS I LIVE WITH	FIVE PERSONS/EVENTS THAT CAUSE FEAR, ANGER OR GRIEF

Wednesday—I will contemplate the diagnostic chart I filled in on Tuesday, praying to see if there are any *obvious* links between Commandments, vices, addictions and persons or events. I draw lines linking the connections *that are clear to me*.

Thursday—I will contemplate the next diagnostic chart of how sin impacted the life of St. Ignatius to see the links in his original (root), core (trunk), and manifest (fruit) sins.

MANIFEST SINS
The Fruit or Ornamentation
(Ignatius' addictive gambling, reactive anger and sexual self-indulgence)
Manifest Fear, Anger, and Grief, moral weaknesses, vices, addictions, and sinful habits that are the
most visible to you.

CORE SINS
The Trunk or Superstructure
(Ignatius' arrogance, blinded conscience and narcissism)
Disobedience and narcissism, along with its fear, anger, and grief, that forms the trunk or superstructure of your daily life, feeding on originating sins and events.

ORIGINAL SINS
The Roots or Foundation
(Original Sin and concupiscence that wounded Ignatius' heart and soul; distinctive family/clan sin and/or early life-events that wounded him spiritually, psychologically and physically)
Ancient, originating events that rooted the patterns of disobedience and narcissism along with its Fear, Anger, Grief.

Friday—I will contemplate the elements from the diagnostic charts I filled in earlier in the week and pray for the grace to see more clearly how sin has impacted me at the roots, trunk and fruit of my life. For each of the blank spaces on the last chart, I will write those elements (at least one each) that I believe are present in my life as Original Sins (root), core sins (trunk) and manifest sins (fruit).

LOOKING FOR LINKS IN MY STORY

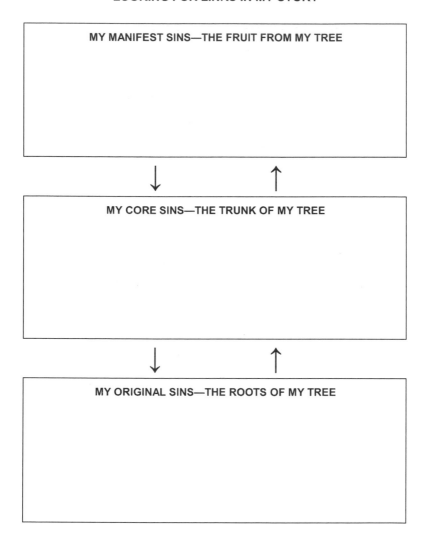

MY MANIFEST SINS—THE FRUIT FROM MY TREE

MY CORE SINS—THE TRUNK OF MY TREE

MY ORIGINAL SINS—THE ROOTS OF MY TREE

I am starting a Relationship that will carry me
for the rest of my life.

All relationships require time and patience.
I will strive for patience and ask for God's help
when I don't understand a lesson.

I will learn the fundamentals and open my heart to God.

I trust that God will lead me.

I believe that my *Sacred Story* will unfold in truth,
in powerlessness and with my patience.

I believe that Jesus awaits me with His grace, mercy and forgiving love.

ᘔ

Week 11

FIRST

I will select my 15-minute quiet times for the week ahead and once again visualize where I will go each day and at what times. I will ask God for the grace to keep those times sacred. I will have my notebook at hand for each prayer period for this week. I will spend no more than 15-minutes in each formal prayer session.

SECOND

My 15-minute quiet prayer this eleventh week is a simple prayer exercise for Sunday through Saturday. I will write a letter to Christ Jesus asking for His help and healing for my life story. The letter is my confession of faith in Him who comes to heal me and forgive me. The letter is also a snapshot of my whole life. It is my opportunity to tell Christ where I have been wounded by sin, life's difficulties, how I struggle for wholeness and why I need Jesus' help and forgiveness. I will ask Jesus to be my Savior.

THIRD

My prayer sessions <u>this week only</u> can be longer than 15-minutes, because I am writing a letter. Nevertheless, I still begin each prayer period by sitting in a comfortable position. I will use my favorite name for Jesus (Christ Jesus, Lord and Savior, Redeemer...), for this week's personal prayer because Christ is the person who won my freedom from sin and death. This week, He is the one to whom I am speaking.

I will awaken to the present moment.

I will take each day and each exercise as it comes.

I cannot do *Sacred Story* better by going faster.

I will ask God to help me.

I will awaken to my spiritual nature and
to the inspirations that inspire faith, hope and love.
I will awaken to the inspirations that
inspire cynicism, impatience and lusts. I will wake up!

Focus Affirmation for Week Eleven
I will say this affirmation aloud once daily:
*Lord Jesus Christ, you experience great joy when I allow you to forgive
my weakness and sinfulness because you lived, died and rose again so
that I might have new life in you.*

ভ

Read this at the beginning of the week

A LETTER TO CHRIST JESUS

You may be wondering how you will make use of the prayer exercises from
the past few weeks. This will become clearer as your journey continues. Have
faith that your efforts will be spiritually fruitful. You are not expected to see the
complete picture in everything you have done so far. We have been on a
treasure hunt of sorts, pulling together many diverse elements of our life story.
The process of piecing the parts together will happen throughout the rest of your
life—both by your careful attention and by the grace of God. So, have patience
and trust. As time goes on, everything you have done up to this point will take on
greater meaning for you (if you follow the lessons in order *and* ask for God's
help).

For this week's exercise to prepare your Whole-Life Confession, you can
refer to some of what you wrote in the last weeks.

What do we mean by a Whole-Life Confession? A Whole-Life Confession is
different from a confession of your whole life. It is not helpful, nor is it required to
twice confess sins and faults you have already confessed. The opportunity of a
Whole-Life Confession is to look at connections and patterns of sin and failure
across *your whole life*—what we have been working on these past weeks. You
are invited to ask for God's help to see a holistic picture of your life—your
story—with Christ as your Divine Physician and healer.

*It must be recalled that this reconciliation with God leads, as it were, to
other reconciliations, which repair the other breaches caused by sin. The*

94

forgiven penitent is reconciled with himself in his inmost being, where he regains his innermost truth. He is reconciled with his brethren whom he has in some way offended and wounded. He is reconciled with the Church.
He is reconciled with all creation.[8]

Think of this confession as your report to Christ—based on your spiritual diagnosis—after these weeks of prayerful reflection. You can confess current issues and past issues that have been overlooked. As you do this, you are telling Christ the chronic *patterns* of sin and weaknesses your prayer and reflection with the help of God's grace has awakened in you. And, importantly, how these issues are *linked* to your life story—your history.

As you look at your life story with Christ, the Divine Physician, address Him directly and acknowledge why you need Him as your Savior. This *could* be the very first time you have reviewed your life, seen clearly why you cannot save yourself, and directly asked Jesus to be your Savior. What a profound grace to know why you cannot save yourself and to ask Christ for this tremendous gift! A profound grace, indeed!

Look at this from Christ's perspective, too. There is no greater gift you give to Christ than your sinfulness and weaknesses as you ask for His healing love, mercy and forgiveness. By doing so, you take seriously the gift of His life, passion, death and resurrection. You are telling Jesus you need His cross to be healed. You are thanking Jesus for suffering and dying for *you* so you can be renewed in Him. This is the real focus of Christian life! Jesus really loves you and wants to hear what you have to say to Him. He waits with compassion and great longing to hear your story. He waits to carry your burdens and to offer you His forgiveness.

The Pharisees and their scribes complained to his disciples, saying, "Why do you eat and drink with tax collectors and sinners?" Jesus said to them in reply, "Those who are healthy do not need a physician, but the sick do. I have not come to call the righteous to repentance but sinners." Lk 5: 30-32

With Jesus as your Divine Physician, a Whole-Life Confession makes *perfect* sense. He understands you and everything about your life. He has an intense desire to hear your life story and wants to respond as your Savior. What follows are a few suggestions to help you prepare for this simple, holy and graced letter. Your letter is a statement of your need and a confession of your sins and patterns of sin, as well as a request for forgiveness, healing and hope:

1.   One picture is worth a thousand words—
Your life is a picture, a story. Write a letter to Christ that is *no more* than 1000 words. If typed, it would be about three and a half pages double-spaced. But you

do not have to write that much. I repeat: write *no more* than 1000 words.

2. *Personal words that are heartfelt—*
Early on you identified the name for God that touches your heart. This week find the name for Christ that speaks to your heart. Perhaps it is Christ Jesus, Lord and Savior or My Lord. You are speaking to the One who won your victory and who came into the world to save you. This week, we want to speak directly to Christ Jesus. Speak to Jesus in the first person: "Please forgive…; I remember; I suffered; please heal me…." Write the confessional story—your history—directly from your heart to the heart of Jesus.

3. *Strive for honesty—*
Strive earnestly for courage and honesty in your letter. The letter is for you and you only, unless you choose to share it in Sacramental Confession. You need not impress anyone. What is significant is your courage and honesty. Be honest too, about the forgiveness you need to extend to others. *Write from your heart.*

4. *You are not climbing Mount Everest—*
PLEASE, pray for the grace not to turn this simple, graced letter/confession opportunity into a huge, exhausting task. You are not climbing a mountain. You are having a conversation with Christ about your life. Hear Him say to you:

Come to me, all you who labor and are burdened, and I will give you rest. Take my yoke upon you and learn from me, for I am meek and humble of heart; and you will find rest for your selves. For my yoke is easy and my burden light.
Mt 11: 28-29

5. *Pray for Patience and Compassion—*
Awakening to your life story will take the rest of your life. It takes a lifetime for Christ's work of healing and forgiveness to embrace your heart and soul. There is no finish line or ultimate enlightenment you can reach on this earth. You will always need healing at deeper levels. You will constantly grow in love and enlightenment, selflessness and humility until the day you pass from this earth. You will not be finished until the day the Divine Physician sits you down at His Eternal Banquet.

But as for the seed that fell on rich soil, they are the ones who, when they have heard the word, embrace it with a generous and good heart, and bear fruit through perseverance. Lk 8:15

6. *Set the scene in your heart's imagination—*
Here is how you might set your heart's imagination as you write: imagine you

have been given the opportunity to be alone with Christ when He is walking from one town to another. You will have 15-minutes with Him…alone. See the road and the other followers walking up ahead of you and the Lord. No one else can hear you. Write your letter as if you are speaking to Christ in this setting. He knows why you want to speak with Him and is ready to hear you. Before you begin talking about your life, He looks you in the eyes and says: "Soon, I will be lifted up on my cross. I am doing this for you so that you can find forgiveness, healing and hope for the sins, weaknesses and suffering you experience in your life. As I conquer all death and sin—as I breathe my last breath—I will hold you and your life story in my heart. You will find victory and eternal life in me and one day be with me in paradise."

Then Jesus said, "Father, forgive them, they know not what they do." Then he said, "Jesus, remember me when you come into your kingdom." He replied to him, "Amen, I say to you, today you will be with me in Paradise." Lk 23: 34, 42-3.

What follows is a template for how you might structure your heart-felt conversation/letter/confession to Christ Jesus, the Divine Physician:

- ✠ "Dear Jesus, I am so grateful for all the gifts you have given to me." (Spend some time writing from your heart why you are grateful. Use Jesus' name often as you write and give *very particular* examples of why you are grateful).
- ✠ "Lord, I am profoundly aware of how some of my past experiences (life history, family, friends, work, school, neighbors) are linked to areas of un-freedom in my life and how these experiences have created embarrassing and/or discouraging habits and rooted patterns of sinfulness." (Spend some time looking back over your life and offer particular examples that capture the links and patterns of sins, addictions, vices, and commandments that cause you to stumble. If you cannot discern patterns yet, simply speak about these areas individually. If there are central people in your life story who are linked to these destructive patterns, mention them to Christ. If you are confused about some of the things you do, tell Jesus what they are and then, ask for His help to better understand why you do what you do. From your heart, ask Christ's grace to gain greater freedom from these sins and patterns of sin, habits and vices).
- ✠ "But Lord, there is one central pattern of sin that causes me the most embarrassment, shame, confusion and discouragement." (Spend some time being very specific in your conversation with Jesus about this pattern of sin in your life and why it is so difficult for you. Tell Jesus the particular circumstances when you seem to fall under its spell the most

and the circumstances that surround your failures. Tell Jesus how you feel when you fail. If there are specific incidents of this pattern of failure that you have not confessed, tell them to the Lord, and ask for His healing and forgiveness).

✠ "Lord Jesus, I have come to realize that I cannot save myself and I ask for your compassion. I ask that you be my Savior. Rescue me and be with me all the rest of my days." (Spend some time speaking with Jesus, in very particular words, about why you have come to realize you cannot save yourself and why you need His grace—why you need Him to be your Savior. Tell Him in very clear words why you know—because of x, y and z—why you cannot save yourself. Tell Him about any persons you cannot forgive and what they did to you. Tell Him why it is difficult for you to forgive them. Tell Jesus that with His grace, you can desire to forgive them, and in time, be able to forgive them. Ask for that grace. Ask the Lord to keep His attention on the core issues in your life (name them) that constantly trip you up, and pray that you never tire in seeking His forgiveness and that you never lose hope in yourself or in Him. Ask the Lord to be your Savior).

✠ "Lord Jesus, I thank you that you have given me the courage to face any fears I had and to trust you with my life in this healing sacrament of your redeeming love." (Close your letter/conversation/confession with very personal words from your heart, thanking Jesus that He has heard your prayer and that He will always be your Savior. With heartfelt words, thank Jesus that He understands your life and ask that He continue to walk with you, give you grace, and be with you till the end of your days. Ask Jesus for the grace to serve Him more each day with everything you think, say and do. Ask for the grace to work for fruit that will endure to eternity).

✠ "Thank you Jesus for being my Savior." (Close your heartfelt letter by thanking Jesus for being your Savior. Ask for His continued grace as He writes your *Sacred Story*).

ও

I am starting a Relationship that will carry me
for the rest of my life.

All relationships require time and patience.
I will strive for patience and ask for God's help
when I don't understand a lesson.

I will learn the fundamentals and open my heart to God.

I trust that God will lead me.

I believe that my *Sacred Story* will unfold in truth,
in powerlessness and with my patience.

I believe that Jesus awaits me with His grace, mercy and forgiving love.

છૂ

Week 12

FIRST

I will select my 15-minute quiet times for the week ahead and visualize where I will go each day and at what times. I continue to ask God for the grace to keep my times of prayer sacred and to seek a place that is technology-free. I will bring my notebook to each prayer period and commit to spending no more than 15-minutes in each formal prayer session.

SECOND

My 15-minute quiet prayer this twelfth week, consists of one simple prayer exercise for Sunday through Saturday.

THIRD

I will keep working on my letter, or if it is complete, I will reflect on what I have written during my prayer times. I will read and reflect with Christ as my companion and stay with my letter to Christ Jesus asking for His help and healing for my life story.

I will awaken to the present moment.
I will take each day and each exercise as it comes.
I cannot do *Sacred Story* better by going faster.
I will ask God to help me.
I will awaken to my spiritual nature and to
the inspirations that inspire faith, hope and love.
I will awaken to the inspirations that
inspire cynicism, impatience and lusts. I will wake up!
Be Not Afraid!
I will not make any decisions that bend into my fears and my anxieties.

They are founded on bad information
and will not lead to my peace.

Focus Affirmation for Week Twelve
I will say this affirmation aloud once daily:
*Lord Jesus Christ, I affirm you will always transform my sin and weakness
into grace and blessings! I will not be afraid!*

ଔ

Read this reflection at the beginning of the week

Your letter to Jesus may or may not be complete. Use your 15-minute prayer times this week to continue the reflection and writing process, or if complete, reflect and pray with the letter. Bring your notebook to your prayer sessions. After each session, write one sentence for what brings you the most hope as you read your letter and one sentence for what causes you the most discouragement as you read your letter.

If you have resolved to bring your letter to confession, make an appointment with a priest for Sacramental Reconciliation. Consciously commit to scheduling the appointment for some time in the next two weeks. If the priest you seek for confession is not familiar with the *Forty Weeks* method, explain to him what it is. Let him know that you would like to read to Christ your confession in this letter form. Tell him that you have spent twelve weeks preparing it and thank him for letting you go to confession in this manner.

ଔ

I am starting a Relationship that will carry me
for the rest of my life.
All relationships require time and patience.
I will strive for patience and ask for God's help
when I don't understand a lesson.
I will learn the fundamentals and open my heart to God.

I trust that God will lead me.

I believe that my *Sacred Story* will unfold in truth,
in powerlessness and with my patience.

I believe that Jesus awaits me with His grace, mercy and forgiving love.

છ૦

Week 13

FIRST
I will select my 15-minute quiet times for the week ahead and visualize where I will go each day and at what times. I will petition the Lord for the grace to keep sacred my times of prayer and strive to pray in a place that is technology-free; a place apart. I will bring my notebook to each prayer period and commit to spending no more than 15-minutes in each formal prayer session.

SECOND
For this week's 15-minute prayer sessions, I have one simple prayer exercise for Sunday through Saturday.

THIRD
I continue to stay with my letter to Christ Jesus asking for His help, insight, patience, grace and healing for my life story. I will either keep writing or speaking to Christ, or sit with my letter in prayer. Since the letter is also a snapshot of my whole life, it is of supreme spiritual worth to be present to Christ with my life story. So I will either continue writing or pray over what I have written and confessed.

I will awaken to the present moment.
I will take each day and each exercise as it comes.
I cannot do *Sacred Story* better by going faster.
I will ask God to help me.
I will awaken to my spiritual nature and to the inspirations
that inspire faith, hope and love.
I will awaken to the inspirations that inspire cynicism,
impatience and lusts. I will wake up!

Be Not Afraid! I will not make any decisions
that bend into my fears and my anxieties. They are founded
on bad information and will not lead to my peace.

ርሄ

Read this at the beginning of the week

We are a people of faith who live in the light of the Cross of Christ, the light of the Resurrection of Christ and the light of the Second Coming of Christ. We are His sisters and brothers. We live because we are loved by God.

During these days as you reflect on your Whole-Life Confession, remember that confession includes grateful praise along with admission of sins and faults. Remember that Christ, the Divine Physician, came so that you can triumph *through* your failings and weaknesses, by His healing and forgiving grace, to produce fruit that endures to eternity. Remember how St. Ignatius marveled once that he did not think, in the entire history of the Church, there was ever someone who sinned as much as he did, who was also given so many graces. "Where sin increased, grace overflowed all the more." (Rom 5:20).

If you have not yet made your confession, you have time to both write a letter and time to go to confession this week. These weeks of prayer are about developing a deeper relationship with God in Christ. Do not surrender to your anxiety or perfectionism that may suggest that you have not done enough of the prayer sessions to make a confession or write a letter. If you feel you are behind, do what you can to keep **moving forward**.

If you have made your confession, use your 15-minute prayer periods this week to be with Christ and the letter you wrote to Him. Bring your notebook to your prayer sessions. After each session, write one sentence for what brings you the most hope as you read your letter, and one sentence for what causes you the most discouragement as you read your letter. Linger over the words and phrases that brought you hope and peace. Remember the experience of your confession and allow its graces to penetrate deeply into your heart.

ርሄ

I am starting a Relationship that will carry me
for the rest of my life.

All relationships require time and patience.
I will strive for patience and ask for God's help
when I don't understand a lesson.

I will learn the fundamentals and open my heart to God.

I trust that God will lead me.

I believe that my *Sacred Story* will unfold in truth,
in powerlessness and with my patience.

I believe that Jesus awaits me with His grace, mercy and forgiving love.

&

Part Two
Learning Sacred Story Prayer

"It was not you who chose me, but I who chose you and
appointed you to go and bear fruit that will remain,
so that whatever you ask the
Father in my name he may give you.
This I command you: love one another."

Jn 15: 16-17

Week 14

FIRST

As I begin Part Two in *Sacred Story*, I consciously determine if it is beneficial to change the number of times I pray daily. I will ask for patience to start each day with renewed commitment, even if I miss a day's prayer. I will bring my notebook to each prayer period. I will begin this week a habit of a simple daily journal. [9] At the end of each day, I will mark one event that increased my faith, hope and love, and one event that decreased my faith, hope and love.

SECOND

I will listen attentively to my experience to discern the two plot lines in my story. I will do this by consciously attending to my fantasies and/or daydreams.

THIRD

As I begin Part Two in *Sacred Story*, I will encounter several more foundational exercises. Like the exercises leading up to a Whole-Life Confession, these additional exercises will help identify important narrative themes in my story that I can bring to my formal times of prayer. The exercises' meaning and energy come from my asking God for help and grace—from my *relationship* with God.

I will awaken to the present moment.
I will awaken to my spiritual nature.
I will not make any decisions based on fear.

Focus Affirmation for Week Fourteen
I will say this affirmation aloud once daily:
My Sacred Story *takes a lifetime to write.*

CB

Read this at the beginning of the week

Take this full week after your Whole-Life Confession for this Ignatian Daydream/Fantasy exercise. It is inspired by St. Ignatius' "awakening" while he was recovering from his battle wound. Now is the perfect time to do this exercise, because after Reconciliation you have much more clarity and peacefulness to see, by grace, the contours of your story.

Ignatius, while recovering from battle, discovered that his daydreams and fantasies were pulling his heart in two different directions. One direction was toward vain, self-serving, self-indulgent exploits rooted in his wounded human nature. The other direction was toward holy aspirations representing his authentic human nature, and the deepest aspirations of his heart. These latter daydreams had been inaudible and out of view most of his life. The black noise of temptations, and the false self-portrait, both deafened and blinded his heart. Aided by grace he awoke to the existence of the fantasies and daydreams, and by grace, discovered that only one of the two storylines expressed his authentic human nature—the deepest dream of his heart.

You will discover that many daydreams and fantasies fight for room in the conscious and unconscious spaces of your heart. No matter their differences, or the fact that they might seem unrelated, they always fall into the two storylines representing the two trajectories of your heart. One set of daydreams or fantasies trend toward infinite Love, holy appetites, integration, humility, reconciliation, hope, peace, wakefulness, sobriety and gratitude. The other set of daydreams/fantasies trend toward finite things, appetites low and earthly, disintegration, narcissism, resentment, cynicism, anxiety, unconsciousness, drunkenness and lack of gratitude.

Begin this week by paying attention to your daydreams and fantasies. Let them see the light of day. You will find their traces everywhere: in things you purchase, or want to buy; in your favorite songs, movies and stories; in radio and TV programs that claim your passionate loyalty; in the lives of artists, athletes, actors, saints, politicians—the heroes you emulate and admire, or those you disdain; in your programs of study and your job applications; in the friends you have, or wish you had; in the things that happened, or things you wish had not happened; in the places you want to visit or make your home, and the places you want to leave and never return; in the worlds you visit in cyberspace, or the one you visit in your inner sacred space; what motivates you to exercise and discipline yourself or what influences you to fall out of shape; in the individuals and groups you love, and those whose love you reject; the people you offer forgiveness, or those you refuse to forgive; in the people you envy, wishing you had their looks, talents, connections, wealth, happiness, or relationships; in what causes you to practice your faith or causes you to forget and forgo its practice; in the persons and events that stir your sexual lusts, or persons and events that stir your childlike innocence; in what opens your wallet to give to the needy, or closes it to their need; in the stories, images and experiences that break your heart, or those that cause your heart to be joyful; in the things that make you cry, or that make you laugh; in the person or group you want to spend the rest of your life with, or the person or group you want to spend the rest of our life avoiding; in what moves your heart to thanklessness, or makes it swell with gratitude.

The Prayer Exercise

Do this exercise in the context of your daily 15-minute prayer sessions, allowing it to permeate your actual daydreams. Your brief journal entry at the end of the day can itemize *just one* thing that brought you hope and peace that day, and *just one* thing that eroded your hope and peace. In light of this fantasy exercise, focus on themes related to the two main daydreams/fantasies that you unconsciously or consciously entertain. An example: "I daydreamed about x today and it brought me joy because..."

Your own daydreams and fantasies may not be so sharply felt but will most likely align with the two themes described below.

Narcissistic Daydreams/Fantasies

Anxiety, fear, lusts, compulsive appetites, resentment and anger, control of others, getting even/ getting back, addictions, lost innocence, aggression and vices populate their story lines. In short, they are narcissistic dreams/fantasies linked to your broken heart and wounded human nature. These daydreams/fantasies generate electrical energy, excitement *and* urges to things low and earthly. They inflate your ego and excite you while you are fantasizing or engaging them, but they leave you dry, empty, hungrier and dissatisfied— even depressed—after the fact. Or out of your sadness, depression, anger, emptiness and dryness, you may turn to them for satisfaction and release—like a narcotic—a painkiller for your heart.

Grateful Daydreams/Fantasies

Peace, calm, self-control, forgiveness, surrendering angers and hatreds, appreciation of beauty and innocence, holy dreams and high ideals, inspirations to selfless love, desires for healing and the joy of making a difference and living a meaningful life are their storylines. These storylines are linked to your God-given human nature, and the deepest dreams of your heart. These daydreams/fantasies generate peace, tears, quiet hope and aspirations to all things innocent, beautiful and noble. They humble your heart and fill you with gratitude while you are fantasizing or engaging them, and they leave you fulfilled, content and satisfied—even joyful—after the fact.

Lord, you will open my lips;
and my mouth will proclaim your praise.
For you do not desire sacrifice or I would give it;
a burnt offering you would not accept.
My sacrifice, O God, is a contrite spirit;
a contrite, humbled heart, O God, you will not scorn.
(Ps 51: 17-19)

SO

NOTES

Week 15

FIRST

I will ask for the grace of patience to start each day with renewed commitment even if I miss a day's prayer. I will have my notebook at hand for each prayer period. I will remember to spend no more and no less than 15-minutes in each formal prayer session.

SECOND

I am listening this week for the way that pride or narcissism takes shape in my daily life. I will do this by engaging an attentiveness prayer that examines the two principal forms of narcissism (passive and aggressive).

THIRD

I will continue to draw consolation from my letter to Jesus and/or my Whole-Life Confession. Also, I can bring insights on narcissism from my daily life into my prayer times. *Sacred Story* prayer is rooted in my asking God for help. Through grace, an intimate relationship between myself and God is being established.

I will awaken to the present moment.
I will awaken to my spiritual nature.
I will not make any decisions based on fear.

Focus Affirmation for Week Fifteen
I will say this affirmation aloud once daily:
Be Not Afraid:
Fear comes from the enemy of my human nature.

ಬ

116

Read this at the beginning of the week

Recall how Ignatius of Loyola discovered a narcissistic pride at the root of all his manifest sins, addictions, spiritual dysfunction and emotional imbalances. In Genesis, pride is the principal sin of Adam and Eve, or as we might define it today, *narcissism*.[10] The serpent tempted both Adam and Eve with eating the fruit of the forbidden tree by telling them that their "eyes will be opened" and they would "be like gods" (Gen 3:5). The rest is the history of sin, sickness, and death.

The immense grief, sorrow and guilt of paradise lost, by human choice, are memories burned deep in the heart of each and every woman and man who has lived, is living, or will ever walk this earth. But praise God, because it is through the wound, guilt, and grief of paradise lost that we come to understand the divisions in our hearts (Jer 17:9). Although our sin separates us from God, it still points out the path that sets each woman and man on a journey back home to God and to our authentic self. St. Ignatius achieved his greatest enlightenment when he identified the pattern of sin in his story. Once he awoke to it, God used him powerfully in the work of redemption. God will do the same for each of us.

Awakening to our prideful narcissism is understood as a positive move toward deeper spiritual growth. It is not a depressing exercise to make us feel bad or fearful. If these negative emotions result from your prayer, set your eyes and heart on Christ Jesus, the Divine Physician. Recall that He looks on you with joy and love, as you discover the things that diminish your hope and spiritual freedom. Allow Christ to work His healing graces in your story. Remember our affirmation for this week: fear comes from the enemy of human nature.

How does narcissism work? Narcissism, or pride, (both words describe the same damaging spiritual darkness) makes *me* the center of the universe and the ultimate arbiter of all truth. Narcissism displaces God in order that I can be "like a god." From that first sin of narcissism flows humankind's banishment from paradise; the advent of pain, sickness and death; the emergence of evolutionary evil in family structures as evidenced by Cain's murder of Abel; and the fracturing of the human community as symbolized in the greed, competition and overweening pride underlying the parable of the Tower of Babel.

Man and woman consciously displaced God as their center and source, and made *themselves* center and source. From this results the fracturing of creation's harmony. A terminal virus of sin now infects the core of all living things. The corruption caused by this virus has even altered life at the cellular, molecular and biological level. Nothing in the created order has been left untouched or unharmed by the virus of this sin (Gen 3:17-19; Rom 8:18-27).

We are all born into it and we all participate in it. Self-centeredness is an equal opportunity employer. All serious Christian prayer disciplines target this core sin so that by the power of Christ's sacrifice, *creation itself would be set free from slavery to corruption and share in the glorious freedom of the children of God* (Rom 8:21).

Prayer Exercise

It is spiritually valuable—*exceedingly so*—to understand what form of prideful narcissism your life circumstances have shaped in you. It might be helpful to realize that no side of pride's face is better than the other. Both are equally difficult to admit! Both forms of prideful narcissism displace God in our lives and serve to mask our wounded human nature—our heart's grief at paradise lost.

With the Divine Physician's grace, ask to understand how you displace God as the center of your life. Ask to become aware of the grief, anger, and fear that grips you, and the void at the center of your heart and soul that only He can heal. The grace of a Whole-Life Confession gives us renewed humility. It fosters a desire to open more to Christ's life and the spiritual growth, insights, freedom, hope and peace it brings!

The following two exercises will help you identify your *type* of prideful narcissism. Spend the prayer periods of three days on each type (Monday, Tuesday and Wednesday OR Thursday, Friday or Saturday). You decide which type to reflect on first and which one second.

Note: this week's prayer exercise is *not* to solve your prideful narcissism problem! That *would* be discouraging (and impossible)! It is enough for now to *identify*, with the Divine Physician's grace, a *type* of narcissism that you judge more present in your story. I emphasize: it was when Ignatius awoke to his prideful narcissism that God was able to really work with him. You will likely discover one or the other of these two principal manifestations of prideful narcissism at the root of all things difficult in your life. Purposely, these two types are defined in *very stark language* so you can distinguish them clearly.

You most likely will not feel them as strongly in your story as they are drawn here. So in your reflection and prayer, attend more to the *type* to which you are susceptible, and not so much the *intensity*. Ask the Divine Physician to guide your prayerful awakening in peace, trust and hope. These two faces of narcissism capture the principal forms of pride that life's circumstances generate in human nature wounded by Original Sin.

ॐ

The Passive Narcissist

Take the prayer periods of three days to pray with the description of *The*

Passive Narcissist. It is vital to understand this type of Original Sin's pride manifesting in human dysfunction. Note briefly in your journal what you consider significant that causes anxiety or hope. Are the Passive Narcissist's qualities ones that typify your negative story?

This type of narcissism rehearses and repeats the anger, fear, anxiety and grief of old wounds and hurts. The passive narcissist complains, is grasping, cynical, and makes excuses for everything except his or her own bad behavior. The passive narcissist draws attention to herself or himself in every thought, word, and deed and says he or she is the center of attention these ways: "see how I have suffered;" "see how I have been victimized" "see how unfairly I am treated;" "see why I behave the way I do;" "see why I am justified in ..." The passive narcissist works hard to blame others for his or her wounds, and labors mightily in every thought, word and deed to make sure others know of their suffering. The passive narcissist takes pride and finds power and comfort in her or his victim status, whether it is real or perceived. The passive narcissist works very hard to maintain her or his victim status and remain powerless, refusing to take responsibility for changing her or his situation because changing the situation means confronting pain and offering forgiveness to those who helped you evolve this way. Changing also means losing your core identity of powerless victim. To lose this identity is to lose power and control. There are three main reasons for this.

First, losing victim status means literally losing power and control of the people and events in one's world. Second, the passive narcissist is disconnected from his or her authentic self. Losing the status of victim initiates an acute and fearful identity crisis because life's meaning and definitions of success have been intimately linked with being a powerless victim. Third, as a result of the loss of power and control and the loss of one's false identity, the passive narcissist will be confronted with the spiritual, psychological and emotional wounds hiding behind the passive narcissism.

During your daily activities, pay attention to sudden anger, anxiety, fear or grief that surfaces. Pray for graced insights to comprehend how sudden anger, temptation, anxiety, fear or grief touch the deep spiritual, emotional and physical wounds and Original Sins in your life. For those events that seem to jump out at you and capture your attention, consciously do this short exercise, speaking to Christ from your heart: Ask to not react but instead to be conscious of what you are reacting to.

✠ Ask to feel the heart's fear, temptation, anxiety, anger and grief present in the reaction.

✠ Ask for knowledge—for graced insight—to begin dismantling this immature, damaging, (aggressive-electrifying or passive-depressing) and self-glorifying process.

✠ Ask who or what initiated this particular pattern of reaction—of overpowering or blaming others—and why?

✠ Ask for courage to face the negative story of being a passive victim, because facing it can cause panic when you are used to being its slave but once confronted, facing it can bring you peace and freedom.

ॐ

The Aggressive Narcissist

Take the prayer periods of three days to pray with the description of *The Aggressive Narcissist*. It is vital to understand this type of Original Sin's pride manifesting in human dysfunction. Note briefly in your journal what you consider significant that causes anxiety or hope. Are the Aggressive Narcissist's qualities ones that typify your negative story?

This type of narcissism rehearses and repeats the anger, fear, anxiety and grief of old wounds and hurts. The wounded, prideful aggressor gets even, is grasping, and determined to best others, and to justify and excuse his or her behavior in the process. The aggressive narcissist draws attention to herself or himself in every thought, word, and deed and says he or she is the center of attention in these ways: "see how special and gifted I am;" "see that you never get in my way;" "see, you will never overpower me;" "see, I deserve what I have, because I earned it;" "see, no one will ever hurt me again."

The aggressive narcissist works hard never to let anyone best him or her, and labors mightily in every thought, word and deed to make sure others get the message of his or her superiority. The aggressive narcissist takes pride, and finds tremendous energy in her or his triumphs over others, real or perceived. The aggressive narcissist works very hard to maintain her or his winner status, for her or his negative story is now totally associated with being the winner. To lose winner status is to lose power and control. There are three main reasons for this.

First, losing winner status means losing the power and control of the people and events in one's world. Second, the aggressive narcissist is disconnected from his or her authentic self. Losing the status of winner initiates an acute and fearful identity crisis because life's meaning and definitions of success have been intimately linked with the story of being the winner. Third, as a result of the loss of power and control and the loss of one's false identity, the aggressive narcissist will be confronted with the spiritual, psychological and emotional wounds hiding behind the aggressive narcissism.

During your daily activities, pay attention to sudden anger, anxiety, fear or grief that surfaces. Pray for graced insights how sudden anger, temptation, anxiety, fear or grief touch the deep spiritual, emotional and physical wounds and Original Sins in your life. For those events that seem to jump out at you, and capture your attention, consciously do this short exercise, speaking to Christ from your heart: Ask to not react but instead to be conscious of what you are reacting to.

✠   Ask to feel the heart's fear, anxiety, anger and grief present in the reaction.
✠   Ask for knowledge—for graced insight—to begin dismantling this immature, damaging, (aggressive-electrifying or passive-depressing) and self-glorifying process.
✠   Ask who or what initiated this particular pattern of reaction—of overpowering or blaming others—and why?
✠   Ask for courage to face the negative story of being an aggressive winner, because facing it can cause panic when you are used to being its slave but once confronted, facing it can bring you peace and freedom.

THE PASSIVE NARCISSIST	THE AGGRESSIVE NARCISSIST
Self-identifies as a *victim*.	Self-identifies as a *winner*.
Is determined to have others notice how special he/she is by *pointing to his/her unfair suffering*.	Is determined to have others notice how special he/she is by *defeating all opponents*.
Is cynical and excuses bad behavior by insisting it is justified because of how much he/she *has suffered*.	Is cynical and excuses bad behavior by insisting it is justified because he/she *has earned it*.
Wallows in self-pity when hurt, whether the hurt is real or imagined.	*Is vindictive* when hurt, whether the hurt is real or imagined.
Blames anyone who criticizes or opposes him/her.	*Threatens* anyone who criticizes or opposes him/her.
Protects him/herself from being hurt again by *keeping wounds as fresh as possible*. If anything is too difficult or painful, he/she will *retreat into those painful memories* and turn *inward, away from others*.	Protects him/herself from being hurt again by *eradicating vulnerabilities*. If anything is too difficult or painful, he/she will act in a *conqueror role* and *dominate* others.
Wins by *emotional manipulation*.	Wins by *direct confrontation*.
Is secretly attached to his/her own *woundedness*.	Is secretly attached to the *power of defeating others*.
Is terrified of *taking control and personal responsibility*, and has difficulty admitting it to him/herself.	Is terrified of *surrendering control and being vulnerable*, and has difficulty admitting it to him/herself.

Why, Lord, do you stand afar
and pay no heed in times of trouble?
Arrogant scoundrels pursue the poor;
they trap them by their cunning schemes.

The wicked even boast of their greed;
these robbers curse and scorn the Lord.
In their insolence the wicked boast:
"God does not care; there is no God."
Yet their affairs always succeed;
they ignore your judgment on high;
they sneer at all who oppose them.
They say in their hearts, "We will never fall;
never will we see misfortune."
Their mouths are full of oaths, violence, and lies;
discord and evil are under their tongues
They wait in ambush near towns;
their eyes watch for the helpless
to murder the innocent in secret.
They lurk in ambush like lions in a thicket,
hide there to trap the poor,
snare them and close the net.
The helpless are crushed, laid low;
they fall into the power of the wicked,
Who say in their hearts, "God has forgotten,
shows no concern, never bothers to look."

Rise up, Lord! God, lift up your hand!
Do not forget the poor!
Why should the wicked scorn God,
say in their hearts, "God does not care"?

But you do see;
you take note of misery and sorrow;
you take the matter in hand.
To you the helpless can entrust their cause;
you are the defender of orphans.
Break the arm of the wicked and depraved;
make them account for their crimes;
let none of them survive.

The Lord is king forever;
the nations have vanished from his land.
You listen, Lord, to the needs of the poor;
you strengthen their heart and incline your ear.
You win justice for the orphaned and oppressed;
no one on earth will cause terror again.

(Ps 10)

&

Week 16

FIRST

I continue to ask for patience to start each day with renewed commitment. I will not be discouraged by the times I have missed prayer, but will instead ask God for help to be more faithful. I will bring my notebook for each prayer and resolve to spend no more and no less than 15-minutes in each prayer period.

SECOND

This week I am invited to learn the components of daily prayer in *Sacred Story*. My fidelity to the linked practice of these daily exercises will produce sustained spiritual growth and enlightenment. Ignatius was a strategist and he understood that spiritual exercises must be regular, focused, and open to grace. It is up to me to ask God for help in using these resources for my healing and spiritual growth.

THIRD

I will continue to draw consolation from my letter to Jesus and/or my Whole-Life Confession.

I will awaken to the present moment.

I will awaken to my spiritual nature.

I will not make any decisions based on fear.

I will practice Sacramental Reconciliation monthly.

Focus Affirmation for Week Sixteen

I will say this affirmation aloud once daily:

The pathway to God's peace and healing runs through my heart's

brokenness, sin, fear, anger and grief.

Read this at the beginning of the week

The most important activity in any day is the time I take to direct my *conscious* attention—my mind and heart—to God in a prayer relationship. Not only is my relationship with God the most important dimension of life, it is also a *relationship* that takes time to build—a lifetime! The depth of the relationship I desire will be evident in my fidelity to my prayer and sacramental life. As Scripture says, where your treasure is, so will your heart be (Mt 6:21).

The *Sacred Story Examen* prayer is a time-proven and highly effective prayer discipline for waking up to God's life in you, and your life in God. Practiced daily, you learn to surrender to God. You will find interior freedom and peace so your life's labor produces fruit that endures to eternity. Ignatius and the early Jesuits used this prayer in conjunction with frequent Sacramental Reconciliation as primary spiritual tools in their pastoral ministries in Europe and the New World.

The combined practice produced tremendous spiritual growth for countless thousands of souls, and still does so today. *Sacred Story* prayer can help you bring this dual spiritual practice into your Christian life to help you encounter Christ daily. It would be hard to find a more effective prayer discipline for this purpose.

This week's prayer disciplines are the support structure to the *Sacred Story* prayer form that you will start next week. It will be a tremendous benefit for you to learn these habits of thought and introduce them into your daily life. One of the chief victories of human nature's enemy in modern times is the violence of hyperactivity and a loss of interior silence.

The prayer disciplines this week, the *Sacred Story* prayer you start next week, and the regular practice of Reconciliation will help you counter this unique modern form of violence and open your heart to the voice of God. These practices are simple, take little time and if done faithfully, will move you forward on the path of integration and holiness with your *Sacred Story*. They are valuable spiritual practices for your life.

You will need this week's reference materials throughout the rest of the 40 weeks and beyond. Use this week's prayer periods to become familiar with them, and **bookmark them** so you can reference them often. Remember that you are not expected to implement these exercises this week.
We will begin implementing them next week.

ȣ

Prayer Exercise for Monday

Reflect on the instructions for the Daily Practice: *Prayer on Waking,* and use the

15-minutes to understand this discipline. Note briefly in your journal what you consider significant. When you begin to incorporate this exercise in your day, you should spend no more than fifteen to thirty seconds with it.

Sacred Story *Daily Practice: Prayer on Waking*
(15 to 30 seconds)

Before arising from your bed, consciously awaken to Creation, Presence, Memory, Mercy and Eternity. Note any significant movements in your heart and mind that come from your dreams. Note the state of your heart regarding any planned events of the day. Pay particular attention to feelings of peace or anxiety that stir in you. Anticipate any challenges that might confront you today, especially those linked to your wounded human nature that might stir fear, anger or grief in you. With gratitude, offer the thoughts, words, and deeds of your day to God.

⅓

Prayer Exercise for Tuesday

Reflect on the instructions for the Daily Practice: *During the Day Awareness Exercise,* and take the 15-minutes to understand this discipline. Note briefly in your journal what you consider significant. This exercise is linked to the exercises on sin, addiction, vices, commandments, narcissism and people in your life narrative.

Sacred Story *Daily Practice: During the Day Exercise Awakening to Sins, Addictions, and Compulsions*
(15 to 30 seconds)

Prepare your heart to watch and listen to your day as it unfolds. Be attentive to the events and circumstances that evoke temptation and incite your attraction to things low and earthly. These are easily recognized because they trigger your angers or addictions, or hook into your vices and the fault lines in your mind and heart. You are, in short, seeking to "wake up" to what makes living the Gospel of Christ Jesus difficult. Discipline yourself to not react to them outwardly.

Be curious about why you are tempted or angry. Remain open to the links between the events that spark your temptations, angers, addictions, narcissism and attractions to things low and earthly. Be conscious of the theme and the fact of the temptation. Wake up, and watch it with Christ so He can teach you how to grow in grace.

When you are tempted or when you fail in the course of your day, Jesus is the Divine Physician who desires to help you. He judges you, but with compassion. He desires you to awaken to patterns of addiction, anger, narcissism and chronic failures that rob you of freedom and peace so they can be healed, so you can be forgiven, so hope and peace may return to your life. Establish this ritual each time you are tempted, and each time you fail by giving in to your core sins, wounds, addictions, angers, and narcissism:

- ✠ **Declare** the specific sin, addiction, narcissistic habit or destructive compulsion as a false lover
- ✠ **Describe** the specific sin, addiction, narcissistic habit or destructive compulsion as coming from the enemy of your human nature
- ✠ **Descend** with Christ into your memory, to see and feel your first experience of this specific sin, addiction, narcissistic habit or destructive compulsion, asking Him to compassionately reveal the stress fractures, loneliness and wounds in your heart that it promised to satisfy
- ✠ **Denounce** the specific sin, addiction, narcissistic habit or destructive compulsion for its ruinous effect in your life
- ✠ **Decide** for Christ to heal this wound, diffuse the stress, anxiety and fear feeding it, and transform its damaging effects on your life into *Sacred Story*

Your goal in this short exercise is to invite God's grace to be present in your most difficult issues. Do the exercise two or three times a day on the most obvious sins, angers and failures. and then move on. Your awakening and healing is on God's schedule, not yours. Over time, this will become a spiritual exercise that comes naturally. It takes people varying amounts of time to make it a habit. But it will become a positive spiritual habit that decreases your fears, reveals your truest self, and deepens your trust in Jesus as your protector and healer. It will also open you to Christ constantly at the most critical moments during your day, reminding you that He is Lord and Savior of your life. Remember, you are not doing this exercise to learn how to save yourself. You are doing it to turn to the Savior who saves, forgives, loves and heals the sins, addictions, angers, and compulsions from which you cannot save yourself!

☙

Prayer Exercise for Wednesday & Thursday

Reflect on the instructions on the following pages for the Daily Practice: *Sacred Story Prayer at Mid-Day and at Night*, and take your 15-minute prayer periods to understand the purpose of this discipline. The content for this main *Sacred Story* prayer will be given to you over the next ten weeks starting in week seventeen. We will take ten weeks to learn the five meditations of Creation, Presence, Memory, Mercy and Eternity and how to combine them into a single 15-minute prayer exercise. While we use the Creation, Presence, Memory, Mercy, Eternity elements below to explain aspects of *Sacred Story* discipline, you will only fully understand these pieces once you have been introduced into their full practice in the next ten weeks. Consider this a preview, and do not be anxious if you "do not get it."

Sacred Story *Daily Practice: Sacred Story Prayer at Mid-Day and Evening*

Find a quiet place apart where you will not be disturbed. Bring with you the particular issues that surfaced in your day related to any specific annoyances or strong emotional events you experienced. Bring also your particular graces and inspirations.

During this time, you may kneel or sit, whichever is better suited to your prayer style, and more conducive to contemplative reflection, prayer, and devotion. Keep your eyes closed, or if opened, in a fixed position, not allowing them to roam.

Take a full 15-minutes for this exercise, no more and no less. You can consciously enter *Sacred Story* prayer for these 15-minute periods in one of two ways. Try both and determine which best suits your character and personality.

First Way: say "Creation" and continue meditating upon this word, as long as you find meaning, connections, delight, and inspirations in considering it and some positive fruit in the graces you seek. The same method of reflection should be followed for each meditation in *Sacred Story* (Presence, Memory, Mercy, Eternity).

Second Way: with each breath or respiration, say interiorly, "Creation," and from one breath to another say this word while you ponder the graces and inspirations you seek. For this same space of time, direct your attention mainly to the meaning of the word and graces you seek, the Person who is addressed, and why you need those graces. Follow this method with the other words (Presence, Memory, Mercy, Eternity) until you finish all the other meditations in *Sacred Story* prayer.

No matter which way you choose, at the beginning and at the end of the prayer time, in your imagination, *see* your whole life in God's hands and say inwardly, while breathing slowly and deeply: "Creation, Presence, Memory, Mercy, and Eternity."

For the body of the 15-minute prayer, after the opening mantra, and before the closing mantra, you can be flexible. On some days, you may spend equal amounts of time on each meditation. On other days, you may spend most of your time on one meditation. Let your heart lead you, based on the events of the day, and the images and emotions that emerge in your reflections.

As the lessons progress, and you learn each meditation in *Sacred Story* prayer, only say the word(s) of the specific lesson for each week. Some weeks you will have only one word. Other weeks you will be combining two or more until you finally combine all five into your completed prayer.

Close the 15-minute *Sacred Story* exercise with one or other of these two prayers:

Our Father
Our Father, who art in heaven, hallowed be Thy name.
Thy Kingdom come, Thy will be done, on earth, as it is in heaven.
Give us this day our daily bread, and forgive us our trespasses,
as we forgive those who trespass against us. Lead us not into temptation, but deliver us from evil. Amen.
(The prayer favored by Ignatius for this discipline)

Suscipe
Take Lord, receive, my liberty, my memory, my understanding, my entire will. Whatsoever I have or hold, You have given to me. I surrender it all back to you to be governed by your will. Give me only Your love and grace. This is enough for me, and I ask for nothing more. Amen.
(The prayer of St. Ignatius that concludes his Spiritual Exercises)

Prayer Exercise for Friday

Reflect on the instructions for the Daily Practice: *At Day's End*, and take your 15-minutes to understand this discipline. Note briefly in your journal what you consider significant.

Sacred Story *Daily Practice: Journal and Day's End Prayer*
(2 minutes—no more)

Write in your journal daily, after you end your last *Sacred Story* 15-minute prayer session. It is not a diary, but a logbook ("jottings," most accurately). What you write should be only single words or short phrases. The goal is to track the most significant events from your days. You are looking, first and foremost, for destructive patterns and trends in your life: patterns of fear, anger and grief, and patterns of sin, compulsion and addiction. In both of these patterns you are also looking for links to persons, events, or issues. On the graced end of the scale, you are looking for gratitude, hope, and peace linked to your *Sacred Story* and the daydreams and fantasies coming from the Divine-Inspirer.

The patterns and trends that are most relevant to *Sacred Story* in awakening to your life as a whole, and growing in interior freedom, are those that help you identify damaging, addictive, sinful habits *at their roots*. This is the principal goal of the *Particular Examen* (*PE*) of St. Ignatius. The *PE* helps individuals name and target the core sins that, more than others, distract us from our lives as *Sacred Story*.

 Be aware of patterns and trends that reveal the triggering mechanisms that make you easy prey to these habits, sins, angers, addictions and vices. Pay attention for patterns and trends that help you 'source' the 'origins' and 'roots' of those habits from your early life. Every day, take one minute before going to bed to write your brief journal entry. Remember your day's awakening exercises, and ask for the grace to be aware of the importance of any significant events that open you to anger, fear, grief or temptations, failures and sins. Ask for God's grace to see your life integrated and holistic as God does. God *longs* for your freedom, forgiveness, peace and healing.

 People who engaged the journal exercises gained much more from the entire *Sacred Story* method than those who did not write in their journal. Those who persevered in the journal practice are the ones who learned to be brief and to do as instructed: write no more than a few words or a short phrase. *You will not succeed in the journal practice if you take more than a minute or two a day to accomplish it!* Be brief, but specific.

Day's End Prayer
(15 seconds)

Upon retiring, listen to your heart for the state of spirit (peaceful or anxious), and what person or event inspires one or the other emotion. Speak a few words to God appropriate to your heart's peace or anxiety, and then invite God into your dreams.

CB

Prayer Exercise for Saturday

Reflect on the instructions for the Daily Practice: *At Week's End and at Month's End*, and take your 15-minutes to understand this discipline. Note briefly in your journal what you consider significant as you come to understand the purpose of this exercise.

Sacred Story *Daily Practice:*
Journal at Week's End Month's End

On Sunday (or Saturday if that is your "weekend"), in place of the day's end journal exercise, review the words and phrases from the preceding week. Ponder the words and phrases and ask to see the story of your whole life (Creation, Presence, Memory, Mercy and Eternity), and notice what particular insights or inspirations arise in you. Do not try to force insights. Most likely you will awaken gradually to patterns and trends.

Read over your journal entries from the week. Write a brief entry that captures any insights you have gained about your life over the course of the week's prayer and reflection process. Be attentive for any connections between persons, events, temptations, sins, fear, anger, grief, and strong emotions.

Pay particular attention to insights that can help you unravel the manifest and root spiritual and psychological stresses (sinful habits and psychological stresses or addictions and vices) that might be linked to significant events from your past history. Write these insights in a new section of your notes (perhaps entitled "Insights and Integration.") Date these reflections so you can watch your progressive growth and awakening.

Journal at Month's End

At the end of a month, in place of the week's end journal exercise, review your summary insights from these end-of-week exercises and look for any patterns that are emerging in your life story, especially those linked to the matrix of spiritual and psychological stresses highlighted by these insights. In your "Insights and Integration section," write short comments ("I think…" "I believe…" "I discovered…") that reveal any changes you experience in your life as a result of grace, healing, forgiveness, or the insights you receive.

It is highly recommended that you initiate a monthly ritual of receiving the sacrament of Reconciliation. This discipline of grace and sacramental accountability will give you energy to engage *Sacred Story* daily, and provide a clear focus for your life-narrative exercises. Those who engage this discipline of monthly Reconciliation, accompanied with *Sacred Story* prayer, advance immeasurably more than those who forgo the graces of this great sacrament of insight and healing. Your journal practice is excellent preparation for Sacramental Reconciliation.

When you receive monthly Reconciliation, consider following the same pattern as when you made your Whole-Life Confession. Write your confession and speak directly to Christ and talk about the events of your life and where you need healing and peace. Do not tire of repeating the same issues, sins and failures. Rely on and ask for the grace to see more and more clearly the roots and origins of the challenges in your life. St. Ignatius even suggested that his followers make a life confession every six months! He said it would help them make a *new book* of their lives. However, monthly Reconciliation is sufficient for measured spiritual, psychological, emotional growth and enlightenment unless you have grave matter that begs immediate attention [11]

The Daily Disciplines at a Glance
THE *SACRED STORY* TEMPLATE

- ✠ ***Prayer upon waking***—Attune to the day ahead and invite God's help
- ✠ ***Exercises during the day***—Awakening to your life
- ✠ **Sacred Story** *prayer*: Mid-day—Creation, Presence, Memory, Mercy, Eternity
- ✠ ***Exercises during the day***—Awakening to your life
- ✠ **Sacred Story** *prayer*: Evening—Creation, Presence, Memory, Mercy, Eternity
- ✠ **Sacred Story** *day journal*—Note significant event(s) of the day
- ✠ ***Prayer upon retiring***—Attune to your heart, invite God into your dreams
- ✠ ***Week's end journal***—Listen for trends, patterns, links
- ✠ ***Month's end journal***—Listen for trends, patterns, links
- ✠ ***Be renewed with monthly Reconciliation***—You will be powerfully graced
- ✠ ***Consult the Affirmations frequently***—Thumbnail discernment aids
- ✠ ***Live your faith***—Engage its spiritual disciplines, serving God and neighbor

ଔ

Lord, you have been our refuge
through all generations.
Before the mountains were born,
the earth and the world brought forth,
from eternity to eternity you are God
(Ps 90: 1-2)

ଓ

Week 17

FIRST
I will ask for patience to start each day with renewed commitment. I will have my notebook at hand for each prayer period and resolve to *spend no more and no less than 15-minutes in each formal prayer session.*

SECOND
I will continue to draw consolation and insight from my letter to Jesus and/or my Whole-Life Confession.

THIRD
This week I am invited to learn the first meditation in *Sacred Story* prayer: Creation. My fidelity to the linked practice of these daily exercises will produce life-long sustained spiritual growth and enlightenment.

.

I will awaken to the present moment.
I will awaken to my spiritual nature.
I will not make any decisions based on fear.
I will practice Sacramental Reconciliation monthly.

Focus Affirmation for Week Seventeen
I will say this affirmation aloud once daily:
God resolves all my problems with time and patience.

ॐ

Read this at the beginning of the week

Awakening to Sacred Story *Prayer—Creation*

Every day, consciously enter *Sacred Story* prayer during your set time(s). For these next weeks, we are building the five meditations of *Sacred Story* prayer. Set aside the other pieces and focus on *Creation* for your 15-minute prayer sessions this week.

Your focus is *Creation*. Remember the structure of the 15-minute sessions you were introduced to last week. Be faithful to the structure. Ignatius was wise in developing the ritual, and rituals are very important. The ritual itself detailed below does not save you. Yet the ritual, *faithfully practiced*, makes it easier for you to open your mind and heart to the One who does save you! Rituals are good.

Remember that the daily practice of *Sacred Story* has six parts:

1. Prayer upon waking
2. "Awareness" exercises during the course of the day
3. 15-minute *Sacred Story* prayer at Mid-day (for this week: **Creation** meditation only)
4. 15-minute *Sacred Story* prayer in Evening (for this week: **Creation** meditation only)
5. *Sacred Story* day journal (immediately following *Sacred Story* evening prayer)
6. Prayer upon retiring

During this week, we are only focusing on *Creation* for the 15-minute prayer periods so you can learn it *by heart*. There are four ways to learn a meditation: a single word; a single phrase; a single description (Prelude); and a single grace for which to pray (Illuminative Grace).

All four elements comprise a single exercise. It seems like a lot at first, but in time you will be able to understand the elements of *Creation* without having to refer to any text. One way to internalize the meaning of the meditation is to read through the prayer exercise text (the phrase, the Prelude, and the Illuminative Grace) and then ponder those ideas while using one of the two ways to focus (letting yourself be led by the inspirations of this word or letting yourself be led by the conversation with the Lord about the graces you seek related to this word).

Remember, eventually we will be mediating on five different words, but only spending significant time with those words that the Spirit is leading us to for that day. This is why it is important for us to learn both the *substance* for each of the words, as well as the standard meditation *process* for the 15-minute periods.

Do not be anxious about learning everything at once – we are going slowly for a reason! This week, focus on internalizing the meaning of *Creation* and learning the rhythm of the 15-minute prayer period.

The meditation text for *Creation* is below (remember, this is the summary of the word, which you will use as a guide during your meditation).

Prayer Exercise—Creation

CREATION

*I believe God created everything in love and for love; I ask for **heart-felt** knowledge of God's love **for me,** and for **gratitude** for the **general** and **particular graces** of **this day**.*

Prelude

God created the universe—all persons and all things—in love and for love. Every *thing*, and every person in creation is linked in Love, through Christ, in whom and for whom everything was made. We are made to reverence God and each other, and to delight in creation as both Divine gift and support for our lives. The God of All knows me personally and loves me, even before I was knit in my mother's womb. So fearfully and wonderfully made am I! (Ps 139: 13-14). My gratitude increases as my awakening to these truths is illuminated.

Illuminative Grace

Here I ask for what I desire: to know and feel God's tender and passionate love and to know myself as beloved—a treasure of God's heart in the grand symphony of creation. I pray for the grace of gratitude. In particular, I pray to know by whom I am created and why I am loved. I pray to know and believe that I am fearfully and wonderfully made.

Review the structure of the 15-minute prayer sessions

You will find these at the **bookmark** you left in Week 16.

ෆ

*When I see your heavens, the work of your fingers,
the moon and stars that you set in place—*

What is man that you are mindful of him,
and a son of man that you care for him?
Yet you have made him little less than a god,
crowned him with glory and honor.
You have given him rule over the works of your hands,
put all things at his feet:
O LORD, our Lord, how awesome is your name
through all the earth!
(Ps 8: 4-6)

❧

Week 18

FIRST

As I engage the *Sacred Story* prayer this week, I may find it helpful to *recommit* to my daily 15-minute sessions. I resolve to spend no more and no less than 15-minutes in each formal prayer session.

SECOND

For week eighteen I am invited to open my heart to Presence, the second meditation in *Sacred Story* prayer. I will strive to trust St. Ignatius' wisdom and engage the prayer disciplines at least once daily as he suggested.

THIRD

Meditation Two—PRESENCE: Use your first prayer session to read Presence and then do the Exercise as suggested during your 15-minute prayer sessions for the rest of the week.

I will awaken to the present moment.

I will awaken to my spiritual nature.

I will not make any decisions based on fear.

I will practice Sacramental Reconciliation monthly.

Focus Affirmation for Week Eighteen
I will say this affirmation aloud once daily:
I will always have difficulties in this life.

ᘓ

Read this at the beginning of the week

Awakening to Sacred Story *Prayer—Presence*

Every day, consciously enter *Sacred Story* prayer during your set time(s) For these next weeks, we are building the five meditations of *Sacred Story* prayer. Set aside the other pieces and focus on *Presence* for your 15-minute prayer sessions this week. Your focus is *Presence*. Remember the structure of the 15-minute sessions you were introduced to last week.

Be faithful to the structure. Ignatius was wise in developing the ritual, and rituals are very important. The ritual itself detailed below does not save you. Yet the ritual, *faithfully practiced*, makes it easier for you to open your mind and heart to the One who does save you! Rituals are good. Review the structure of the 15-minute prayer sessions. You will find these at the bookmark you left in Week 16.

Awakening to Sacred Story*—Presence*

Prayer Exercise: Presence

PRESENCE

*I believe God is **present** in **each moment** and **event** of my life, and I ask for grace to **awaken, see** and **feel** where and*
how God is present.

Prelude

The eternal God can only be experienced in the here and now, for everything in the universe is sustained by God's love in the present moment. When I worry about the past, or fret about the future, my consciousness of God, of creation, and of my deepest desires, is blocked. My challenge is to anchor both heart and mind **firmly** in the present: in each thought, word, and deed, as the story of my life evolves, in each moment, in God's presence.

Illuminative Grace

Here I ask for what I desire: to be present and awake to every feeling, thought, word and deed—in the present moment. I beg for the grace to wake up to God's presence in every person, experience, event—good or ill—that I encounter in my day.

CB

How lovely your dwelling,
O Lord of hosts!
My soul yearns and pines
for the courts of the Lord.
My heart and flesh cry out
for the living God.
As the sparrow finds a home
and the swallow a nest to settle her young,
My home is by your altars,
Lord of hosts, my king and my God!
Blessed are those who dwell in your house!
They never cease to praise you.

(Ps 84: 2-5)

SO

Week 19

FIRST
As I engage the *Sacred Story* prayer this week, I will make a point of reviewing my prayer discipline and make any necessary changes to be more faithful to the daily disciplines I have committed to. I also resolve to spend no more and no less than 15-minutes in each formal prayer period.

SECOND
For week nineteen I am combining meditations one and two in the *Sacred Story* prayer: Creation and Presence. I will enter my prayer at least once daily as St. Ignatius suggested.

THIRD
Meditations One and Two—*Creation* & *Presence*: I will commit to reviewing the prayer structures from Week 16.

I will awaken to the present moment.
I will awaken to my spiritual nature.
I will not make any decisions based on fear.
I will practice Sacramental Reconciliation monthly.

Focus Affirmation for Week Nineteen
I will say this affirmation aloud once daily:
There are just two ways to cope with my difficulties.
One leads to life, one to death.
I will choose life.

ભ્

Read this at the beginning of the week

Review the structure of the 15-minute prayer sessions. You will find these at the bookmark you left in Week 16. For this week, you are combining the first two meditations in *Sacred Story* Prayer: Creation and Presence. Use your 15-minute prayer sessions this week to pray these two meditations together, following the wisdom you learned in Week 16 for this practice.

Awakening to Sacred Story—*Creation, Presence*

Prayer Exercise: Creation, Presence

CREATION

*I believe God created everything in love and for love; I ask for the grace of a **heart-felt** knowledge of God's love **for me,** and for **gratitude** for the **general** and **particular graces** of **this day**.*

Prelude

God created the universe—all persons and all things—in love and for love. Every *thing*, and every person in creation is linked in Love, through Christ, in whom and for whom everything was made. We are made to reverence God and each other, and to delight in creation as both Divine gift and support for our lives. The God of All knows me personally and loves me, even before I was knit in my mother's womb. So fearfully and wonderfully made am I! (Ps. 139:13-14). My gratitude increases as my awakening to these truths is illuminated.

Illuminative Grace

Here I ask for what I desire: to know and feel God's tender and passionate love, and to know myself as beloved—a treasure of God's heart in the grand symphony of creation. I pray for the grace of gratitude. In particular, I pray to know by whom I am created and why I am loved. I pray to know and believe that I am fearfully and wonderfully made.

PRESENCE

*I believe God is **present** in **each moment** and **event** of my life, and I ask for grace to **awaken, see** and **feel** where and how God is present.*

Prelude

The eternal God can only be experienced in the here and now, for everything in the universe is sustained by God's love in the present moment. When I worry about the past, or fret about the future, my consciousness of God, of creation, and of my deepest desires, is blocked. My challenge is to anchor both heart and mind **firmly** in the present: in each thought, word, and deed, as the story of my life evolves, in each moment, in God's presence.

Illuminative Grace

Here I ask for what I desire: to be present and awake to every feeling, thought, word and deed—in the present moment. I beg for the grace to wake up to God's presence in every person, experience, event—good or ill—that I encounter in my day.

CB

LORD, who may abide in your tent?
Who may dwell on your holy mountain?
Whoever walks without blame,
doing what is right,
speaking truth from the heart;
Who does not slander with his tongue,
does no harm to a friend,
never defames a neighbor;
Who disdains the wicked,
but honors those who fear the LORD;
Who keeps an oath despite the cost,
lends no money at interest,
accepts no bribe against the innocent.
Whoever acts like this
shall never be shaken.
(Ps 15)

SO

NOTES

Week 20

FIRST

I resolve to ask God for help to be faithful to my prayer disciplines. I also resolve to spend no more and no less than 15-minutes for these times of prayer.

SECOND

For week twenty I am invited to enter the third meditation of Memory. As St. Ignatius suggested, I will engage my formal prayer at least once daily.

THIRD

Meditation Three—*Memory*: Use your first prayer session to read Memory and then do the Exercise as suggested during your 15-minute prayer sessions for the rest of the week.

I will awaken to the present moment.
I will awaken to my spiritual nature.
I will not make any decisions based on fear.
I will practice Sacramental Reconciliation monthly.

Focus Affirmation for Week Twenty
I will say this affirmation aloud once daily:
"Impossible" is not a word in God's vocabulary.

ങ

Read this reflection at the beginning of the week

Awakening to Sacred Story *Prayer—Memory*

Every day, consciously enter *Sacred Story* prayer during your set time(s). For these next weeks, we are building the five meditations of *Sacred Story* prayer. Set aside the other pieces and focus on *Memory* for your 15-minute prayer sessions this week. Your focus is *Memory*.

Be faithful to the structure. Ignatius was wise in developing the ritual, and rituals are very important. The ritual itself detailed below does not save you. Yet the ritual, *faithfully practiced*, makes it easier for you to open your mind and heart to the One who does save you! Rituals are good. Review the structure of the 15-minute prayer sessions. You will find these at the bookmark you left in Week 16.

Awakening to Sacred Story*—Memory*

Prayer Exercise—Memory

MEMORY

*I believe every violation of love committed by me and against me **is in my memory**, and I **ask God to reveal them to me**, especially those that have manifested themselves today, **so I can be healed**.*

Prelude

I hold in my heart, by the power of God's grace, the memory of every action—of every thought, word and deed—done to me and done by me, that has eroded my innocence. I affirm that these unloving thoughts, words and deeds have spiritual, physical, and emotional consequences that wound me, others, and creation and for which Christ had to suffer for my redemption. I believe all these unloving actions have both generational and evolutionary consequences. At the root of my own narcissism are some events that more than others, have more significantly distorted my heart and mind. These events cripple my desire and my ability to love selflessly and to freely forgive others.

Illuminative Grace

Here I ask for what I desire: to become conscious of my lost innocence; the grace to see and the power to touch the Original Sins and wounds, especially the most vital ones, which shape in me an anti-story instead of a *Sacred Story*. I ask for the grace of an illumined conscience to know intimately how these wounds and sins connect to **everything** I do that makes life burdensome; to know how and why these wounds so often compel me to violate God's life in myself, others and creation. I ask God for the grace to wake up so I can see, feel, and name these thoughts, words, and deeds, and bring them to the light of day, to be healed by the Divine Physician.

ೞ

Oh, that today you would hear his voice:
"Harden not your hearts as at Meribah,
as in the day of Massah in the desert,
Where your fathers tempted me;
they tested me though they had seen my works."
If today you hear his voice,
harden not your hearts.
(Ps 9: 8-9)

ഇ

151

Week 21

FIRST

As I engage the *Sacred Story* prayer this week, I will continue to ask God's help to be faithful to my commitment. I will also resolve to spend no more and no less than 15-minutes in each formal prayer session as St. Ignatius suggested.

SECOND

For week twenty-one I am invited to pray with the first three meditations in the *Sacred Story* prayer. As St. Ignatius suggested, I will commit to entering my prayer at least once daily.

THIRD

Meditation One, Two and Three— *Creation, Presence, Memory*: Use your first prayer session to read the Reflection and then do the Exercise as suggested during your 15-minute prayer sessions for the rest of the week.

I will awaken to the present moment.

I will awaken to my spiritual nature.

I will not make any decisions based on fear.

I will practice Sacramental Reconciliation monthly.

Focus Affirmation for Week Twenty-One
I will say this affirmation aloud once daily:
Sacred Story *leads to my freedom and authenticity,*
but does not always make me feel happy.

cs

Read this at the beginning of the week

Review the structure of the 15-minute prayer sessions. You will find these at the bookmark you left in Week 16. For this week, you are combining the first three meditations in *Sacred Story* Prayer. Creation, Presence and Memory. Use your 15-minute prayer sessions this week to pray these three meditations together, following the wisdom you learned in Week 16 for this practice. You can also refresh your memory on the Preludes and Illuminative Graces of these three meditations if you find it helpful.

Awakening to Sacred Story—*Creation, Presence, Memory*

Prayer Exercise—Creation, Presence, Memory

CREATION

I believe God created everything in love and for love; I ask for the grace of a **heart-felt** *knowledge of God's love* **for me,** *and for* **gratitude** *for the* **general** *and* **particular** *graces of this day.*

PRESENCE

I believe God is **present** *in* **each moment** *and* **event** *of my life, and I ask for grace to* **awaken, see** *and* **feel** *where and how, especially in this present moment.*

MEMORY

I believe every violation of love committed by me and against me **is in my memory**, *and I* **ask God to reveal them to me**, *especially those that have manifested themselves today,* **so I can be healed**.

Come, let us sing joyfully to the Lord;
cry out to the rock of our salvation.
Let us come before him with a song of praise,
joyfully sing out our psalms.
For the Lord is the great God,
the great king over all gods,
Whose hand holds the depths of the earth;
who owns the tops of the mountains.
The sea and dry land belong to God,
who made them, formed them by hand.
(Ps 95: 1-5).

SO

Week 22

FIRST
I will preview my week and visualize the places and times for my prayer. They will be places apart—technology-free zones. I also resolve to spend no more and no less than 15-minutes in each formal prayer session as St. Ignatius suggested.

SECOND
For week twenty-two I am invited to pray the fourth meditation in *Sacred Story* prayer: Mercy.

THIRD
Meditation Four— *Mercy*: I will begin my week reviewing the prayer structure from Week 16 and practice the prayer on Mercy for the rest of the week's prayer periods.

I will awaken to the present moment.
I will awaken to my spiritual nature.
I will not make any decisions based on fear.
I will practice Sacramental Reconciliation monthly.

Focus Affirmation for Week Twenty-Two
I will say this affirmation aloud once daily:
*My life's greatest tragedies can be transformed
into my life's major blessings.*

 C3

Read this at the beginning of the week

Awakening to Sacred Story *Prayer—Mercy*

Every day, consciously enter *Sacred Story* prayer during your set time(s). For these next weeks, we are building the five meditations of *Sacred Story* prayer. Set aside the other pieces and focus on *Mercy* for your 15-minute prayer sessions this week. Your focus is *Mercy*.

Be faithful to the structure. Ignatius was wise in developing the ritual, and rituals are very important. The ritual itself detailed below does not save you. Yet the ritual, *faithfully practiced*, makes it easier for you to open your mind and heart to the One who does save you! Rituals are good. Review the structure of the 15-minute prayer sessions. You will find these at the bookmark you left in Week 16.

Awakening to Sacred Story*'s Meditations—Mercy*

Prayer Exercise—Mercy

MERCY

*I believe that **forgiveness** is the only **path to healing and illumination**. I beg for the **grace of forgiveness**, and the **grace to forgive**, especially for the general and particular failures of this day, and from my past.*

Prelude

The path to Christian holiness and an illumined consciousness runs through the darkest memories and deeds of your life, strangely enough. These memories and deeds corrupt your innocence and blind your vision to the sacredness of all life. These memories and deeds can, by choice, act as a wall blocking the peace that leads to holiness and highest consciousness, or as a gate opening to them. The gate is unlocked by forgiveness and compassion; both received from God, and then extended to all those entwined with the lost innocence that broke your heart: those who hurt you, those whom you hurt, and the gifts of creation that you abused or misused as a result. This miracle of peace and enlightenment is attainable through Christ, who bore in love the wounds of every sin and dark deed since time immemorial. Christ has the power to transform darkness, sin and death into grace for the salvation of the world.

Illuminative Grace

Here I ask for what I desire: for the grace to forgive any person who wounded my innocence, or who broke my heart. I pray to not only forgive them, but to have compassion and mercy on them. I ask for the grace of mercy and forgiveness for those whose hearts I have broken, and whose innocence I have wounded, and the gifts of creation that I have misused. I beg to know personally the One who absorbed in His heart and body every wound and every sin of this dark evolution across the millennia. I beg for the dual knowledge of sin and mercy as it affects my life story. I beg for patience, knowing that accepting and offering mercy and forgiveness leads me to holiness. This awakening to highest consciousness takes a lifetime.

଼

Fill us at daybreak with your mercy,
that all our days we may sing for joy.
Make us glad as many days as you humbled us,
for as many years as we have seen trouble.
Show your deeds to your servants,
your glory to their children.
(Ps 90: 14-16)

଼

NOTES

160

Week 23

FIRST

I will assess my fidelity to the 15-minute prayer periods and make the adjustments necessary to be more faithful. I resolve to *spend no more and no less than 15-minutes in each formal prayer session.*

SECOND

For week twenty-three I am invited to combine meditations one through four in the *Sacred Story* prayer. I will enter my prayer at least once daily as St. Ignatius suggested.

THIRD

Meditation One, Two, Three and Four— *Creation, Presence, Memory and Mercy*: I will use my first prayer session to review the daily prayer structure and then use my 15-minute prayer periods for the rest of the week for the combined prayer.

I will awaken to the present moment.
I will awaken to my spiritual nature.
I will not make any decisions based on fear.
I will practice Sacramental Reconciliation monthly.

Focus Affirmation for Week Twenty-Three
I will say this affirmation aloud once daily:
*Times of peace and hope always give way
to times of difficulty and stress.*

ॐ

Read this reflection at the beginning of the week

Review the structure of the 15-minute prayer sessions. You will find these at the bookmark you left in Week 16. For this week, you are combining the first four meditations in *Sacred Story* Prayer: Creation, Presence, Memory and Mercy. Use your 15-minute prayer sessions this week to pray these four meditations together, following the wisdom you learned in Week 16 for this practice. You can also refresh your memory on the Preludes and Illuminative Graces of these three meditations if you find it helpful.

Awaken to **Sacred Story:** *Creation, Presence, Memory, Mercy*

Prayer Exercise—Creation, Presence, Memory, Mercy

CREATION

I believe God created everything in love and for love; I ask for the grace of a **heart-felt** *knowledge of God's love* **for me,** *and for* **gratitude** *for the* **general** *and* **particular** *graces of this day.*

PRESENCE

I believe God is **present** *in* **each moment** *and* **event** *of my life, and I ask for grace to* **awaken, see** *and* **feel** *where and how, especially in this present moment.*

MEMORY

I believe every violation of love committed by me and against me **is in my memory**, *and I* **ask God to reveal them to me**, *especially those that have manifested themselves today,* **so I can be healed**.

MERCY

I believe that **forgiveness** *is the only* **path to healing and illumination.** *I beg for the* **grace of forgiveness**, *and the* **grace to forgive**, *especially for the general and particular failures of this day, and from my past.*

ॐ

My heart is steadfast, God;
my heart is steadfast.
Let me sing and chant praise.
Awake, lyre and harp!
I will wake the dawn.

I will praise you among the peoples, Lord;
I will chant your praise among the nations.
For your mercy is greater than the heavens;
your faithfulness, to the skies.

Appear on high over the heavens, God;
your glory above all the earth.
Help with your right hand and answer us
that your loved ones may escape.
(Ps 108: 2-7)

℘

Week 24

FIRST

As I engage the last meditation in *Sacred Story* prayer this week, I will review my commitment to develop a rhythm that will carry me the rest of my life. To help me with that commitment, I resolve to spend no more and no less than 15-minutes in each formal prayer session.

SECOND

For week twenty-four I am invited to pray meditation five in the *Sacred Story* prayer: Eternity. As St. Ignatius suggested, I will enter my prayer at least once daily for 15-minutes.

THIRD

Meditation Five—*Eternity*: I will use my first prayer session to review the daily prayer structure from Week 16 and then use my remaining 15-minute prayer periods to pray Eternity.

I will awaken to the present moment.

I will awaken to my spiritual nature.

I will not make any decisions based on fear.

I will practice Sacramental Reconciliation monthly.

Focus Affirmation for Week Twenty-Four
I will say this affirmation aloud once daily:
*Times of difficulty and stress always give way to
times of peace and hope.*

cs

Read this at the beginning of the week

Awakening to Sacred Story *Prayer—Eternity*

Every day, consciously enter *Sacred Story* prayer during your set time(s). For these next weeks, we are building the five meditations of *Sacred Story* prayer. Set aside the other pieces and focus on *Eternity* for your 15-minute prayer sessions this week. Your focus is *Eternity*.

Be faithful to the structure. Ignatius was wise in developing the ritual, and rituals are very important. The ritual itself detailed below does not save you. Yet the ritual, *faithfully practiced*, makes it easier for you to open your mind and heart to the One who does save you! Rituals are good. Review the structure of the 15-minute prayer sessions. You will find these at the bookmark you left in Week 16.

Awakening to Sacred Story*'s Meditations—Eternity*

Prayer Exercise—Eternity

ETERNITY

*I believe the grace of **forgiveness opens my heart,** making my every thought, word and deed bear **fruit that endures to eternity**. I ask that everything in my life serve Christ's Great Work of Reconciliation.*

Prelude

The *Sacred Story* of all history, revealed on the last day, will show that the lost innocence and the broken hearts of humankind inaugurated the Great Work of Reconciliation. Because of Christ's mercy, each of us is now being invited to take our part in this work. The grace of mercy and forgiveness, received and offered, is the reconciling work that brings true progress to the world; it is the only work that brings fulfillment and bears fruit that endures to eternity. A holy life and the highest consciousness attainable come in personally knowing the One who both reconciles my life, and reconciles all creation. In this reconciling Love, I daily discern how to direct each thought, word, and deed, to eternal glory—to the Divine work of reconciliation.

Illuminative Grace

Here I ask for what I desire: to be graced daily with a profound consciousness of Christ Jesus' healing love, personally experienced, that will so enlighten my heart and mind that my every thought, word and deed can serve His Great Work of Universal Reconciliation.

166

I will listen for what God, the Lord, has to say;
surely he will speak of peace
To his people and to his faithful.
May they not turn to foolishness!

Near indeed is his salvation for those who fear him;
glory will dwell in our land.
Love and truth will meet;
justice and peace will kiss.
Truth will spring from the earth;
justice will look down from heaven.

Yes, the Lord will grant his bounty;
our land will yield its produce.
Justice will march before him,
and make a way for his footsteps.
(Ps 85: 9-14)

ΒΟ

Week 25

FIRST

As I combine all five meditations in *Sacred Story* prayer this week for the first time, I will review my commitment and imagine a rhythm that will carry me for the rest of my life. To help me with that commitment, I again resolve to spend no more and no less than 15-minutes in each formal prayer session.

SECOND

For week twenty-five I am praying meditations one through five in the *Sacred Story* prayer. I will enter my prayer at least once daily as St. Ignatius suggested.

THIRD

Meditation One, Two, Three, Four and Five—*Creation, Presence, Memory, Mercy* and *Eternity*: I will use my first prayer session to review the daily prayer disciplines from Week 16. I will use the remainder of the week's 15-minute prayer periods for the combined prayer exercise.

I will awaken to the present moment.
I will awaken to my spiritual nature.
I will not make any decisions based on fear.
I will practice Sacramental Reconciliation monthly.

Focus Affirmation for Week Twenty-Five
I will say this affirmation aloud once daily:
I will not tire of asking God for help because God delights in my asking

൫

Read this at the beginning of the week

Review the structure of the 15-minute prayer sessions. You will find these at the bookmark you left in Week 16. For this week, you are combining the five meditations in *Sacred Story* prayer: Creation, Presence, Memory, Mercy and Eternity. Use your 15-minute prayer sessions this week to pray these five meditations together, following the wisdom you learned in Week 16 for this practice. You can also refresh your memory on the Preludes and Illuminative Graces of these three meditations if you find it helpful.

Awakening to Sacred Story—*Creation, Presence, Memory, Mercy & Eternity*

Prayer Exercise—Creation, Presence, Memory, Mercy & Eternity

℅

CREATION

*I believe God created everything in love and for love; I ask for the grace of a **heart-felt** knowledge of God's love **for me,** and for **gratitude** for the **general** and **particular** graces of this day.*

PRESENCE

*I believe God is **present** in **each moment** and **event** of my life, and I ask for grace to **awaken, see** and **feel** where and how, especially in this present moment.*

MEMORY

*I believe every violation of love committed by me and against me **is in my memory**, and I **ask God to reveal them to me**, especially those that have manifested themselves today, **so I can be healed**.*

MERCY

*I believe that **forgiveness** is the only **path to healing and illumination**. I beg for the **grace of forgiveness**, and the **grace to forgive**, especially for the general and particular failures of this day, and from my past.*

ETERNITY

*I believe the grace of **forgiveness opens my heart**, making my every thought, word and deed bear **fruit that endures to eternity**. I ask that everything in my life serve Christ's Great Work of Reconciliation.*

CB

May God be gracious to us and bless us;
may his face shine upon us.
So shall your way be known upon the earth,
your victory among all the nations.
May the peoples praise you, God;
may all the peoples praise you!
The earth has yielded its harvest;
God, our God, blesses us.
May God bless us still;
that the ends of the earth may revere him.
(Ps 67: 2-4, 7-8)

ED

Week 26

FIRST

I visualize the week ahead and plan how I will engage my 15-minute prayer times. I resolve in my heart to allow God to help me be faithful to these set times of prayer. To increase my fidelity, I also resolve to spend no more and no less than 15-minutes in any formal prayer period.

SECOND

For week twenty-six I am invited to continue a life-long process of praying the five meditations of *Sacred Story* prayer. I will enter this prayer at least once daily as St. Ignatius suggested.

THIRD

I will personalize Meditations One, Two, Three, Four and Five: *Creation, Presence, Memory, Mercy* and *Eternity*.

I will awaken to the present moment.

I will awaken to my spiritual nature.

I will not make any decisions based on fear.

I will practice Sacramental Reconciliation monthly.

Focus Affirmation for Week Twenty-Six
I will say this affirmation aloud once daily:
The urge to stop Sacred Story *practice*
always comes before my greatest breakthroughs.

ങ

Ongoing Awakening to Sacred Story *Prayer*

A very significant exercise for us in the first weeks of *Sacred Story* was finding the personal name for God that touches our hearts. Praying to God by saying this name often continues to be a powerful spiritual experience. Personalizing prayer and our relationship with God is an essential step in deepening our understanding of, and belief in, the God who is lovingly present to us each day of our lives.

Take what you are learning from praying with your personal name for God to understand why it is important to personalize the five meditations of *Sacred Story*. This week, you are invited to write your own single sentence for each of the meditations in *Sacred Story*. You are invited to continue working on this exercise until you "know" each of your sentences "by heart." In this exercise, you are personalizing the *Sacred Story* of creation, the Fall and our redemption in Christ to your own life story.

Engage all the other disciplines associated with *Sacred Story* prayer as part of your daily practice: *On Waking, During the Day Consciousness Exercise, Journal,* and *On Retiring Exercise*. Personalize *Creation, Presence, Memory Mercy* and *Eternity* for the 15-minute sessions this week.

Prayer Exercise—Continue praying your 15-minute Creation-Presence-Memory-Mercy-Eternity prayer & complete writing your own one-sentence version of each meditation of *Sacred Story* prayer. Use the blank space provided on the next page or write the sentences in your personal journal.

CREATION

PRESENCE

MEMORY

MERCY

ETERNITY

ᚖ

Come, children, listen to me;
I will teach you fear of the LORD.
Who is the man who delights in life,
who loves to see the good days?
Keep your tongue from evil,
your lips from speaking lies.
Turn from evil and do good;
seek peace and pursue it.

The eyes of the Lord are directed toward the righteous
and his ears toward their cry.
The Lord's face is against evildoers
to wipe out their memory from the earth.

The righteous cry out, the Lord hears
and he rescues them from all their afflictions.
The Lord is close to the brokenhearted,
And saves those whose spirit is crushed.
(Ps 34: 12-19)

ᚖ

Week 27

FIRST

I will visualize my prayer times this week and resolve to spend no more and no less than 15-minutes in each formal prayer session.

SECOND

For week twenty-seven I am invited to continue developing a life-long process of praying the five meditations of *Sacred Story* prayer. As St. Ignatius suggested, I will enter my prayer at least once daily.

THIRD

Meditation One, Two, Three, Four and Five: *Creation, Presence, Memory, Mercy* and *Eternity.*

I will awaken to the present moment.

I will awaken to my spiritual nature.

I will not make any decisions based on fear.

I will practice Sacramental Reconciliation monthly.

Focus Affirmation for Week Twenty-Seven
I will say this affirmation aloud once daily:
*God gives me insights, not because I am better than others,
but because I am loved.*

෫

Read this at the beginning of the week

Ongoing Awakening to Sacred Story *Prayer*

Sacred Story prayer is designed to carry us through our Christian journey to our heavenly home. It is also designed to open us to grace so our story is shaped more and more by Christ's *Sacred Story*. Living our story in Christ is a labor of love accomplished as we awaken to the truths of Creation, Presence, Memory, Mercy and Eternity.

Let us resolve this week to continue our journey by praying with Creation, Presence, Memory, Mercy and Eternity. By our openness and God's grace, our history and the history of the Church and world *are* changing. Make an act of faith this week that this is indeed true.

We also engage all the other disciplines associated with *Sacred Story* prayer as part of our daily practice: *On Waking, During the Day Consciousness Exercise, Journal,* and *On Retiring Exercise*. Continue to use your personalized prayers of *Creation, Presence, Memory, Mercy* and *Eternity* for the 15-minute sessions this week.

Prayer Exercise—Continue praying your 15-minute Creation-Presence-Memory-Mercy-Eternity prayer & complete your own one-sentence version of each meditation of *Sacred Story* Prayer.

Use the template from last week for this exercise.

ɔ3

Many are the troubles of the just one,
but out of them all the Lord delivers him;
he watches over all his bones;
not one of them shall be broken.
Taste and see the goodness of the Lord.
(Ps 34: 20-21)

ʒɔ

NOTES

Part Three
Entering the
School of Discernment

"Beloved, do not trust every spirit but
test the spirits to see whether they belong to God,
because many false prophets have gone out into the world."
1 Jn 4: 1

The Spiritual World

Spiritual discernment is challenging for a reason. Due to Original Sin, we have lost our capacity to readily distinguish truth from falsehood. To enter the path of discernment, we need to understand God and the universe God created. It is a universe that is both physical and spiritual. To help you enter the "school of discernment," *Sacred Story* prayer proposes a *relational* model (or *paradigm*) for God, human persons, and the created universe. Let us take a few moments to explore this *relational paradigm*.

First, we affirm a simple Truth: God is Love. The essence of God *as* Love is God as Perfect Relationship. God is a Trinity of perfect, loving relationship. The Trinity—Father, Son and Spirit—are three totally distinct, unique *persons* with no boundaries to their *giving* and *receiving* love. God *is* Love. It is a Love without beginning or end. God *is* Perfect Relationship. Love is *always* about relationship. The loss of love is *always* about the breaking of relationship. So everything not of God is anti-relationship, what Scripture calls the spirit of anti-Christ, "which is to come, but is already in the world" (1 Jn 4: 3).

Second, God "created mankind in his image; in the image of God He created them; male and female he created them" (Gen. 1:27). God *willed* human nature's form, freely creating persons as a perfect relationship of body and spirit.[12] The *human nature* God willed is the person as an *embodied spirit.* Human nature as *embodied spirit* is fashioned in God's own image. Consequently, persons are made to share in the Love that the Trinity enjoys—unique beings created to freely *give* and *receive* love with no boundaries.

For the human person, *perfect love* is the experience of being a *completely unique* individual. And in that uniqueness, being *completely transparent* to one's beloved, who is also completely unique. Perfectly transparent in the *giving* and *receiving* of love: perfectly giving; perfectly accepted; perfectly loved; perfectly loving; and eternally cherished! This *giving and receiving* of love, with no boundaries, was intended in God's plan to be realized between the persons and their Creator, and between the persons themselves. The *relational paradigm* of the Trinity is enriched immeasurably by God's free act of creation.

183

Third, the story of Paradise in the Book of Genesis reveals the state of *perfect relationship* between our first parents and God. This state of intimacy with God enabled a state of perfect justice and righteousness—a paradise! As long as our first parents remained in this state of spiritual intimacy with the Divine—as long as the state of perfect justice held—they were free from sickness and death.[13] This state of immortality was possible as long as they allowed God to be the very center of their lives—as long as they stayed in perfect, intimate relationship with God. In this state of perfect intimacy—their hearts undivided—they *knew themselves*. They had perfect interior harmony between their body and spirit. *Authentic!*

Because they were innocent and radically transparent to their Creator, they cherished each other as sacred in God's eyes. As incarnate spirits they shared intimate knowledge, respect, trust, complementarity, uniqueness, separateness and transcendent love. And they *understood* the creation. They had perfect relationship with creation because they understood it as God's gift. God gifts the human persons with the *power to name* the plants and animals. We understand that this gift of "naming" includes the knowledge of creation's rhythms. They would understand *how* creation works to their benefit and their delight and for their enjoyment. The gift of Love freely given to our first parents by God was to expand in cosmic harmony.

The tragedy of Original Sin severs the perfect relationship between the incarnate spirits and the Creator:

"When they heard the sound of the Lord God walking about in the garden at the breezy time of the day, the man and his wife hid themselves from the Lord God among the trees of the garden." (Gen 3:8)

The perfect relationship they had enjoyed now becomes filled with blame and grief. They will fight each other and their offspring will fight them. Their perfect relationship with creation is now also cursed (Gen 3:17-19) and they lose immortality. They are vulnerable to sickness and disease. Free will, essential for love, also allows persons to sever their relationship with Love, with God. Relationship violated and severed is the *true face of sin*.

This is why abandonment and loneliness are the heart's deepest fears. As the most profound misery caused by sin, it is what Christ suffered on the cross, for all of humanity for all time, to a degree unimaginable: *My God, my God, why have you abandoned me?* Love itself, suffered love's complete absence (Ps 22: 1; Mt 27: 45-46).

But God's work in creation cannot be undone by sin. The *original* unity is lost forever, but out of this tragedy God creates an even more astonishing good. God would not create such beauty without a way to rectify even this tragedy with something more glorious. We are now invited to accept the mission of participating with Christ in His grand work of Reconciliation. We do this by opening to life as *Sacred Story*. We allow God to work His miracle of healing and forgiveness for the hope that we, as brothers and sisters of Christ and children of God, are destined to share:

I consider that the sufferings of this present time are as nothing compared with the glory to be revealed for us. For creation awaits with eager expectation the revelation of the children of God; for creation was made subject to futility, not of its own accord but because of the one who subjected it, in hope that creation itself would be set free from slavery to corruption and share in the glorious freedom of the children of God. We know that all creation is groaning in labor pains even until now; and not only that, but we ourselves, who have the first fruits of the Spirit, we also groan within ourselves as we wait for adoption, the redemption of our bodies. For in hope we were saved. Now hope that sees for itself is not hope. For who hopes for what one sees? But if we hope for what we do not see, we wait with endurance. In the same way, the Spirit too comes to the aid of our weakness; for we do not know how to pray as we ought, but the Spirit itself intercedes with inexpressible groanings. And the one who searches hearts knows what is the intention of the Spirit, because it intercedes for the holy ones according to God's will. (Rm 8: 18-27)

Your discernment is made easier if you can see everything in light of the *paradigm of perfect relationship*—given, lost, and being restored in Christ:

1) Perfect relationship of incarnate spirits in our unity of body and spirit.

2) Perfect relationship of created, incarnate spirits with our Creator God.

3) Perfect relationship of incarnate spirits with each other as unique individuals.

4) Perfect relationship between incarnate spirits as male and female called to fruitful, respectful, loving and joyful reverence.

5) Perfect relationship between created, incarnate spirits with the earth given for our delight, refreshment and sustenance.

6) Perfect relationship with the Church, the *Body of Christ*, as the community formed by Him for the work of Reconciliation, leading to a new heavens and a new earth.

Every thought, word and deed that seeks to *affirm the meaning* of perfect relationship and the human nature *willed* by God, everything that is working to heal damaged relationships, is a work of the Divine-Inspirer; God the Creator.

Every thought, word and deed that moves to *alter the meaning* of perfect relationship and the human nature *willed* by God, everything that is further undermining damaged relationships, is a work of the counter-inspirer; "the enemy of human nature," *who from the beginning, is a murderer and a liar—the father of lies* (Jn 8: 43-45).

As you enter the school of spiritual discernment, keep your heart and mind focused on the *relational paradigm*. You are seeking the knowledge of your identity as a child of God, but informed by the truth of perfect relationship. Your authentic identity is a human nature, *willed* by God, as *unity* of body and spirit. You seek also the knowledge of your authentic God-given human nature as it has been violated and broken by Original Sin. And you seek this knowledge in light of what Christ is offering: by His life, death and resurrection, you are offered *the beginning* of the full healing that will be completed in the world and the life to come.

In short, you are seeking the knowledge of perfect relationship and how in your own life and the world, that perfection has been broken but can also be restored, healed and redeemed by the Divine Physician. You are also seeking knowledge of the thief and the robber—*the enemy of human nature*—who seeks to distort what authentic relationship is, and to hide from you the Truth of God and your authentic human nature. You are seeking to discern the two plot-lines in your story: the one that leads to curse and death and the one that leads to life and blessings. Ultimately, you are seeking to know truth from falsehood in *all* of your thoughts, words and deeds.

ଔ

So Jesus said again, "Amen, amen, I say to you, I am the gate for the sheep. All who came [before me] are thieves and robbers, but the sheep did not listen to them. I am the gate. Whoever enters through me will be saved, and will come in and go out and find pasture. A thief comes only to steal and slaughter and destroy; I came so that they might have life and have it more abundantly. I am the good shepherd. A good shepherd lays down his life for the sheep.

(Jn 10: 7-11)

ଓ

state of Human Nature w/ Original Sin

Closer to God

Jesus

God
Father - Son - Holy Spirit

Love — Perfect Relationship

Life

Life

Human
Body-Spirit

Choices

Free Will

Attacks
Death

Enemy
Accuser
Liar

Death
sinful
Habits

Farther away
from God

Authentic — perfect interior harmony between soul and God

Love of God

187

Week 28

FIRST

I will visualize the week ahead and imagine where and when I will find a technology-free zone for my times of prayer. As before, I resolve to spend no more and no less than 15-minutes in each formal prayer session.

SECOND

I realize I am developing a deep, personal relationship with Christ. My life-long process of praying *Sacred Story* prayer is a commitment to my relationship with Christ. As St. Ignatius found so fruitful, I will enter my prayer at least once daily.

THIRD

This week I enter the school of spiritual discernment. It is essential for my progress in *Sacred Story* to understand how the spiritual world works. The lessons on discernment will span twelve weeks. My goal is to lay a foundation to *understand* Ignatius' guidelines for discerning the difference between the "voice" of God and the "voice" of the *enemy of human nature*. I will resolve not to become discouraged. The school of discernment requires spiritual exercise. Learning to distinguish the difference between the voice of God and the voice of the enemy of human nature takes practice. Most importantly, it requires listening, time, trial and error, prayer, patience and God's grace.

I will awaken to the present moment.
I will awaken to my spiritual nature.
I will not make any decisions based on fear.
I will practice Sacramental Reconciliation monthly.
Focus Affirmation for Week Twenty-Eight
I will say this affirmation aloud once daily:

The insights and graces I need to move forward in life's journey
unfold at the right time.

ↂ

Read this at the beginning of the week

Cultivate the interior freedom to continue pondering the reflections as they link to your own life. Understand them as an essential component to living your *Sacred Story* prayer.

Awakening to Sacred Story *Discernment Guidelines*

Introduction

As we begin discernment, continue with your daily prayer disciplines and the five meditations of *Sacred Story*. The materials for this third part of *Sacred Story* are not new elements to integrate into the five-part prayer discipline you are practicing. The discernment lessons are designed for you to learn more about how the spiritual world works. They are also an invitation for you to comprehend more fully the spiritual influences that are shaping your *Sacred Story*. Resist the temptation to incorporate these lessons on spiritual discernment into the structure of your prayer. See them more as *essential* guidelines that will help you enter more fully into the daily disciplines of *Sacred Story*.

If you are praying the *Sacred Story* prayer faithfully, you will naturally encounter the dynamics taught in these guidelines on spiritual discernment. There is a reason for this. If you think and pray about *Creation, Presence, Memory, Mercy* and *Eternity* in your *Sacred Story* every day, the spiritual world awakens to you. The God of Grace who seeks to support you with Divine inspirations, and the enemy of your human nature who seeks to disrupt your life with counter-inspirations, will both become apparent. If you seek daily to grow in faith, you will consciously encounter the spiritual world that supports your growth and the spiritual world that wants to disrupt your growth. While both forces have always been present in your life's story, you may have never before consciously noticed their activity.

These lessons on discernment will help you navigate these two spiritual currents so you can more readily move forward in your *Sacred Story*. If you do not now understand everything you are reading, you will one day *understand everything* in these lessons *if* you remain faithful to your prayer disciplines in the context of practicing your faith.

The first lesson examines God's *intentional* creation of *human nature* as a *unity* of spirit and body. We also examine why God *willed* the form of our human nature and created us as *embodied spirits*. Read the lesson several times this week and reflect on it. These *truths* need to be rediscovered and consciously reflected upon to help bring clarity to our lives. We are all influenced by the secularism of our age, to a greater or lesser degree, and need to wake up to what is "real." Because what is "real" may seem like spiritual fairy-tales. But the principles of discernment we present here are the *time-tested doctrines of our faith.* If you do not believe or accept these fundamental Christian truths, Ignatius' discernment guidelines will make no sense whatsoever.

Church Tradition affirms that *human nature*, as a *unity* of spirit and body, was *willed* by God. We are *human* because our physical body is animated by an immortal, rational soul. No other creature is gifted with a rational soul to animate its physical body. Why did God *will* our human nature as a *unity of physical body and rational soul*? So God could be intimate with us. God communicates with our human nature by means of our spiritual soul. Complete intimacy with God is our destiny, our glory and the purpose of our creation. Only a being with a spirit can know and love. A spirit's two chief faculties are the intellect (which knows) and the will or heart (which loves). Human beings are spiritual since humans both know and love.

Church Tradition also affirms that God created human beings as immortal beings. This is known as the condition of *original holiness* or *original justice*. The state of original justice means that the physical body and spiritual soul of our first parents was in complete harmony. The state of original justice afforded our first parents complete *self-mastery*. That a state of sinlessness allowed all our thoughts, words and deeds to be in complete harmony with the Divine.

We were without sin and thus without suffering, disease or death. Immortality was the result of the total intimacy our first parents shared with God. Without complete spiritual intimacy with God, immortality would not be possible. Our first parents were *at one in themselves, at one with each other and creation*, and *at one with God*. Our spiritual nature, completely intimate with God, perfectly guided the lower nature of our material body. We call this period of history "Paradise" or original justice.

Our first parents were *knowing beings* (*Homo Sapiens*). They knew themselves, God and the purpose of creation's gift. They were the apex of God's creation and were given dominion to act as co-creators with God. To be co-creators means they were given power to cultivate and care for the earth and to name all living creatures (Gen 2:15-20). As woman and man, they have the power to give birth to other beings that will have an eternal destiny. Their role as co-creators can be accomplished with total integrity and justice because of their complete *self*-mastery. The triple corruption (1 Jn 2:16) of human nature "that subjugates us to the pleasures of the senses, covetousness for earthly goods, and self-assertion, contrary to the dictates of reason" had not yet poisoned

God's plan for humanity and creation.

The Tradition affirms that sin *entered into creation* originally from a spiritual entity, Lucifer, and the other spirits who *irrevocably* rejected God. Thus, sin first enters into God's creation in the *spiritual* realm, through a *spiritual act* of the will. It was an act of disobedience. Lucifer is the embodiment of sin which is hatred of God and God's creation. Lucifer's hate, pride and envy seek to destroy

---

Why Did God Allow Us to Disobey and Suffer?

God is love. Love always offers a choice to accept or reject Divine love. If the woman and man cannot freely reject God's offer of life and love, God violates the freedom of the beings made in the Divine image. Yet God would not have allowed this freedom if it would undo his plan for humankind. Our promise is that Jesus' Redemption will open a new heavens and a new earth with more blessing and glory than the first creation.

---

everything God creates. Lucifer operates through a gateway from his spiritual realm to the material realm so as to *infect creation* and activate its destruction. His *gateway* is the spiritual nature of our first parents. The perfect expression of hatred toward God is to destroy the beautiful, innocent immortals created to share in God's life.

Lucifer's malevolent design starts by sabotaging the unity of human nature as a perfect relationship of body and spirit. His seduction begins by inviting persons to worship themselves instead of God. From this perversion of God's design, all other relationships will shatter. Lucifer's hope is that the virus of self-love—of narcissism—and the rejection of God's love that it manifests, will eventually evolve to destroy humanity and creation itself.

The time of paradise was real, and the plan to destroy paradise was also real. The plan to destroy creation required separating our first parents from their *total intimacy* with God. Here is the allegorical description in Genesis of the Original Sin that describes this heartrending primordial event:

Now the snake was the most cunning of all the wild animals that the LORD God had made. He asked the woman, "Did God really say, 'You shall not eat from any of the trees in the garden'?" The woman answered the snake: "We may eat of the fruit of the trees in the garden; it is only about the fruit of the tree in the middle of the garden that God said, 'You shall not eat it or even touch it, or else you will die.'" But the snake said to the woman: "You certainly will not die! God knows well that when you eat of it your eyes will be opened and you will be like gods, who know good and evil." The woman saw that the tree was good for food and pleasing to the eyes, and the tree was desirable for gaining wisdom. So she took some of its fruit and ate it; and she also gave some to her husband, who was with her, and he ate it. (Gen 3: 1-6).

This account is an allegory, a symbolic description of a real event that Tradition calls the Original Sin. We will never know the exact context for the Original Sin that ruptured God's plan for humanity and creation itself. And we cannot know the way the enemy of human nature insinuated itself into the consciousness of our first parents to get them to reject God and to make themselves gods, "masters of the universe."

Yet the Genesis account provides valuable spiritual and theological material for reflection about the nature of temptation and the horrifying fall from grace that has *evolved* over time because of God's displacement from the center of human hearts. We see it in insatiable greed and grinding poverty; personal

---

What is Sin?

Every sin, in its essence, is a perversion and erosion of the perfect love and relationship that God gave to human persons as gift, life and truth. And every sin in evil's evolution mimics the Original Sin. Each sin— whether it be a thought, word or deed—spreads the virus of anti- Christ—anti-relationship as narcissism—to destroy human nature made in the Divine image. Creation's perversion and destruction is the goal of evil's architect—the one St. Ignatius calls *the enemy of human nature.*

---

hatred and fratricidal war; the violation of the innocent in abuse and human trafficking; the legal murdering of children in the womb; the discarding of the weak, the vulnerable and the aged; the lonely and despairing exploited by predators of all sorts; intellectual and scientific arrogance that subverts human nature and the created order; self-serving political and financial collectives whose power is destabilizing and destroying families, nations, and creation itself.

Dissecting the story, we can imaginatively enter into this frightening and grief-filled catastrophe and see it with new eyes, through the relational paradigm: the plan of human nature's enemy to destroy the perfect ordering in Love of all relationships, and to destroy God's creation.[14]

1. Violation of Obedience and the birth of a divided conscience

In the state of original justice, the woman and the man were completely intimate with God. Their spiritual nature was ordered solely to the Divine and this gave them self-mastery over their lower physical nature. They also had the gift of immortality because they *listened only* to God. The Latin root for *obey* means

193

"to listen deeply." Lucifer inserts himself between our first parents and God. He did this by engaging them in seemingly innocent conversation. They violated obedience to God by elevating the voice of Lucifer to a status equal to God. This foreshadowed unspeakable tragedy and loss. Turning from God to *listen* and *speak* to Lucifer constitutes the *first stage* of Original Sin.

2.   Violation of Chastity and the birth of illegitimate desires

In a state of original justice and with trusting innocence, the man and woman obeyed God, knowing the truth of their being, God and creation. Engaged in conversation with the prince of lies, they were invited to *see with new eyes* what before held no interest, or incited any desire. But now, their hearts (consciences) were divided. They could not properly reason nor could they maintain self-mastery over their physical nature. Cut off from God, their spiritual nature experienced the lust of *self*-assertion. They now contemplate (*see with new eyes*) an illegitimate desire opposed both to God and to their own human nature. All illegitimate desires are described in Tradition as appetites linked to the seven capital vices (pride, envy, anger, gluttony, greed, sloth, gluttony). This is the *second stage* of Original Sin.

3.   Violation of Poverty and the taking of what does not belong to me

Their total intimacy with God severed, the woman and the man had new desires and contemplated an electrifying, exciting and seemingly glamorous choice: to be like gods, knowing good and evil. God had told them that they would die if they ate *this* fruit. But Lucifer soothed with lies to trick them into taking what they must have known "in their hearts" was wrong. The *third stage* in Original Sin is this: *to experiment* and *find out for yourself* who is telling the truth. And so our first parents took what they did not need and what did not belong to them. Devastation, heartache, and unspeakable tragedies followed.
First,
By choice and/or habit, the heart—conscience—is distant from God. I think I am following my own plans, but I am easily and subtly influenced to choose against God and my authentic self. I disobey my conscience. This lack of obedience ("deep listening") begins with my *self*-assertion. I make myself the final arbiter of truth. I break relationship with God and become independent of God, serving self over God.

Second,
In this *self*-assertion, I open myself to all manner of illegitimate desires and I *entertain* them. All these illegitimate desires are in their essence, perversion and erosion of authentic relationships. Illegitimate desires are deemed "objectively

wrong" by the Commandments, the Gospel and Tradition, but I judge them *appropriate options* because "I decide" what I will and will not do. In so doing I violate chastity. Violations of chastity are perversions and erosions of perfect relationship.

Third,

I move from considering options to experimenting and trying what I like because "it's my life." In this I violate poverty by taking what does not rightfully belong to me. Violations of poverty are perversions and erosions of relationship because I take what I do not need or is not mine

Before the incarnate God-man Jesus begins His public ministry, He confronts this triple sin of our first parents. He confronts the temptation of Lucifer to turn the stones into bread. In this He confronts the violation of poverty by refusing to take what is not offered Him by the Father: 'One does not live by bread alone, but by every word that comes forth from the mouth of God.' (Mt 4:4).

Next He confronts the violation of chastity and illegitimate desires by refusing to gain attention by plunging from the temple parapet: "Again it is written, 'You shall not put the Lord, your God, to the test.'" (Mt 4:7).

Finally, He confronts the violation of obedience and the divided conscience it wrought by refusing to serve Lucifer and rule on this earth. "At this, Jesus said to him, 'Get away, Satan! It is written: "The Lord, your God, shall you worship and him alone shall you serve."'" (Mt 4:10).

Sacred Story prayer journey challenges you to awaken to the voice of God in your own unique history, calling you to the poverty, chastity and obedience that can bring peace and repair sin's damage. To do this effectively, it is essential to learn the language of discernment. The Discernment Guidelines presented in the coming weeks are modeled on St. Ignatius' classic *Rules* for spiritual discernment. For thirty years Ignatius made decisions based on *self-assertion*, with little thought of God. Both the desire and the choice to advance spiritually were totally new for him.

Ignatius' awakening forced him into uncharted terrain where he did not know how to navigate. He was not *spiritually literate*. He did not know himself—his authentic self—because he lived controlled by sensual lusts and the desires of riches, honors of the world and pride. All are values readily celebrated by our culture today. God instructed Ignatius in discernment during his conversion journey. In his awakening process he writes: "what is the new life we are living?" In this phrase he was discovering what Nicodemus was told by Jesus: *Amen, amen, I say to you, no one can see the kingdom of God without being born from above."* (Jn 3:3)

Ignatius, in being born from above, was reconnected by grace to his spiritual nature and to God. He was awakening to realities he could not have known previously. He was learning that there were "two voices" and learning how to distinguish between them. By understanding the discernment guidelines that God revealed to Ignatius, we can awaken more easily to our authentic human nature. To prepare ourselves, we will learn a new language of discernment and discover in our own life history the two voices "inspiring" us— one voice working to help us unite our spiritual and physical nature, and one voice working to keep us separated from God and divided within ourselves. You will learn how to distinguish the voice of God from the voice of the enemy of human nature in your thoughts, words and deeds.

☙

But they soon forgot all he had done;
they had no patience for his plan.
In the desert they gave in to their cravings,
tempted God in the wasteland.
They exchanged their glory
for the image of a grass-eating bull.
They forgot the God who had saved them,
who had done great deeds in Egypt,
They sacrificed to demons their own sons and daughters,
Shedding innocent blood,
the blood of their own sons and daughters,
Whom they sacrificed to the idols of Canaan,
desecrating the land with bloodshed.
They defiled themselves by their actions,
became adulterers by their conduct.
Save us, Lord, our God;
gather us from among the nations
That we may give thanks to your holy name
and glory in praising you.
(Ps 13-14, 20-21,38-39,47)

❧

Week 29

FIRST
I will visualize the week ahead to imagine where and when I can find a place apart—a technology-free zone—for my 15-minute periods of formal prayer.

SECOND
This week, I continue the life-long process of praying meditations one through five in the *Sacred Story* prayer. I resolve to enter my prayer at least once daily as St. Ignatius suggested.

THIRD
I continue my lessons in spiritual discernment. This week, I will come to understand how the world changed by the rupture of sin, and study God's plan to help us find our way home.

I will awaken to the present moment.
I will awaken to my spiritual nature.
I will not make any decisions based on fear.
I will practice Sacramental Reconciliation monthly.

Focus Affirmation for Week Twenty-Nine
I will say this affirmation aloud once daily:
My personal engagement with Sacred Story *accomplishes, through Christ, a work of eternal significance.*

ᙅᙖ

Read this at the beginning of the week

Awakening to Sacred Story *Discernment Guidelines*

Introduction

Take time, at your convenience outside of your prayer periods, to read and reflect on this second lesson in discernment. The lesson will examine two elements. First, the consequences of our first parents' decision to violate the freedom bestowed upon them by displacing God from the center of their lives. Second, God's rescue plan to redeem us.

God *desired* that we be free and that we use that freedom to remain linked to God, our source of life. The *complete unity* of our higher spiritual nature with God is what *made* us human. This complete spiritual unity with God also bestowed balance and control over our lower physical nature. We controlled our bodily appetites. This complete unity of our higher spiritual nature with God also made us, *body and soul*, immortal. It was Paradise.

Covering Their Nakedness

In Genesis 3: 7, Adam and Eve "see" their nakedness and "cover" themselves. Their *seeing* and *covering* demonstrates that their separation from God awakens them to know and feel that they no longer have control over their physical nature. They can objectify each other—use each other—and in their loss of innocence, are shamed by this discovery. Now begins the history of psychological and physical exploitation linked to the very gift God created to give life: human sexuality. The enemy of human nature knew this tragedy would result and relishes the agony it causes. The perfect complementarity of human nature created in the Divine image, male and female, is shattered by narcissism. But God has a plan to rescue us and make all things new. It begins with the miracle of the wine at the Wedding at Cana that signifies the super abundance of grace that God pours out upon the covenant of marriage through Christ's life. (Jn 2: 1-12).

The woman and the man silenced God's voice as the center of their consciences and replaced it with their opinions. In silencing God's voice, they cut the lifeline of God's grace. As a result, human nature, as an *integrated unity* of spirit and body, was shattered. The higher spiritual nature no longer guided the lower physical nature. The immortality of human nature as body and soul is lost. With their appetites cut off from the Divine spiritual compass, paradise was lost.

199

Before our first parents used free choice to make themselves the center of their own universe—to make themselves gods—spiritual discernment was not necessary. They knew the true God, they knew who they were, and they knew instinctively how to act with integrity and holiness. *Truth* was instinctive based on the complete harmony they shared with God. Discernment was automatic. Using their freedom to *self*-assert, harmony with God was broken and so was their human nature. *Human nature* is now at war with itself and with God. The human heart has difficulty hearing God's voice. Even when God's voice is heard, it is difficult to act upon.

We cannot determine at what point in the two hundred thousand year history of modern humans this rupture took place, but we affirm that it did occur. As a result, God's plan to save humankind and creation began. Our Judeo-

---

What is Truth?

"For this I was born and for this I came into the world, to testify to the truth. Everyone who belongs to the truth listens to my voice." Pilate said to him, "What is truth?"
Jn 18: 37-8

At the beginning of the Third Millennium, many believe truth is relative. Even before the Third Millennium commenced, many pointed out that the greatest threat to the Faith is not atheism but relativism. Jesus tells Pilate that he was born and came into the world to testify to the truth—the truth about God, the truth about human nature, and the truth about salvation. Truth does exist and discernment's goal is to help us distinguish truth from falsehood in our *Sacred Story*.

Christian faith is a *revealed religion*. This means that God *reveals* it to us; we did not *create* it. In the rupture caused by Original Sin, we lost the ability to instinctively know the truth about God, our human nature and creation. God must reveal the idea of truth, good and evil, to His beloved creatures that are now subject to corruption, disease and death. It is no wonder that the First Commandment states: "I am the Lord your God; you shall not have strange gods before me."

The Ten Commandments reveal *the* moral truths: about God; about woman and man's proper relationship to God, and their relationship to each other and to creation. God is *revealing* the knowledge of truth lost in paradise. God chose the Jewish people for this mission. The whole history of Israel is preparing for the coming of the Messiah who will save us from the devastation caused by Original Sin. Sin closes hearts to the truth and so even the Chosen People rejected God's messengers, the prophets. Christ fared no better and was executed. The Pharisees, with darkened consciences, even accused Jesus of collaborating with Satan (Mt 12:24).

Sacred Story prayer journey links you to the entire history of salvation. In your prayer and in your discernment, you participate in the holy labor of returning body and soul to God. You join Christ's great work of Reconciliation by your engagement. It is a labor to be sure, as St. Ignatius learned. He lived for thirty years with his lower appetites in near complete control of his life. His awakening was guided by God and began while recuperating from battle. Ignatius was graced to notice a difference between two sets of fantasies or daydreams.

In the first daydream/fantasy, he imagines himself successful in marrying King Ferdinand and Queen Isabella's daughter. He describes this later as a *vain fantasy*. In the second daydream/fantasy, he imagines himself making a pilgrimage to Jerusalem and living like the saints.[15] Both daydream/fantasies make him feel good while he entertains them. But on deeper reflection, the afterglow of the first daydream leaves him *dry and dissatisfied* while the afterglow of the second daydream/fantasy leaves him feeling *content and peaceful*. With this awakening, he begins a life-long practice of spiritual discernment.

What did he learn in this lesson? That *the feelings* associated with even *imagined* actions can reveal the truth about our identity. Learning to pay close attention to our feelings (our affective-emotional life) can reveal the signature of God in our authentic identity *and* the signature of human nature's enemy in our false identity. Ignatius was utterly amazed at this discovery. Never before had he noticed this subtle difference in his affective-emotional feelings.

As his Christian conversion deepens, St. Ignatius learns that there are three ways the human person can be "inspired." Inspirations can come from God, from the enemy of human nature and from oneself. Next week, we will look at these three in more depth.

The *first* goal of spiritual discernment is *to learn* truth vs. falsehood about your human nature, your identity as a child of God, and about God and His creation. The *second* goal of spiritual discernment is *to choose* thoughts, words and deeds that express your authentic identity as a child of God. You are called to surrender *self*-assertion in favor of humility so your life's labor—your *Sacred Story*—produces fruit that endures to eternity.

Awaken this week to the truth that you are *both body and spirit*. You have a higher spiritual nature and a lower bodily nature. At one point they were an integrated unity but now, they are divided (Jer 17:9). God desires to heal you spiritually, (*Lord, I am not worthy to have you enter under my roof; only say the word and my servant will be healed*. Mt 8:8), so that you can be at peace and gain eternal life. The enemy of human nature seeks to keep you spiritually distant from God so that your lower nature (your base appetites) guide your thoughts, words and deeds, robbing you of peace and eternal life.

Both God and the enemy of human nature are working to achieve these very different ends. This is nothing to be afraid of because you have given your heart to Christ. Christ will guide you to safety and holiness just like He did St. Ignatius. All the great teachers of the Church reinforce these central spiritual truths. .[16]

Human Nature and Authentic Identity

Films, songs, books and newspapers often define *human nature* positively *and solely* as our lower appetites. How these lower appetites might be divided from our spiritual nature and from Divine influence is usually ignored. Today, many definitions of human nature are influenced by the theories of Sigmund Freud. Freud believed that sexual drives/desires are the root of all human psychological activity. *Being authentic* often means discerning one's identity mainly by expressing one's sensual appetites. Yet to discern one's *authentic identity* requires being spiritually grafted to Christ. Only then can one discern both the higher calling we have as daughters and sons of God, and our true human nature. This "being born from above" reveals the truth about God, our authentic identity and our mission to love as Christ loved.

ଓଃ

And the Word became flesh and made his dwelling among us,
and we saw his glory, the glory as of the Father's only Son,
full of grace and truth.
(Jn 1:14)
God is Spirit, and those who worship him must worship in Spirit and truth."
(Jn 4:24)
"If you remain in my word, you will truly be my disciples, and you will
know the truth, and the truth will set you free."
(Jn 8:31-32)
Jesus said to him, "I am the way and the truth and the life.
No one comes to the Father except through me."
(Jn 14:6)

ଞ

Week 30

FIRST

I resolve to spend no more and no less than 15-minutes in each formal prayer session. As before, I will visualize the week ahead and imagine where I can find a technology-free zone for my prayer

SECOND

I continue the process of praying meditations one through five in the *Sacred Story* prayer and, as St. Ignatius suggested, I will enter my prayer at least once daily. This prayer, like the rosary, will never grow old. It will take on more and more meaning, helping me deepen my faith and my wisdom and awaken me to God's truth and love.

THIRD

I will continue to open my heart to the lessons on discernment as I try to understand the three different sources of inspiration that can influence my thoughts, words and deeds.

I will awaken to the present moment.
I will awaken to my spiritual nature.
I will not make any decisions based on fear.
I will practice Sacramental Reconciliation monthly.
I will ask Jesus for help when I am troubled.
I will thank Jesus daily for life's gifts.

Focus Affirmation for Week Thirty
I will say this affirmation aloud once daily:

Inspirations can have a divine or a demonic source. I pray for the grace to remember how to discern one from the other.

ଔ

Read this at the beginning of the week

Awakening to Sacred Story *Discernment Guidelines*
Guidelines for Fundamental Healing and Spiritual Growth

Introduction

Take time, at your convenience outside of your prayer periods, to read and reflect on this third lesson in discernment. We will examine the three distinct sources of inspiration that can guide our thoughts, words and deeds.

Inspirations affecting your human nature (spirit-body) can originate from three different sources according to St. Ignatius.[17]

1. Inspirations can originate with yourself.
2. Inspirations can originate from a Divine source: the *Divine-Inspirer*.
3. Inspirations can originate from a demonic source, the *enemy of human nature*: the *counter-inspirer*.

There are three sources of spiritual inspiration, but only two spiritual states. St. Ignatius names the two states *consolation* and *desolation*. Next week we will explore these two spiritual states in more depth.

Spiritual consolation is when one *experiences*, to a greater or lesser degree, an increase in faith, hope and love. Spiritual desolation is when one *experiences,* to a greater or lesser degree, a loss of faith, hope and love.

Sources of Inspiration

✦ Human nature as spirit/body
✦ The *Divine-Inspirer*
✦ The *counter-inspirer*

Types of Inspiration

✦ Consolation—increase of faith, hope and love
✦ Desolation—loss of faith, hope and love

Sources of Inspiration

To affirm that our human nature can be the source of inspirations makes perfect sense. We have our own thoughts and convictions and act on them. Such thoughts originate from within our being in several ways.

First, we can let our body make decisions. We can be led by our sensual appetites and "give into them" with little or no conscious thought about the consequences. Sometimes that "giving in" is due to sickness or addictions. But it is the appetites doing our "thinking" and "inspiring" our actions.

Second, we can be inspired by what we might call *embedded strengths/gifts* in human nature from our Creator OR from *embedded*

Evil's Work is More Hidden than Sensational

Don't go looking for *Exorcist*-movie drama in your spiritual discernment. The counter-inspirer accomplished his greatest damage in the Original Sin when human nature was crippled. He knew you would be subject to disease and death, and that the anger, cynicism, sickness, war, poverty and injustice in human society would chip away at belief. The loss of faith, hope and love would result, and belief in a "God of love" would diminish. Kindness avoided, forgiveness withheld and self-centered behavior work to diminish faith, hope and love. All have conspired to create the evolution of darkness present in our history. *Exorcist*-movie evil does exist but serves the counter-inspirer's work mostly by making us blind to evil's greatest work: crushing the human spirit and making us believe that evil is more powerful than God and love. Yet, the enemy of human nature—the counter-inspirer—has already lost his battle in Christ's victory. Be Not Afraid!

---

diseases/weaknesses in human nature marred by Original Sin. Consolation from an *embedded strength/gift* in human nature from our Creator could be a bodily feeling that "life is good" after an excellent workout. It might also be a spiritual feeling of being happy to be alive, that "life is beautiful" when looking at a baby or a beautiful sunset.

Desolation from an *embedded disease/weakness* in human nature marred by Original Sin might be a bodily feeling that "life is miserable" when you have a cold, flu or some type of bodily injury. It might also be a spiritual feeling that "life is difficult, burdensome and not fair" if you are hurting in a relationship or suffering due to early life events.

If you are inspired spiritually by either the Divine-Inspirer or the counter-inspirer, the inspiration will be communicated to you through your higher spiritual nature which was willed by God to guide your lower spiritual nature. We will look at this reality in coming weeks.[18]

You may continue your reflections on these spiritual realities by reading a homily by St. Bernard of Clairvaux and a short section from Vatican II's *Gaudium et Spes*: The Pastoral Constitution on the Church in the Modern World.[19]

☙

My eyes long to see your salvation
and the promise of your righteousness.
Act with mercy toward your servant;
teach me your statutes.
I am your servant; give me discernment
that I may know your testimonies.
(Ps 119: 123-25)

❧

Week 31

FIRST

I will visualize my week to imagine where I can find a technology-free zone to spend my 15-minutes prayer sessions.

SECOND

I continue the life-long process of praying meditations one through five in the *Sacred Story* prayer. I commit to enter my prayer at least once daily as St. Ignatius suggested. This prayer will carry me for life. It will deepen my faith and my wisdom and awaken me to God's truth and love.

THIRD

This week I will continue to seek knowledge of spiritual discernment, by examining two benchmark rules: Spiritual Consolation and Spiritual Desolation.

I will awaken to the present moment.
I will awaken to my spiritual nature.
I will not make any decisions based on fear.
I will practice Sacramental Reconciliation monthly.
I will ask Jesus for help when I am troubled.
I will thank Jesus daily for life's gifts.

Focus Affirmation for Week Thirty-One
I will say this affirmation aloud once daily:
Christ, who has walked before me, shares my every burden.

Christ, who has walked before me,
will help me resolve every crisis.
Christ, who has walked before me, knows my every hope.

ᛣ

Read this at the beginning of the week

Awakening to **Sacred Story** *Discernment Guidelines*
Guidelines for Fundamental Healing and Spiritual Growth

Introduction

Take some time this week to read and reflect on this fourth lesson in discernment. We will examine the two types of inspiration that can guide our thoughts, words and deeds. First, a brief review of the past three weeks.

God willed that human nature be a perfect unity of body and soul. The gift of this blessed unity of human nature in paradise made us immortal. The turning from God, which we call Original Sin, broke the perfect unity of human nature:

God Is Healing Our Broken Human Nature

Original Sin crippled our human nature. None of us will achieve perfection this side of eternity. Yet knowing that human nature was "perfect" once and will be perfect again informs the Church's interpretation of holiness. God's grace fosters healing in our souls, enabling us to gain a measure of mastery over the lusts and desires of our bodily nature. It also enables us to grow in forgiveness, selflessness, and charity. All of us are called to cooperate with God's grace for this healing and holiness. We are all encouraged by Christ not to be afraid but to be patient as the process of healing takes a lifetime.

---

body and soul. Lust for power, dominance and unbridled physical desires of our bodily nature (concupiscence) do battle with our spiritual nature. In this battle our authentic identity was distorted. Our conscience was clouded and we lost sight of right and wrong. Disease, strife, suffering and death resulted. Original Sin broke our perfect unity with God's loving will. Also broken was the unity between male and female and their harmony with creation. Paradise was an ecstasy of harmonious relationships. Original Sin broke all relationships. Most tragically, it broke our hearts.

The revelation of the Ten Commandments to the people of Israel was one

210

of the most significant gifts from God to help us re-learn "right relationship." In the New Covenant, Christ is the ultimate revelation of God. Christ's life and message is the most perfect expression of how each of us is called to live. This is why we call Judeo/Christianity a "revealed religion." We did not come to the truth by our own reasoning processes. It had to be revealed to us. The teaching Church has been entrusted with interpreting, passing on and holding secure for all people the authentic message of Christ and the revealed Truths of God. It is the same Church that Ignatius served and loved. His discernment rules are spiritual guidelines that help us understand the revealed truth of "right relationship" in our own lives according to the revealed truths entrusted to the teaching Church.

Ignatius' discernment wisdom, in his rules, is discovered when individuals begin to pay close attention to inspirations that we identify through *affective feelings*. We are "inspired" in thoughts, words and deeds from three sources: our own human nature (body and soul); the Divine-Inspirer; and human nature's enemy, the counter-inspirer. These "inspirations" have one of two effects on us, they either create spiritual consolation or spiritual desolation. This week we begin looking at these two types of inspiration.

Two Benchmark Guidelines for Spiritual Discernment

To help your awakening and initiation into spiritual discernment, two benchmark guidelines will be beneficial in many life situations. It is important to understand that Divine inspiration, or consolation, does not always *feel good*. Equally important is to realize that an unholy inspiration, or spiritual desolation, does not always *feel bad.* We will explore this seeming paradox in a later lesson. For now it is sufficient to absorb the two benchmark guidelines and to understand that both are intended to influence the direction of our life towards or away from God in *every* thought, word and deed.

Benchmark One: Authentic divine inspirations called consolations will have specific features. Consolations will:

1) Increase the heart's love for God and others

2) Increase the virtues of docility, humility and self-generosity

3) Not run contrary to the truths and teachings of Scripture, the Tradition and the teaching Church[20]

211

Consolation can be the consequence of the Divine Physician's Spirit working in you. This form of consolation helps strengthen your heart and soul, encouraging you to turn to God. Consolation helps you to choose thoughts, words and deeds that express your authentic human nature made in the Divine image.

Consolation can also be the consequence of the body/spirit aspect of your Divinely-shaped human nature. God created your human nature as a gift in the Divine image and likeness. In spite of Original Sin's impact, cooperating with God's grace activates embedded life forces of your Divinely-shaped human nature, helping to heal biochemical, physiological and emotional imbalances; energizing you; and enabling thoughts, words and deeds that express your authentic human nature.

Benchmark Two: Authentic counter-inspirations called desolations will have specific features. Desolations will:

1) Increase narcissism, displacing God and others

2) Decrease docility and humility, and increase pride and self-satisfaction

3) Arouse hungers and desires that, although they feel good, will typically contradict the truths and teachings proposed by the Scripture, Tradition, and the teaching Church. This is because the author of counter-inspirations is opposed to Christ and will lead you away from life and truth. Counter-inspirations will produce desires *that feel authentic* because they are linked to *fallen* human nature's physical lusts and spiritual pride. They are the familiar default drives of a broken heart and a broken human nature.

Desolation can be the consequence of the enemy of human nature working in you. This form of desolation helps weaken your heart and soul, encouraging you to turn from God. Desolation helps you choose thoughts, words and deeds that are opposed to your Divinely-shaped human nature.

Desolation can also be the consequence of your own fallen human nature. God created your human nature as a gift in the Divine image and likeness. Yet, because of Original Sin's impact, not cooperating with God's grace erodes embedded life forces of your Divinely-shaped human nature, helping to destroy biochemical, physiological and emotional balance; de-energizing you; and increasing thoughts, words and deeds that are in opposition to your authentic human nature.

It is time for the Lord to act;
they have disobeyed your law.
Truly I love your commandments
more than gold, more than the finest gold.
Thus, I follow all your precepts;
every wrong way I hate.
(Ps 119: 126-28)

Week 32

FIRST

I resolve to spend no more than 15-minutes in each formal prayer session and to do so in some place apart; a technology-free zone.

SECOND

For the sake of God's greater glory, I continue a life-long process of praying with meditations one through five in *Sacred Story* prayer. I enter my prayer at least once daily as St. Ignatius suggested. This prayer will carry me for life. It will deepen my faith and my wisdom and awaken me to God's truth and love.

THIRD

By God's grace, I continue opening my heart to learn spiritual discernment. This week I explore definitions of spiritual consolation and spiritual desolation as Divine inspiration and counter-inspiration.

I will awaken to the present moment.
I will awaken to my spiritual nature.
I will not make any decisions based on fear.
I will practice Sacramental Reconciliation monthly.
I will ask Jesus for help when I am troubled.
I will thank Jesus daily for life's gifts.

Focus Affirmation for Week Thirty-Two
I will say this affirmation aloud once daily:
Christ, who has walked before me, knows everything I suffer.
Christ, who walks before me, will always lead me home to safety.

∞

Read this at the beginning of the week

Awakening to Sacred Story Discernment Guidelines
Guidelines for Fundamental Healing and Spiritual Growth

Is Prayer Helping or Hurting?

Some might say: "Until I started this prayer, I never felt bad, but now I do. I wonder if it is hurting instead of helping." If you find yourself asking the same question, you probably were feeling bad before you started the prayer discipline. You just were not aware of the pain or of your true feelings. There are many ways for us to "self-medicate" our pain, whether that pain is spiritual, emotional, or physical. The process of spiritual awakening brings to the light *pre-existing* spiritual conditions, that previously we were simply not conscious of. Now that you are becoming more aware, and actually *feeling* what is happening, you can ask for God's help and God can help you. Sometimes the presence of discomfort and pain is the first step to healing. Welcome it and invite Christ Jesus to heal your life and heart!

Introduction

Take some time this week to read and reflect on this fifth lesson in discernment. We will examine the Divine inspiration of spiritual consolation and the counter-inspiration of spiritual desolation. Start paying attention to your affective moods to *feel* the states of consolation and desolation in your story. This process requires a graced awakening, so ask God for the "eyes to see" your story through the lens of these spiritual lessons. Be patient as you slowly learn this way of understanding your story.

Guidelines for Fundamental Healing and Spiritual Growth

The practice of *Sacred Story* prayer makes one aware of the spiritual forces at work in one's life and in the world. Ignatius became a master at discerning these spiritual movements. He left guidelines for understanding how they work. You have learned already that there are three distinct sources influencing your thoughts, words, and deeds:

1)   your own emotional, psychological, and intellectual make-up shaped by concupiscence and your unique history

216

2) the Divine inspiration of consolation working to draw your thoughts, words, and deeds in the direction of your authentic human nature

3) the counter-inspirations of the enemy of your true human nature, seeking to pull you away from your authentic self

God (Divine-Inspirer) and the enemy of human nature (counter-inspirer) each seek ultimate influence over how your history unfolds: God for eternal love and life, the enemy of human nature for eternal despair and death; God for eternal relationships; the enemy of human nature for eternal loneliness.

Both God and the enemy of human nature are aware of your strengths, weaknesses, wounded memories, hopes, dreams, and fears. God desires to stir your conscience towards freedom and light, and bring you healing and hope.

God will build on your strengths, inflaming your holy desires and healing what is hurt and broken. The enemy of human nature seeks to silence your conscience and hide it in shadows. He will work to magnify your problems, diminish your holy desires and inspire hopelessness.

We identify and distinguish Divine inspirations from counter inspirations by their *intellectual* and *affective* traits, or signature characteristics. Ignatius defines two distinct types of inspiration. The first type, caused by Divine inspiration of the Spirit, he calls *consolation*. The second type, caused by the counter inspiration of the enemy of your human nature, he calls *desolation*.

Divine Inspiration: Consolation defines the feelings and thoughts of a healing heart returning to God and/or residing in God. God always inspires movement towards reconciliation and union. The signature characteristics of Divine Inspiration include being passionate for God and loving all things in God; tears of remorse and sadness when you fail, yet feeling loved by God despite your failures. You may experience tears of love for Christ who suffered the consequences of all sin, including your own. It is every increase in love, hope and faith that magnetizes your heart towards holy things; and all experiences of peace and quiet in the presence of your Creator. The Divine inspiration of consolation is manifest in humility that views eternal life, lasting love, and faith in God as the hope of the single-hearted, and the ultimate goal of those "willing to risk seeing reality as it truly is."

Counter Inspiration: Desolation defines feelings and thoughts that are the direct opposite of consolation's Divine inspiration. The signature characteristics of counter inspiration are darkness and confusion of a broken and wounded heart, soul, and spirit; magnetic and compulsive attractions to sensual and base appetites; restlessness, anger, cynicism, and temptations that make all things geared towards faith, hope and love appear dull, absurd and even destructive to your heart. You will feel a lazy, lukewarm and sad spirit as if separated from God. The counter inspiration of desolation is everything that magnetizes a broken heart towards cynicism, lusts, isolation, anger, despair and aloneness. The counter inspiration of desolation is manifest in an unyielding pride that views eternal life, lasting love, and faith in God as illusions of the simple-minded, and the result of those "unwilling to risk seeing reality as truly it is."

Spiritual Pleasure and Success

Illicit pleasures of our higher spiritual nature often reside in our attitudes like one's personal definition of success. I can be comforted by my own self-righteousness and contemptuous of others.

The Pharisee took up his position and spoke this prayer to himself, 'O God, I thank you that I am not like the rest of humanity—greedy, dishonest, adulterous—or even like this tax collector. I fast twice a week, and I pay tithes on my whole income"(Lk 18: 11-12).

The Pharisee, while fulfilling the *rule of law*, was trapped in a false identity. Spiritual attitudes (world views and our definitions of success) need discernment to determine whether or not they are of God. Just because they are legal, does not mean they are *of* God!

Consolations can make you *feel bad* when they move you toward your authentic human nature. The bad feelings caused by movement toward authenticity are something that applies equally to both your lower physical nature and higher spiritual nature. If you are accustomed to physical pleasures or lifestyles and relationships that fall outside the boundaries of the Commandments and/or Church teaching, the inspiration to cut loose from those pleasures can make you feel distress and anxiety. Remember that Ignatius panicked and felt distress when he realized that he would have to live without the pleasures of his first thirty years for the rest of his life.

The distress you feel when moving toward authenticity in your physical nature is also true when you are moving toward authenticity in your spiritual nature. If you are accustomed to spiritual pleasures that fall outside the boundaries of the Commandments or Church teaching, such as a false definition of success that has shaped your life, you may similarly feel distress, panic or anxiety when contemplating a change. This is because you are uncertain of what lies beyond the false definition of success. It may feel like a frightening void.

Thus the movement toward authenticity can create fear and distress for both your physical and spiritual natures. The fear aroused by the invitation to live authentically needs to be strongly confronted, because you are being invited towards life, not death. You must learn to resist the fear when moving toward authenticity as defined by the Commandments and Church teaching.

Counter inspirations called desolations can make you *feel good* even if they move you away from your authentic human nature. The *good feelings* caused by movement away from authenticity apply equally to both your lower physical nature and higher spiritual nature. If you are accustomed to physical pleasures that fall outside the boundaries of the Commandments and/or Church teaching, the inspiration to stay committed to those pleasures can make you feel relief— *feel good.*

The relief you feel when moving away from authenticity in your physical nature is also true when you are moving away from authenticity in your spiritual nature. If you are accustomed to spiritual pleasures that fall outside the boundaries of the Commandments and/or Church teaching, like a false definition of success that has shaped your life, you may similarly feel relief—*feel good*—in remaining committed to that false identity.

The inspiration to "stay just where you are" will most likely be supported by many *logical* justifications for why it is best not to change course. By staying put, you have consciously or unconsciously been manipulated by your fears. The fears aroused by the invitation to live authentically need to be strongly confronted because you are being invited towards death, not life. You must learn to resist the fear when moving away from authenticity as defined by the Commandments and Church teaching.

This is an important discernment lesson. It is critical to understand that inspirations caused by the Divine Inspirer, as well as those inspired by the counter-inspirer, can both *feel good* or *feel bad*, depending on your lifestyle and the corresponding state of your heart and soul.

So, always pay attention to *definitions of authenticity* regarding human nature as defined by the Commandments and Church teaching. It is advisable to *keep an eye on the direction the inspirations lead*, (away from authenticity or towards authenticity) more than whether inspirations make you *feel good* or *feel bad*.

ଔ

From wanton sin especially, restrain your servant; let it not rule over me.
Then shall I be blameless and innocent of serious sin.
The precepts of the Lord give joy to the heart.
(Ps 19: 14)

ଔ

Week 33

FIRST

As before, I will visualize the week ahead and imagine where I can find technology-free zones for my 15-minutes of formal prayer each day. I will consider changing the number of prayer sessions each day (from one to two or from two to one). I will make a conscious choice to adjust my prayer schedule, if I judge it a wise decision that will deepen my daily commitment to Christ.

SECOND

I pray for the grace to make a life-long commitment to daily pray movements one through five in the *Sacred Story* prayer. I will enter my prayer at least once daily as St. Ignatius suggested. I recognize that this prayer will carry me for life, deepening my faith and wisdom, and awakening me to God's truth and love in every thought, word and deed.

THIRD

I continue to ask God's grace to understand spiritual discernment in my life. This week I will explore definitions of spiritual consolation and spiritual desolation as embedded attitudes or lifestyles that can shape my *Sacred Story*.

I will awaken to the present moment.

I will awaken to my spiritual nature.

I will not make any decisions based on fear.

I will practice Sacramental Reconciliation monthly.

I will ask Jesus for help when I am troubled.

I will thank Jesus daily for life's gifts.

Focus Affirmation for Week Thirty-Three

I will say this affirmation aloud once daily:

I will strive to curb temptations to react to people and events.
I will ask myself what causes my anger
and irritation at people and events.
I will seek to identify the source of my anger and irritation.

CB

Read this at the beginning of the week

Awakening to Sacred Story *Discernment Guidelines*
Guidelines for Fundamental Healing and Spiritual Growth

Introduction

Take some time this week to read and reflect on this sixth lesson in discernment. We examined the Divine inspiration of spiritual consolation and the counter inspiration of spiritual desolation last week. This week we focus on identifying the ways in which these spiritual states manifest as lifestyles. Continue to pay attention to your affective moods to *feel* the states of consolation and desolation in your story. Look too for embedded lifestyle attitudes that bear the signature characteristics of consolation and desolation.

Consolation and desolation manifest as lifestyles. We can consciously or unconsciously live a life that is either aligned with life *or* death. The book of Deuteronomy powerfully captures this reality. God placed before the people Israel two distinct choices:

See, I have today set before you life and good, death and evil. If you obey the commandments of the LORD, your God, which I am giving you today, loving the LORD, your God, and walking in his ways, and keeping his commandments, statutes and ordinances, you will live and grow numerous, and the LORD, your God, will bless you in the land you are entering to possess. If, however, your heart turns away and you do not obey, but are led astray and bow down to other gods and serve them, I tell you today that you will certainly perish; you will not have a long life on the land which you are crossing the Jordan to enter and possess. I call heaven and earth today to witness against you: I have set before you life and death, the blessing and the curse. Choose life, then, that you and your descendants may live, by loving the LORD, your God, obeying his voice, and holding fast to him. For that will mean life for you, a long life for you to live on the land which the LORD swore to your ancestors, to Abraham, Isaac, and Jacob, to give to them (Dt. 30: 15-20).

Cling to God

222

If we have become insensitive to God's presence, we can be moving away from the Author of Life in our *Sacred Story*. We may not be aware of this because of a silenced conscience. If you live in a culture or a sub-culture that is also insensitive to the Author of Life, you can be doubly challenged to find the path back to life. If you are sensitive to the Author of life, then your *Sacred Story* is moving in the direction of producing fruit that endures to eternity. This will be true even if you live in a culture that is insensitive to life's Author. A culture oriented away from God can make choosing the good more difficult, but Christ guarantees the fruit produced. He promises:

What Are Inordinate Attachments?

If we lack freedom before created *things*, St. Ignatius says we have an *inordinate attachment*. I can be *inordinately* attached to wealth, age, health, people, material goods or a definition of success for my life. An inordinate attachment can be almost anything I control (or want to control) that affects my *Sacred Story*. The goal is not to get rid of the things that are inordinate attachments. Ignatius tells us that we want to get rid of the *attachment* to the things. I may have $100 and be inordinately attached to it. Ignatius would advise that I neither keep *nor* give the money away, but pray for the spiritual freedom to *either* keep it or let it go. My discernment to keep or surrender is made according to whatever action advances me further along the path of my *Sacred Story*. The Foundations Prayer from Week Twenty-Three E&W, articulates this principle of spiritual freedom from attachments.

Blessed are you when they insult you and persecute you and utter every kind of evil against you [falsely] because of me. Rejoice and be glad, for your reward will be great in heaven. Thus they persecuted the prophets who were before you (Mt 5: 11-12).

We can also choose to align ourselves with sub-cultures that are counter to the life proposed by the Commandments, Scripture and the teaching Church. It is difficult to be objective about anti-Gospel lifestyles when we are immersed in these sub-cultures simply because we become habituated to them.

These self-selected sub-cultures can diminish one's ability to gain objectivity or to discern effectively. These anti-Gospel sub-cultures can be economic, political, artistic, ethnic, intellectual, sexual, athletic, addiction-based, and Web-based, just to name a few. The main challenge is that we can cocoon in these cultures, allowing their definitions of happiness, success, the good, the beautiful, and the moral to isolate us from the data coming from deep in our heart, or from any other source.

This process of cocooning marks the impenetrable individualism of the present age. For these reasons, *consolation* and *desolation* can be described more comprehensively as *lifestyles* so one can measure the arc of one's life—one's life-*style*—against the traditional categories Ignatius defined as the signature characteristics of human nature's Author or its enemy.

Thus your individual *lifestyle* can be discerned as either influenced by the Divine-Inspirer or the counter-inspirer. You can identify the trajectory of your story first by reflecting on how you live. If your story and the *balance* of thoughts, words and deeds are aligned with the Commandments, Scripture and the teaching Church, then you are *choosing life*. If not, then it is time to pray for light.

CB

Divine Inspiration as a Lifestyle

Are you *evolving* under the Divine inspirations aligned to thoughts, words and deeds harmonious with the Scripture, Commandments and the teaching Church? If so, the Divine author of your human nature will provide "heart-verification" to alert you to thoughts, words and deeds that can move you off the true path. The Divine-Inspirer will awaken your reason and stir your conscience.

When this happens you will feel sadness, anxiety, grief and remorse, the result of thoughts, words, and deeds that lead away from God. God grants these feelings if you are moving towards the counter inspirations of anti-love—anti-Christ. Such feelings can be difficult and intense. Yet they are a gift and a certain reminder that engaging the Gospel values of your Faith belief and practice, will bring you the peace and hope you seek.

Counter Inspiration as a Lifestyle

Are you *evolving* under the counter inspirations opposed to love? Are your thoughts, words and deeds opposed to the Commandments, Scripture and the teaching Church? The enemy of your human nature is able to hold you in the grip of your disordered appetites by deceit and false appearances. What leads you away from God, from Love, appears pleasurable, and is presented as good, life-giving, fashionable, enlightened and sophisticated.

Leading away from the sheltering safety of God's love and your authentic human nature, these thoughts, words and deeds, as excessive appetites, are aptly named *false loves*, and false loves speak powerfully to broken hearts. If you are in the grip of the counter inspirations of these false loves you will feel aversion to engaging the Gospel values or be hostile to the Commandments and guidelines of the teaching Church. You will experience difficulty practicing and persevering in your faith.

This is an important discernment lesson. Think of Divine inspiration (spiritual consolation) as a healthy lifestyle that may not feel healthy because *it is not* supported by the culture or sub-cultures in which you live. Think of counter inspiration (spiritual desolation) as an unhealthy lifestyle that might not feel unhealthy because *it is* supported by the culture or sub-cultures in which you live. So as you learned last week, always *keep an eye on the direction the inspirations lead*, more than whether inspirations make you *feel good* or *feel bad*.

If you want to map some of the influences in your life, make a small chart of the various sub-cultures where you spend most of your time each week: corporate culture, work environments, Internet, social groups and associations, exercise or athletic environments, groups aligned with arts and or entertainment, political parties, and the cultures of film, television and or radio where you spend time. Next to each sub-culture, write what you believe is its *signature characteristic* regarding its *overall* influence on your lifestyle. Does the sub-culture support Divine inspiration or support counter inspiration? In other words, is the sub-culture congruent with the values of Scripture, Tradition and the teaching Church?

Some of these sub-cultures may be fixed parts of your life due to career, family, or region. Others may be affiliations by personal choice. Do some of the sub-cultures force you to conceal your religious beliefs? Do you have what St. Ignatius defines as an inordinate attachment to any of these sub-cultures and the values they espouse? Does your affiliation with the sub-culture move you further along in your *Sacred Story* or obstruct your movement? Does your affiliation with the sub-culture increase the ease or difficulty of developing your authentic human nature as guided by the Commandments and Church teaching?

ය

Set a guard, Lord, before my mouth,
keep watch over the door of my lips.
Do not let my heart incline to evil,
to perform deeds in wickedness.
On the delicacies of evildoers
let me not feast.
Let a righteous person strike me; it is mercy if he reproves me.
Do not withhold oil from my head
while my prayer opposes their evil deeds.
(Ps 141: 3-5)

න

Week 34

FIRST

I will visualize my week ahead to identify places I can find technology-free zones for my 15-minutes of prayer each day. I am also learning that my resolution to spend no more and no less than 15-minutes in those prayer periods increases my fidelity to the practice.

SECOND

I will continue this thirty-fourth week by praying the five meditations of *Sacred Story* prayer. As St. Ignatius suggested, I enter my prayer at least once daily. Each time I pray my heart opens more fully and I am carried forward in my *Sacred Story.*

THIRD

I will ask God to help me understand the school of spiritual discernment. This week I will ponder St. Ignatius' wisdom on how I ought to act when influenced by the desolation of counter-inspiration.

I will awaken to the present moment.
I will awaken to my spiritual nature.
I will not make any decisions based on fear.
I will practice Sacramental Reconciliation monthly.
I will ask Jesus for help when I am troubled.
I will thank Jesus daily for life's gifts.

Focus Affirmation for Week Thirty-Four
I will say this affirmation aloud once daily:

I will give thanks for what angers and upsets me; identifying their source will set me free.
I will strive to listen, watch and pray; listen, watch and pray.
I will listen, watch and pray!

CR

Read this at the beginning of the week

Awakening to Sacred Story *Discernment Guidelines*
Guidelines for Fundamental Healing and Spiritual Growth

Introduction

Take some time this week to read and reflect on this seventh lesson in discernment. Last week we examined the Divine inspiration of spiritual consolation and the counter inspiration of spiritual desolation as embedded in our lifestyles. This week we will consider St. Ignatius' wisdom on how we can help diffuse the impact of counter inspiration's desolation when in its grip.

Guidelines for Fundamental Healing and Spiritual Growth

Diffusing Counter Inspirations

Personal sin, addictions, and emotional/psychological wounds make a person vulnerable to spiritual desolation. When gripped by spiritual desolation, your faith, hope and love is diminished. Ignatius offers indispensable guidance when you are under the influence of counter inspirations and are spiritually desolate, discouraged, hopeless and frustrated. If you closely adhere to these guidelines and act on them, *you will avoid much pain and grief in your life*. Do not despair if you do not understand the guidelines now. There will come a time when this wisdom will help you.

Ignatius offers four principles for how we ought to act when tempted by the counter inspirations of desolation.

1) *When spiritually desolate and experiencing a loss of faith, hope and love, NEVER change course away from the positive resolutions and decisions you reached while under the influence of the Divine inspiration of consolation. Never change course when in desolation!*

When you suffer the anxieties and the pressures of counter-inspirations' desolations, **do not change course!** Human nature's enemy feeds on spiritual/emotional wounds and on broken hearts. The counter inspirations may seem logical but they **never lead to freedom, peace, or your heart's healing.** None of the choices and decisions influenced by the counter inspirations of desolation, **no matter how utterly logical they might appear,** will ever increase faith, hope or love. One must be vigilant when tempted by an urgent or compelling need *to act immediately.* When you feel compelled by an anxious urgency to reach a decision or engage an action, *it is a clear sign* of counter inspirations at work.

2) *During times of desolation, redouble efforts to open and orient your heart to God. Use prayer, examination of conscience, and perhaps some simple penance or fasting to seek God's grace (Mk 9:29).*

Counter inspirations make it difficult to *see and feel* authentic human nature. Amplifying positive efforts on spiritual fronts might feel incredibly difficult. Yet St. Ignatius' experience demonstrated that we need, at these times, *extra exercise* of spirit and body to resist desolation. A determined spirit is necessary during such times. Also, be attentive to thoughts, words, or deeds that are based on *inaccurate* assessments of your authentic human nature. Allow the times of desolation to instruct you!

Watch for Obsessive Thinking

You are *always* either in a state of consolation or desolation. These lessons are teaching you to *notice* these two spiritual states that have been with you all your life. If you find yourself becoming obsessive about tracking what state you are in at each moment of the day, then you have succumbed to counter-inspirations. Strive for an alert heart and mind. Pray to avoid an obsessive attitude. Being aware will serve your spiritual growth. Being obsessive will harm your spiritual growth.

---

3) *God provides the essential support and grace necessary to withstand these times of trial and purification.*

The support you need will come from your natural abilities, assisted by Divine grace. You may feel completely overwhelmed by temptations, or the darkness of spirit associated with disordered attractions and compulsive behaviors. Yet there is sufficient grace for salvation, even if the *logic* of the counter inspiration indicates otherwise! Jesus, the Divine Physician, is *very close to you* during these times of purification. When you encounter the full force and darkness of counter inspirations, be assured that God is present to you even though you may not feel God's presence.

Do not be deceived by the feelings, no matter how strong or mocking they might appear. This is especially true when your weaknesses, shame and failings are painfully highlighted. Through trial and error, St. Ignatius learned that God is *not* absent. Trust Ignatius' wise counsel and affirm your faith in God during times when you do not feel the Spirit. Instead, consciously *thank God, who in complete faithfulness,* will embrace you. Thank God *aloud* and affirm God's salvific role in your *Sacred Story.*

4) *Intentionally strive to cultivate patience and persevere in the religious practices of your faith when influenced by the desolation of counter-inspiration.*

When to Make Decisions

Counter-inspirations are usually accompanied by anxiety, electrical excitement and a compelling urge to act quickly and definitively. Never make decisions when you sense these emotional states.

Divine-inspirations are usually accompanied by a deep and abiding peace and calm with no urge to act quickly or definitively. Only make decisions during times of Divine-inspiration's peace and calm.

Learning the difference between these two spiritual states of heart/mind will serve you very well. It is hard to resist the compulsive urge to act quickly when in the grip of counter-inspiration's anxieties. Resist! You will save yourself a great deal of pain the enemy of human nature desires to inflict on you.

The Divine inspiration of consolation always returns. In the interim, use the means of prayer, penance, and self-examination to resist and gain the most from these times of trial. To counter the anxiety you may experience, embrace desolations as an opportunity to deepen your maturing life with God. Be not afraid.

Considerable spiritual and human progress, as well as illumination, will result from your patience and perseverance during these trials. In time you will discover that these times of stress, endured in faith, can produce the enlightenment, healing, peace and hope you seek. *Therefore, do not fear them.*

Say aloud the one thing that makes you question God's love for you. Now hear the Lord say: "Nothing in the past or the future; no angel or demon; no height or depth; nothing in all of creation will ever separate you from my love in Christ Jesus." (Rom 8:38-39).

CB

Let your work be seen by your servants and your glory by their children; and may the gracious care of the Lord our God be ours; prosper the work of our hands for us! Prosper the work of our hands!

Ps 90: 16-17

SO

Week 35

First
I resolve to spend no more and no less than 15-minutes in each formal prayer period. At the beginning of the week, I will visualize where each will be, in some place apart: a technology-free zone.

Second
For this thirty-fifth week, I resolve by God's grace, to commit for life to praying meditations one through five in the *Sacred Story* prayer. As St. Ignatius suggested, I will enter my prayer at least once daily. Also, I may find it necessary to recommit to the simple, daily journal exercises explained in Week 16.

Third
I ask God's grace to deepen my knowledge of spiritual discernment as this week I consider the three sources of desolation identified by St. Ignatius.

I will awaken to the present moment.

I will awaken to my spiritual nature.

I will not make any decisions based on fear.

I will practice Sacramental Reconciliation monthly.

I will ask Jesus for help when I am troubled.

I will thank Jesus daily for life's gifts.

Focus Affirmation for Week Thirty-Five
I will say this affirmation aloud once daily:
Everyone has been mortally wounded spiritually, psychologically, and physically by Original Sin and the loss of paradise.

Journeying with Christ to the roots of my
sins and addictions will help break their grip.

℘

Read this at the beginning of the week

Awakening to Sacred Story _Discernment Guidelines_
Guidelines for Fundamental Healing and Spiritual Growth

A Review of the Journal Exercises
Before proceeding, it is important to revisit the *indispensable practice* of the daily, weekly and monthly journal or logbook exercises. Early in the *Sacred Story* prayer journey, you wrote two things that surfaced in your life each day: something that brought encouragement and something that upset you or generated fear, anger or grief. By briefly focusing every day on these two categories, you will be recording the necessary data that will help you to understand Ignatius' spiritual discernment *Rules* in your own story and life history. Every day, write one experience that increases faith, hope and love. Write a second experience that decreases your faith, hope and love.

Make sure you write a complete sentence. For example: "The Sunday homily about forgiveness helped me understand God's mercy and brought me hope." Or: "The Sunday homily about forgiveness upset me and made me wonder if God can ever forgive some of the things I have done." The first experience increases faith, hope and love; the second diminishes faith, hope and love.

These *short* statements are different than a diary or a regular journal. The statements help to *track trends* in your spiritual life. Done faithfully, you will begin to identify the signature of God's grace in your particular joys and encouragements, and the signature of the enemy of human nature's presence in your particular temptations and discouragements. For this week, every day, write two experiences you noticed from each source (instead of the usual one experience from each source). This exercise ought to be no more than one minute in length, as explained in the lesson from Week 16.

At the end of each week, identify the most significant consolations and desolations. Write two short sentences at week's end that capture what you observe to be *the most significant* statement on each side of the spiritual divide: spiritual consolation and spiritual desolation.

At month's end, review your weekly summaries of consolations and desolations. Sort through those eight statements (four consolations and four desolations), and identify the two that you consider have *most increased* and *most decreased* your faith, hope and love. These monthly summary statements, for both consolation and desolation, might be a new statement that is a *composite* of the four you wrote. Or it may be *one* of the four you wrote that stands out as the most important in each category (consolation or desolation).

An analogy from the medical world might help. Imagine I am diabetic. Daily (or perhaps hourly) I have to monitor my blood sugar. I will become quite attentive to foods and drink that increase or decrease my blood sugar.

In like fashion, this simple writing exercise, done faithfully—daily, weekly and monthly—will provide spiritual illumination on what increases and decreases your faith, hope and love. Graced insights will reveal how God and the enemy of your human nature work in *your* life history. Grace will attract you toward peace and hope, while the enemy's influence will manifest in discouragement and despair.

Three Reasons for Spiritual Desolation

Introduction

Take some time this week to read and reflect on this eighth lesson in discernment. Last week we examined four important ways to respond during a time of counter-inspiration's spiritual desolation. This week we consider three reasons Ignatius gives for *why* we experience spiritual desolation.

Personal sin, addictions, and your emotional/psychological wounds make you vulnerable to spiritual desolation. When gripped by spiritual desolation, faith, hope and love diminish. Ignatius offers indispensable guidance to assist you through the temptations of these counter-inspirations.

Recall that when you are spiritually desolate, you will experience discouragement, hopelessness and frustration. By close attention to these guidelines, and applying them daily, *you will avoid much pain and grief in your life*. Do not despair or get frustrated if you do not understand the guidelines now. There will come a time when this wisdom will be crystal-clear.

God allows us to experience desolation to orient our hearts toward genuine love and our true human nature. We experience counter-inspiration's desolation for one of three reasons:

1) *Desolation is directly related to wrong choices in thoughts, words, and deeds made under the influence of the false logic of the counter-inspirations.*

God removes the divine inspiration of consolation *as a holy warning* that you are straying from your authentic human nature. God acts this way to stir your conscience to remind you to return to authenticity. God allows the loss of consolation so you can *feel* the consequences of your thoughts, words, and deeds associated with counter-inspirational choices. Such false choices will, in due course, destroy relationships, creation, human life, faith, hope and love.

Essentially, your false choices erode and destroy the very things that God provides so you can find fulfillment, communion, and peace in this life, and eternal joy in the next. Our own choices and the consequences of those choices lead us to experience the reality of counter-inspiration's desolation.

> 2) *God allows desolation, which is directly linked with your human growth and spiritual progress, to awaken your whole being—spirit, mind and body—to its spiritual, emotional and psychological wounds.*

Desolation reveals the ways in which your destructive desires and habits have taken root in your spirit, mind and body. Desolation is evidence of how your wounds contribute to the division of your being. Spiritual progress and forward movement in your life story is only possible when you awaken and confront this damaging pattern.

We need to be courageous. Identifying and uprooting these appetites and habits can be likened to spiritual surgery. Because this awakening, and the spiritual renewal and healing it initiates can, at times, be painful and intense, resulting in one *feeling* hopeless and/or abandoned. But recall that your spiritual maturity cannot be evaluated by unpleasant feelings. Take courage and walk forward, trusting in God.

It is essential that you allow these deeply rooted destructive tendencies to surface, so that a new consciousness and freedom can be born. Giving God permission to move forward with your spiritual growth is the only way these habits, grounded in counter-inspirations, can be uprooted, diffused and healed.

Ignatius taught that God supports us most especially during these times when we can *feel* lost. At times, we might feel condemned by the darkness in our being: heart, mind and body. These can be present events, or ones we experience through memories. St. Ignatius advised, based on his own experiences of these intense moments, that God's grace is enough to support one.

You can have *feelings* of desolation associated with the awareness of your disordered appetites and a human nature wounded by sin. The feelings do not indicate how God *views* and *feels* about you. Since these *feelings* offer a false reading of your authentic human nature, do not be fooled into believing that God does not love and cherish you because you *feel* and experience these periods of darkness.

You are completely distinct from the darkness or the disordered, shameful appetites that you experience. God loves you and supports your most authentic self as you suffer the stripping away of the pain, sin, narcissism and wounds that hide your authentic human nature.

Feelings of darkness are associated with your false self: the false loves; the broken heart and dreams; the narcissism and pride; the extravagant appetites and the destructive drives associated with your spiritual and psychological wounds. With your cooperation, God is gradually uprooting these from your heart.[21]

3) *Third, counter inspirations of desolation may appear during times of spiritual advancement.*

After a period of purification marked by desolation, your heart finds peace in the Divine inspiration of consolation. During these graced rests, you may be tempted to believe the illusion that you have arrived and/or reached the end of your spiritual journey. You experience this state of calm and peace as definitive, and feel that you have achieved sanctity, completion, and holiness.

During these times, *and almost imperceptibly*, a spirit of pride and self-sufficiency takes hold in your heart. When this happens (when, not if!) the counter inspirations of desolation return *as a warning*. This happened to St. Ignatius once. He felt that he was among the just, and that his spiritual growth was complete, but having experienced desolation, he realized that he was actually *only beginning* on the road to salvation.

Everything achieved up to this point has occurred through God's grace, and through your cooperation with that grace. Grace has reunited you with God, and as a result the virtues of humility, trust, and dependence are beginning to develop.

God allows desolations as a warning to remind you that although you have grown in authenticity and holiness, you are still susceptible to the narcissism and destructive pride that will halt all your progress towards further union with God. Be watchful for the first signs of narcissism and pride. They usually manifest when you start to fall away from your spiritual disciplines and other practices of your Faith. You might say to yourself: "I am healed;" or, "I don't need those practices anymore;" or "at least I don't heed them as much as I used to!" You are deceiving yourself, and being deceived, to believe such things.

Therefore, cultivate humility during the consoling times of the Divine inspiration. Use your periods of consolation as a preparation for the times of desolation. Be *aware and awake*, always anticipating the return of desolation.

Plan ahead for when desolation makes its return. During your time of consolation, remember how helpless you felt during your time of desolation. This serves as a reminder that *God is the only one* who stabilizes your heart with the Divine inspiration of consolation.

When the counter inspiration of desolation returns, pray to understand which of Ignatius' three reasons might be its origin. When under the influence of desolation, hold steady! Nurture humility and patience, doing everything possible to orient your thoughts, words, and deeds towards an awareness of God's presence in your life. Recall Creation, Presence, Memory, Mercy and Eternity.

Remember that God holds you fast during the Divine inspirations of consolation, and holds you even closer during the cleansing times of desolation. Affirm your faith in God. Hold fast to the spiritual disciplines offered here as well as the other practices of your Faith. Seek stability and fidelity in times of peace and calm as well as in times of turbulence and struggle.

03

Behold, the eye of the Lord is upon those who fear him,
upon those who count on his mercy,
To deliver their soul from death,
and to keep them alive through famine.
Our soul waits for the Lord, who is our help and our shield.
May your kindness, O Lord, be upon us
who have put our hope in you.
(Ps 33: 18-22)

80

Week 36

FIRST

I resolve to spend no more than 15-minutes in each formal prayer session and to visualize my week ahead for where these will be. I will choose a place apart.

SECOND

I continue praying meditations one through five in the *Sacred Story* prayer in this thirty-sixth week. I enter my prayer at least once daily as St. Ignatius suggested. If I have not been faithful to my journal exercises, I will recommit to this very important discipline.

THIRD

I ask God's grace to deepen my understanding of spiritual discernment as I consider two of the three strategies the enemy of human nature employs to stall my spiritual growth.

I will awaken to the present moment.
I will awaken to my spiritual nature.
I will not make any decisions based on fear.
I will practice Sacramental Reconciliation monthly.
I will ask Jesus for help when I am troubled.
I will thank Jesus daily for life's gifts.

Focus Affirmation for Week Thirty-Six
I will say this affirmation aloud once daily:
I will not waste time worrying about my sins and failures.
I will use my time wisely and ask God to help
me understand the source of my sins and failings.

I will trust that Christ came to heal all my wounds.

೦෪

Read this at the beginning of the week

Awakening to **Sacred Story** *Discernment Guidelines*
Guidelines for Fundamental Healing and Spiritual Growth

Introduction

Take some time this week to read and reflect on this ninth lesson in discernment. Last week, we examined the three principal reasons we experience counter inspiration's spiritual desolation. This week we look at two of the three attack strategies used by the enemy of human nature to obstruct our spiritual progress.

All three strategies use elements of our life story as weapons against us: our unconscious fears; our psychological and spiritual vulnerabilities; and our long-standing addictive, compulsive and/or sinful habits. These sinful habits do not make us happy. But they are familiar behaviors and the *pain of the familiar* is often preferred to *the fear of the unknown.*

Ignatius learned these three attack strategies from his own experience of being deceived during his conversion process. Learn from his hard-earned wisdom. You might be at a place in your life where you have not yet encountered any of these tactics. If that is the case, the explanations may not make sense now, but they will in time. Notice again that *fear* is the common basis for all lines of attack.

Be Not Afraid!

The enemy of our human nature likes to conceal himself and manipulate us with our conscious and unconscious fears. It is a carefully planned strategy. The strategy of the enemy is to "play" on our greatest vulnerabilities, even menace us and taunt us with them.

A part of the carefully designed strategy is to keep us bending to our fears. The more we bend to them, the stronger the fears become the next time we consider opposing them. This is why it is imperative to call fear's bluff and confront the fear—whatever fear it may be. "Be not afraid" is one of the most common phrases in Old and New Testament. God uses hope. The enemy uses fear. Discern the difference in their "voices."

Three Strategies of the Enemy of Human Nature: To Confound, Frighten, and Deceive Individuals Committed to Spiritual Growth

When you engage your faith practice daily, the enemy of human nature can employ three subtle and malicious lines of attack to discourage you. He will use the weaknesses associated with your vices, your extravagant appetites, your compulsive drives, your spiritual/psychological wounds, and your broken heart. This week we will consider the first two of the three strategies:

1) *Fear and panic attacks are strategically employed to block growth.*

If you stay committed to the process of uprooting vices, sins, addictions and destructive habits from your life and heart, you may be attacked with waves of fear and panic to turn you away from the healing process. If you waver in your commitment to the healing process, the fear and panic can intensify exponentially. In the extreme, you can be paralyzed by unrelenting terror and withering dread.[22]

Directly confront the menacing fear. If you hold steadfast to the commitments associated with your spiritual and psychological growth, the panic and fear will eventually abate. If you consistently confront the fears and hold fast to the healing process, you will notice that the strategy of "fear and dread" is just that: a strategy. As a ploy, the fear and the dread is never realized. Nonetheless, it is maliciously effective *if and when* you surrender to it.[23]

2) *Narcissism and false values masquerade as true love and authentic values.*

Those committed to allowing vices, addictions, sins and destructive habits to be uprooted from their life and heart will also confront other tricks. The enemy can also portray narcissism as authentic love and vices as positive values. These are tactics of the father of lies to deceive you. The enemy of human nature knows that every heart searches for true love. But every heart is also divided and broken by the effects of its multiple spiritual and psychological wounds. The counter-inspiration of desolation blinds your heart's perception of what is spiritually and humanly authentic, and what leads to eternal life. Your heart can be easily fooled and tempted by false promises of love. All false loves are illicit because they are *lusts* masquerading as *love*. False loves are like mirages for parched and anxious hearts hoping to quench their thirst and find comfort. Instead of providing lasting peace, these illicit loves—illusions really— merely intensify longings, self-deception, self-preoccupation, and narcissism, ultimately leading to spiritual and psychological death.

It is easy to observe the corrosive effects of sins and addictions in other individuals and other groups. But when you are in their grip, it is difficult to imagine these sins and addictions as anything other than a precious lifeline. God

243

clearly sees the corrosive and poisonous effects of false loves on persons, families, societies and nature. But those in their grip are seduced into believing in false love's comforts, because all false loves can appear as *good*, *life-giving*, and *natural*. The deception to believe false loves as good, life-giving and natural is complicated by evil's evolution: in political and financial collectives; in educational systems and philosophies; in family structures and social networks; in culture and entertainment. Evil's evolution in all of these can support and reward those trapped in the deception.

The varieties of deception and seduction are as numerous as the ways a heart can be broken. God will not sanction these lusts because they issue from a violated heart and lead to your heart's further violation. Once acted upon, you will most assuredly violate the hearts of others. God is Love: the origin, the end, and the defender of the human heart. While God is infinitely merciful with our struggles, God cannot sanction anything that breaks your heart, destroys your authentic human nature, or leads to your spiritual death.

Bring all false loves to full consciousness. Examine them in light of the writings of saints, doctors of the Church, and the mystical Christian traditions of West and East. Identify and name your sins, addictions, and habits truthfully as false lovers. Speak about these false loves with a spiritual guide who holds sacred the Tradition and the Gospels.

You will not be convinced of these false loves' unholy origin until you are honest about them. Examine your false lovers in the light of day, not by the cover of night. Here, in the light of grace, they will be revealed as neither true servants of the heart nor pathways to the Divine. By exposing them, you will not lose love and life as you fear. You will find, eventually, the path to Love itself: the Christ who is worthy of your total devotion and self-surrender.

When you are in the grip of false loves, activate Ignatius' *Truth Paradigm* (as we first learned in Week 16). With Christ at your side consciously take these steps:

Declare to Christ the specific sin, addiction, or destructive compulsion and name it as a false lover.

Describe to Christ the specific sin, addiction or destructive compulsion as coming from the enemy of your human nature.

Descend with Christ into your memory to see and feel your first experience of this specific sin, addiction or compulsion. Ask Christ to compassionately reveal the stress fractures, loneliness and wounds in your heart it promised to satisfy.

Denounce with Christ as your witness, the sin, addiction or destructive compulsion for the ruinous effect in your life, others' lives and society.

Decide for Christ to heal this wound, diffuse the stress, anxiety and fear feeding it, and transform its damaging effects on your life into *Sacred Story*.

Love Can Miss the Mark

The most common word in Greek for sin is *hamartia*, meaning to *miss the mark*. If we define sin primarily by what it does—destroy relationships—then sin means *missing the mark* in both our understanding and practice of "right relationship." Let's take a recurrent song lyric theme: "How can something that feels so right, be so wrong?" If the love this lyric expresses stands outside Gospel values, then "what feels so right" can be an experience of love that *feels* better than the lovelessness one had previously experienced. Or a variation on this lyric: "Feels so good to be loved so bad." This expression demonstrates the "false love" of lust that has become an addiction. Both types of love might *feel* better than what one had previously experienced. But both loves *miss the mark* on the true love God wants for us. They will not ultimately bring us to the fullness of our authentic human nature. This is why they are "wrong" in God's eyes and why Jesus does not bless them. Jesus wants much more for the Father's beloved children.

CZ

For I know well the plans I have in mind for you—plans for your welfare and not for woe, so as to give you a future of hope. When you call me, and come and pray to me, I will listen to you. When you look for me, you will find me. Yes, when you seek me with all your heart.

(Jer 29: 11-13)

ℰ

Week 37

FIRST
Visualizing the week ahead, I will decide where to spend my 15-minutes in each formal prayer period. As before, I will select a place apart, a technology-free zone.

SECOND
I will continue this thirty-seventh week by praying meditations one through five in the *Sacred Story* prayer. I will enter my prayer at least once daily as St. Ignatius suggested. I will make a firm commitment to the simple, daily journal exercises because they are an invaluable part of awakening to my *Sacred Story*.

THIRD
I will ask God's grace to help me master spiritual discernment. This week, I am invited to understand the third of the three strategies the enemy of human nature employs to stall my spiritual growth.

I will awaken to the present moment.
I will awaken to my spiritual nature.
I will not make any decisions based on fear.
I will practice Sacramental Reconciliation monthly.
I will ask Jesus for help when I am troubled.
I will thank Jesus daily for life's gifts.

Focus Affirmation for Week Thirty-Seven
I will say this affirmation aloud once daily:
*I alone control Christ's ability to transform
my life into a* Sacred Story.

The process begins when I ask for the grace to honestly
name my sins and addictions.
The process continues when I invite Christ
to illuminate my narcissism.
Only God's grace and mercy can write my Sacred Story.

ℭ

Read this at the beginning of the week

Awakening to Sacred Story *Discernment Guidelines*
Guidelines for Fundamental Healing and Spiritual Growth

Introduction

Take some time on the weekend or during the week to read and reflect on this tenth lesson in spiritual discernment. Last week we examined two of the three attack strategies used by the enemy of human nature to obstruct spiritual progress. All three strategies use elements of our life story as weapons against us: our unconscious fears, our psychological/spiritual vulnerabilities, and our long-standing habits. These habits do not create long-lasting happiness, but they are familiar. The boredom and/or pain of the familiar is often preferred to the fear of the unknown.

This week we examine the third attack strategy used by the enemy of human nature to obstruct our spiritual progress. Just as in the first two lines of attack, *fear* is the weapon used here by the enemy of human nature.

3) *When you commit to uprooting sin, addictions, and vices from your body and soul, you will be assaulted by attacks directed at the spiritual and psychological wounds that make you most vulnerable.*

The enemy of human nature can viciously attack where your wounds have left you most vulnerable. Those wounds might be spiritual, emotional, psychological, or moral. Core spiritual and psychological injuries to your heart and mind affect your capacity for self-transcendence. They make it difficult to love selflessly and achieve higher consciousness. A wall, built with emotional and intellectual counter-inspirations, is erected around the injuries, darkening your conscience. It is characteristic of the enemy of human nature to reinforce these emotional and intellectual defenses.

The enemy's purpose is to keep your emotional and intellectual defenses firmly in place; to keep your conscience dark and your true human nature *hidden*. The enemy's assault is felt as a bolstering and intensification of powerful emotional and intellectual defenses, leading you deeper into self-centered, self-absorbed, self-defended, self-justifying and narcissistic thoughts, words and deeds.

You become more proud. You are adamantly convinced and hardened in your judgments about the meaning of life, truth and beauty. These hardened convictions often contradict the Scriptures, received Tradition, the teaching Church and the mystical Christian traditions of West and East.

The defense measures of hardened convictions share the various qualities of desolation's counter inspiration.[24] The strategic attacks by the enemy of human nature keep you attached to self-oriented, defensive thoughts, words, deeds and habits, re-enforcing rigid reasoning systems and disordered attachments.

The enemy of human nature's chief goal is to *permanently camouflage* your heart's spiritual, emotional and psychological wounds. He does this to hide them from an awakened conscience, so you never notice *where or why* you need healing. Jesus made reference to these forms of defensive structures. They keep people from believing in Him, even if He should rise from the dead (Lk 16:31), and they grieved Jesus because they harden hearts (Mk 3: 5).

In our daily press, we can observe evidence of this tactic of the enemy of human nature. In one report, a teenager won a court case, forcing a public high school to remove a banner in the school's gym that referred to "Our Heavenly Father." The student, a baptized Roman Catholic, stopped believing in God at ten years of age when their mother fell ill. "I had always been told that if you pray, God will always be there when you need Him," the student said. "And it didn't happen for me, and I doubted it had happened for anybody else. So yeah, I think that was just like the last step, and after that I just really didn't believe any of it."

Much of the media framed the story as a legal and constitutional fight to prevent state-sponsored religion. But another plotline can be detected in this story. The student is opposing religious expression because of deep childhood wounds. The student's mother fell ill and "God did not listen" to a prayer for healing. At the bottom of this story is a deeply wounded heart. On the surface we see a determined and fearless youth standing up against the wrath of classmates and townspeople to defend constitutional rights.

The student is a self-described atheist and revered as a hero by many (including much of the media). This student could be at the beginning of a life-long crusade. And the enemy of human nature would urge this person on in that fight. The enemy will do anything to keep this person distracted from the interior wound so it cannot be healed. This fight will appear noble to the individual and to others. However, through the lens of *discernment*, the person is blind to the emotional and intellectual defense systems that have been constructed. Those defenses of pride, intellectual justification, and defiance conceal the fear and pain of a ten-year old child's broken heart.

Many people, fighting apparently noble causes, are terrified, wounded children running away from their pain. Further, the defense structures erected to protect the wound are hard to penetrate. Pride, rigid determination, anger, and attitudes of "crusader justice" conceal the fearful and wounded heart within. One thinks of St. Paul's attacks on the Church before his conversion. At the opening of the Acts of the Apostles, Saul witnessed the murder of Stephen. Later he started a crusade to crush all followers of the Way:

Now Saul, still breathing murderous threats against the disciples of the Lord, went to the high priest and asked him for letters to the synagogues in Damascus, that, if he should find any men or women who belonged to the Way, he might bring them back to Jerusalem in chains.
Acts 9:1-2

The enemy of human nature manipulated Saul's anger to legitimize murder. His homicidal rage was cloaked in religious justifications to stomp out all who followed the Lord Jesus. Fear was likely at the root of Saul's rage. It is possible that fear was also a driving force in St. Ignatius' life. Against the advice of the other knights, Ignatius forced the hand of his commander to engage a futile battle that nearly ended his life.[25]

Much of the violence perpetrated between persons, groups, and countries in our own day is generated by wounded hearts seeking revenge for their suffering. Violence, be it economic, academic, physical, psychological, or verbal, can be self-justified and is often hidden behind nationalism, false religion, laws, cultural norms and/or mob mentality.

Observe how the enemy of human nature instigates intellectual arguments, fosters a sense of injustice, and promotes defiance against legitimate authority. Ask the Lord, "What motivates *my* crusade (or crusades)? Where do I hurt? Help me to heal, and forgive me in the same way that I seek to forgive others. Help me spend the energy of my life to produce fruit that endures to eternity."

For he is our God,
we are the people he shepherds,
the sheep in his hands.

Oh, that today you would hear his voice:
Do not harden your hearts as at Meribah,
as on the day of Massah in the desert.
There your ancestors tested me;
they tried me though they had seen my works.
Forty years I loathed that generation;
I said: "This people's heart goes astray;
they do not know my ways."
Therefore I swore in my anger:
"They shall never enter my rest."
(Ps 95: 7-11)

NOTES

Week38

FIRST
I resolve to spend no more and no less than 15-minutes in each formal prayer period.

SECOND
As before, I continue this thirty-eighth week by praying meditations one through five in the *Sacred Story* prayer, entering my prayer at least once daily as St. Ignatius suggested. I reaffirm the importance of the simple journal exercises and my monthly practice of Sacramental Reconciliation.

THIRD
I will ask God's grace to keep my mind and heart open as I learn the ways of spiritual discernment in my *Sacred Story*. This week I am invited to reflect on the second series of discernment rules given by St. Ignatius. This second series of rules details temptations of a more subtle nature. Here the enemy of our human nature manipulates our undetected narcissism to obstruct or disrupt our spiritual growth.

I will awaken to the present moment.
I will awaken to my spiritual nature.
I will not make any decisions based on fear.
I will practice Sacramental Reconciliation monthly.
I will ask Jesus for help when I am troubled.
I will thank Jesus daily for life's gifts.

Focus Affirmation for Week Thirty-Eight
I will say this affirmation aloud once daily:

253

I will strive daily to pick up the cross, for it leads to my life.
The closer I get to holiness, the more I will
see and feel sin's disorder in my life.

␊

Read this at the beginning of the week

Awakening to Sacred Story *Discernment Guidelines*
Guidelines for Integrated Healing and Spiritual Growth

Introduction

Take some time this week to read and reflect on this eleventh lesson in discernment. Last week we finished a study of St. Ignatius' first set of rules on discernment. The first set of rules is called *Guidelines for Foundational Healing and Spiritual Growth*. They are *foundational* rules because they are directed towards those who can be more easily distracted from their spiritual journey with sensual pleasures and delights by the enemy of human nature. These rules help build the *foundation* of one's faith journey. The enemy of human nature seeks his victories at this level by fanning our cowardice and fear in the face of surrendering addictive and sinful thoughts, words and deeds.

This week we examine St. Ignatius' second set of discernment rules. We call these *Guidelines for Integrated Healing and Spiritual Growth*. They apply to those persons who the enemy of human nature distracts from their spiritual journey with attacks to the reasoning processes. These rules are termed *integrated* because they facilitate healing of our human nature as a unity of body and spirit. The enemy of human nature seeks his victories at this level by creating illusions, and hiding the truth of our thoughts, words and deeds.

This week we consider five of the seven guidelines for discerning the difference between the Divine-Inspirer's and the counter-inspirer's tactics at this more subtle, nuanced level of spiritual development.

The Guidelines for Integrated Healing and Spiritual Growth are essential for discerning counter inspirations of a more subtle nature.

They are applicable when a person has matured to the point where vices, sinful habits, addictions, and extravagant appetites are no longer effective temptations to lure one from God.

When a certain level of spiritual, emotional and psychological maturity has been reached, the enemy of human nature can best deceive with seemingly good, holy thoughts and feelings. He mimics the Divine-Inspirer. He is no longer successful in undermining your authenticity and innocence with temptations to false pleasures and obvious discouragements. *Direct* appeals to narcissistic pride are no longer effective. Instead, the enemy resorts to twisting new and holy inspirations and habits against you, based on the *undetected roots* of your narcissism.

The enemy of human nature will then disguise counter inspirations by having them appear as Divine-inspirations. Ignatius first discovered these new, indirect temptations in the midst of his battle with the crippling guilt of his scruples. The obsessive habit of re-confessing his past sins *appeared* as a good thing to do. The habit appealed to someone *serious* about spiritual growth. But the habit appealed especially to Ignatius' desire to be in *control* of his life and save himself.

In his former way of living, Ignatius tried to win fame at the battle of Pamplona by attempting to conquer the French almost single-handedly. Later, in his Christian life, his narcissism appeared under the "holy" guise of winning fame by conquering his sinfulness through his own agency. A different battle; but the same concealed narcissism and pride at work.

Ignatius was miserable and experienced the constant re-confessing as damaging. Yet he would not relinquish the obsessive habit *even when told to do so* by his spiritual director. Ignatius seemed to be held bound by a "pious" and "holy" habit. In fact, he was bound by his narcissism and determination to save himself instead of allowing Christ to be his Savior. The enemy's counter inspirations that characterized this episode were invisible to Ignatius, most likely because surrendering the habit would mean a loss of control and a threat to his pride.

Ignatius was given grace to see the deception by observing the direction it was taking him: away from God. He realized that the *inspiration* was to "stop" the new life he was living. The enemy of our human nature can inspire desires and choices that are non-harmful or even objectively good. They *appear as if* they will help us evolve towards more perfect Love and life.

Thus in Ignatius' situation, conscientious confession would *appear* to be a good choice to root out past sins and vices. But to someone susceptible to damaging scrupulosity, it could be the perfect tactic to turn them from the path of faith and trust in God! And the enemy of human nature will search for any and all vulnerabilities to subvert our journey in faith.

Spiritual and religious persons are especially vulnerable to these more subtle temptations. The narcissism of these persons is concealed in a pious façade. A partial conversion has not sufficiently targeted the narcissistic pride that guides this person's life. Those not sufficiently purified parade about like a just and righteous person. The truth is they are proud and arrogant. Jesus reserved some of His most serious criticisms for these religious hypocrites. (Lk 18:9-14).

Some things that are good, or appear as good, can gradually lead you away from the good you intend. They lead you away from God toward disintegration, separation, and death. This is exactly what happened to Ignatius. He was so disgusted with the trials and traumas of his obsessive re-confessing of past sins that he was suddenly inspired to be done with the new life he embraced. As far as Ignatius was concerned, if he could not convert himself, and do it his way, he would not do it at all. This is narcissistic pride, plain and simple.

A habit that appeared noble was silently, slowly, and maliciously eroding his confidence in himself and his confidence in God, and threatened the new way of life he had chosen. If the enemy of human nature could not lure Ignatius with the obvious vices and sins of his former life, then the enemy would manipulate Ignatius' new and holy inspirations, linking them to his yet undetected narcissistic pride. The enemy turned Ignatius' good habit against him.

It can be difficult to differentiate between Divine inspirations and counter-inspirations, especially because a counter-inspiration can *appear* as a genuine good, or *feel* authentic. Ignatius offers these guidelines of discernment:

First, the Divine-Inspirer works to give you true joy and happiness. This is accomplished by eliminating all sadness and upset caused by the enemy of your human nature. The counter-inspirer works against such joy and happiness. He does this most successfully by using false reasoning, subtleties, and layers of deceptions. The enemy's arguments will be logical, yet leave you feeling anxious, discouraged, hopeless and possibly cynical.

Second, the Divine-Inspirer alone can work *directly* on your heart and soul. The Divine-Inspirer can touch your soul at will. What does the Divine-Inspirer promote by these spiritual visits?

- ✠ Increases love of God and love of innocence
- ✠ Increases humility, selflessness, and surrendering control of your life to God
- ✠ Fosters a docile spirit: a spirit capable of listening deeply, accepting and affirming as true the Commandments, the teachings of Christ, and those divinely revealed and definitively proclaimed matters of belief held by the Church[26]

Inspirations with these signature characteristics can be verified as coming directly from the Divine-Inspirer.

Third, both the Divine-Inspirer and the counter-inspirer can *inspire,* but with *opposite goals*. The Divine-Inspirer seeks to promote genuine human freedom, authenticity, and spiritual/psychological growth in harmony with your authentic human nature. The counter-inspirer seeks to erode genuine human freedom and to disintegrate your spiritual and psychological health. The goal is to further damage your authentic human nature.

Fourth, the counter-inspirer can mimic some of the influences of the Divine-Inspirer in thoughts, feelings, and desires. However his purpose in doing so is to gradually lead you in the wrong direction: similar to Ignatius' experience with his damaging habit of re-confessing old sins.

Fifth, distinguishing the difference between Divine and counter inspirations requires you to develop the habit of examining the *overall trajectory* of your thoughts and desires. If the beginning, middle, and end are all directed to what is genuine and right, the inspirations are from the Divine-Inspirer. If the trajectory of the desires and thoughts lead to:

- ✠ something contrary to the Commandments or the precepts of Christ;
- ✠ or they distract and weaken your aspirations for selflessness;
- ✠ or they in some way diminish the good plans and goals you had previously established;

then it is *very clear* they are a product of the counter-inspirer. The goal of the enemy of human nature is to lead you away from genuine progress, authenticity, innocence, humility, obedience and peace **and** conceal his presence as he does so.

Ignatius was distracted by his re-confession habit, and his aspirations for following the path of conversion were undermined by it. When he realized this, he identified the influence of the counter-inspirer, and surrendered the damaging habit. This choice began the process of dismantling his narcissistic pride *at its root.*[27]

Ignatius once remarked that human beings are no match for the subtle temptations of the enemy of human nature. But God is! God is indeed a match for the enemy's temptations. *Never dialogue with the enemy of your human nature.* Speak only to Christ, and let Christ deal with the enemy of your human nature. Trust your life, your heart and your soul to Christ.

LORD, guide me in your justice because of my foes;
make straight your way before me.

For there is no sincerity in their mouth;
their heart is corrupt.
Their throat is an open grave;
on their tongue are subtle lies.
Declare them guilty, God;
make them fall by their own devices.
Drive them out for their many sins;
for they have rebelled against you.

Then all who trust in you will be glad
and forever shout for joy.
You will protect them and those will rejoice in you
who love your name.
For you, Lord, bless the just one;
you surround him with favor like a shield.
(Ps 5: 9-13)

ଅଠ

Week 39

FIRST
I resolve to spend no more and no less than 15-minutes in each formal prayer period.

SECOND
I ask God's grace to help me commit to a life-long habit of praying the five meditations of *Sacred Story* prayer. With God's grace, I will be able to enter my prayer at least once daily as St. Ignatius suggested. God's grace will also help me to commit to my simple journal exercises and a monthly practice of Sacramental Reconciliation.

THIRD
I am invited to continue reflecting on spiritual discernment by concluding the series of St. Ignatius' rules on integrated healing. This second series of rules takes into account temptations of a more subtle nature. Here the enemy of my human nature manipulates undetected narcissism to interfere with my spiritual growth.

I will awaken to the present moment.
I will awaken to my spiritual nature.
I will not make any decisions based on fear.
I will practice Sacramental Reconciliation monthly.
I will ask Jesus for help when I am troubled.
I will thank Jesus daily for life's gifts.

Focus Affirmation for Week Thirty-Nine
I will say this affirmation aloud once daily:

The more I experience sin's disorder, the more tempted I will be to disbelieve my life as Sacred Story.
The way through the temptation is to surrender my powerlessness to God.

૭ૹ

Read this at the beginning of the week

Awakening to Sacred Story *Discernment Guidelines*
Guidelines for Integrated Healing and Spiritual Growth

Introduction

Take some time on the weekend or during the week to read and reflect on this twelfth lesson in discernment. Last week our study of St. Ignatius' second set of rules on discernment examined five guidelines to utilize with temptations of a more subtle form. This week we examine the sixth and seventh guidelines. Remember these rules apply to those distracted from the spiritual journey by the enemy of human nature with attacks targeting their reasoning processes with illusions of truth, but not truth itself. We call these *integrated* rules because they facilitate healing of our human nature as a unity of body and spirit.

Review the introductory narrative from Week 38. These *Guidelines for Integrated Healing and Spiritual Growth* are essential for discerning counter inspirations of a more subtle nature. They are applicable to those who have matured to the point where vices, sinful habits, addictions, and extravagant appetites are no longer effective in to luring one away from God.

Sixth, develop the habit of tracing the trajectory of the thoughts and desires that have led you away from God and away from your authentic self. Do not become discouraged. This discipline takes practice. You will fall for the bait countless times. When you do, examine the initial inspiration and follow it through the whole course of your deliberations. Notice how you were initially inspired, but then gradually, step by step, lost your peace of soul.

Notice how your former holy commitments and resolutions were undermined. From this objective vantage point, reflection will enable you to identify the particular strategy the counter-inspirer uses in your life story. This vigilance will help you develop spiritual radar for these deceptive tactics. You will also learn to identify your personal vulnerabilities that the enemy of your authentic human nature manipulates.

At this level of conversion, the enemy's tactics work on your concealed pride, vanity, and narcissism—the Original Sin of the human family. When you think or feel: "I do not need God"; or "I will control my own life"; "I will set my own rules"; or "I will be my own savior" and you feel proud about it, rest assured, the enemy of human nature *is* at work!

Seventh, when you are progressing towards authenticity, innocence and genuine human freedom, the effects of the Divine-Inspirer are gentle and produce delight. A sense of electrical energy, anxious excitement, or a restless need to make hasty decisions is totally absent. Instead, a calm patience and tranquility abides. When making progress towards authenticity, you can detect the effects of the counter-inspirer by the rush of electrical energy, anxious excitement, or restlessness to make hasty decisions.

But, you need to awaken to *both* the **feelings** (anxious or calm) and the **trajectory** (towards or away from authenticity) to accurately *interpret* what the feelings are signaling.

So, if you are moving *toward* God, the enemy of your human nature will inspire "black noise," creating anxious thoughts and urgent feelings. The enemy wants to discourage you from turning to God.

And, if you are moving *away* from God, God will inspire with alarm bells that you are entering dangerous territory. It can feel like the same anxiety and urgent feelings described above, but this time, it is your awakened conscience that God uses to alert you of an inauthentic trajectory.

If you are moving *away* from God, the enemy of your human nature will inspire with thoughts that are appeasing, reassuring your complacency and attempting to *conceal* your movement away from God, and your authentic human nature.

When the inspiration produced in your heart and soul comes directly from the Divine-Inspirer, you cannot be deceived or led astray. You will come to know the inspirations of the Divine-Inspirer *because of the effects* on your heart and soul. These inspirations produce an intense sense of devotion and love of God and of innocence. They produce a sense of selflessness and willing surrender of your life to God's control. The inspirations help you understand and trust received Tradition, the Commandments, and the precepts of Christ as proclaimed by the Church.

However, you can be led astray in the *after-glow* of such inspiration and grace. You can be led astray by your own ideas or by the influence of the counter-inspirer. Be highly attentive during the time *following* Divine inspirations. Be cautious and make no revisions, commitments, or plans during this time *unless* you are clear as to the source of the inspiration.

The Divine-Inspirer will lead you further along the path of love, innocence, humility, and self-surrender. The counter-inspirer will work toward disintegration and a weakening of your previous commitments and holy resolutions. The counter-inspirer will pull you further down the path of pride, and encourage you to justify your angers. The enemy of human nature will inspire you to cling to whatever difficulties you have with Gospel values as proposed by the Church.

Conclusion

Understand now, how St. Ignatius' Divine inspiration to reform his life was corrupted into a damaging habit of confessing old sins. The counter-inspirer accomplished this by manipulating Ignatius' narcissistic nature and long-standing vulnerabilities. If Ignatius had been deceived into walking away from his conversion journey, the Church would have been deprived of the gifts of his spirituality and the many saints who achieved holiness through it.

This was the counter-inspirer's hope for Ignatius. It will be the counter-inspirer's hope for you as well. The counter-inspirer understands the great good that you can accomplish for the Kingdom of Christ, and will work to sabotage it *at all costs*. While we are incapable of matching the subtleties of the enemy of human nature, we can rest in the assurance that God is capable of battling our ancient enemy.

The Divine-Inspirer will always offer the graces and insights to lead you home. God's victory is assured for you in Christ's birth, life, death and resurrection. Have hope in Him. He will help you just as He helped St. Ignatius. You will achieve the goal of love, the goal of forgiveness, and through your life's *Sacred Story*, the goal of service to the Great Work of Reconciliation that Christ has invited you to share with Him.

As you work with God's grace to let your life be transformed into *Sacred Story*, never be discouraged by your failings, sins and weaknesses. The Divine Physician will never tire of forgiving you. Never tire of coming to Him for forgiveness. In this radical, loving trust, you encounter the unfathomable and unbounded mercy of God.

ര

Hallelujah!
Praise the Lord, my soul; I will praise the Lord all my life,
sing praise to my God while I live.

Put no trust in princes,
in children of Adam powerless to save.
Who breathing his last, returns to the earth;
that day all his planning comes to nothing.

Blessed the one whose help is the God of Jacob,
whose hope is in the Lord, his God,
The maker of heaven and earth, the seas and all that is in them,
Who keeps faith forever, secures justice for the oppressed,
who gives bread to the hungry.
The Lord sets prisoners free; the Lord gives sight to the blind.
The Lord raises up those who are bowed down;
the Lord loves the righteous.
The Lord protects the resident alien,
comes to the aid of the orphan and the widow,
but thwarts the way of the wicked.
The Lord shall reign forever,
your God, Zion, through all generations!
Hallelujah!
(Ps 146)

ഔ

Week 40

FIRST

I resolve to spend no more and no less than 15-minutes in each formal prayer period.

SECOND

I ask God's grace to help me commit to a life-long habit of praying the five meditations of *Sacred Story* prayer. With God's grace, I will be able to enter my prayer at least once daily as Ignatius suggested. God's grace will also help me to commit to my simple journal exercises and a monthly practice of Sacramental Reconciliation.

THIRD

This week I am invited to conclude my lessons on St. Ignatius' rules for spiritual discernment. This final section offers special discernment advice for those times that my deepening conversion to life as *Sacred Story* may prompt life changes of one sort or another.

I will awaken to the present moment.
I will awaken to my spiritual nature.
I will not make any decisions based on fear.
I will practice Sacramental Reconciliation monthly.
I will ask Jesus for help when I am troubled.
I will thank Jesus daily for life's gifts.

Focus Affirmation for Week Forty
I will say this affirmation aloud once daily:

*It is never too late to open my heart to Christ
and live my life as* Sacred Story.

☙

Read this at the beginning of the week

Additional Guidelines on Life Choices

Introduction

Take some time on this week to read and reflect on this thirteenth lesson in discernment. Last week we completed the study of St. Ignatius' second set of rules on discernment. These examined the sixth and seventh guidelines that indicate the presence of temptations of a more subtle form in our lives. This week we conclude the study of discernment by examining the guidelines St. Ignatius offers to those who, open to God's grace, contemplate making life choices.

These rules may not be applicable at this point in your spiritual journey. These guidelines will be helpful whenever you are required to make decisions based on faith in the future. The enemy of human nature is always at work to derail our conversion process, but we are not to be afraid. The Lord is our strength and shield. We must simply learn to be gentle as doves and wise as serpents (Mt 10:16).

As your conversion deepens, grace illumines your mind and heart. What had been in darkness is now revealed. You begin to awaken, to see the true nature of reality, the world, and your authentic human nature. *Grace alone* facilitates this journey out of spiritual unconsciousness and the darkened conscience of counter inspiration. As you continue to awaken, you will discover why narcissism and pride are so much more difficult to identify and eliminate than the sins of the flesh.

The pain of Original Sin, early life trauma and lost innocence encourages your narcissism. The narcissistic ego is closed to the Spirit. This ego rationalizes and legitimizes whatever it needs to fill its painful void. It is the ancient wound created by the self displacing God as the heart's center. The defenses that hide your narcissism match the intensity of the hidden pain at the center of your heart. You defend the use of vices and addictions because they protect you from feeling the pain in your heart, and keep you from turning to God for help and healing.

Your *Sacred Story* begins when you accept the Divine Physician's grace to honestly name your sin and let the heart's healing begin. You need God's grace, to both break through and dismantle your defenses. This is the true path to mystical awakening. There are no shortcuts. There is no other way home. You have a unique path to holiness that no one else in all of history can follow. It is God's path for you. It is linked to the unique circumstances of your life. Let the Divine Physician heal you and lead you to wholeness and holiness.

The humility Ignatius discovered in surrendering control of his life—surrendering his pride and narcissism—allowed him to envision a new life, *in and for Christ*, that he had never known before. This awakened consciousness has its own graces and difficulties, as Ignatius well-discovered. These graces abound regardless of one's state of life and vocation. These graces bring illumination and clarity. They illumine the true portrait of your free and authentic *self*. They open you to the world, your Catholic faith, and the creator God. They reveal your past and present commitments, and your choices—both well and ill conceived. This is where Ignatius found himself after his spiritual and psychological trials at Manresa.

The grace of conversion transforms and heals divided hearts. The values you previously espoused that were contrary to the Gospel give way to thoughts, words, and deeds that open you to opportunities never before imagined or thought possible. Purifying graces rush in with new opportunities for your life, filling the void of a heart on the mend. What else would you expect when your heart is touched directly by Divine grace? When your heart is flush with the energy, enthusiasm, and the vitality of God, Ignatius has clear advice.

Ignatius advises that a person in this stage of integrated conversion and healing, who has received these graces of illumination, must consider them very attentively. One needs to cautiously distinguish the initial consolation from the period that follows. In the *afterglow* of these illuminations and insights, when the consolations themselves have ceased, the soul is still passionate. It has been blessed with graces and these graces have an *afterglow*. In the time of the *afterglow*, the heart and soul often forms resolutions and plans that are not directly inspired or granted by God.

These ideas and resolutions can emanate from your own reasoning, creating ideas based on your own judgments. Or these resolutions can be the direct inspiration of the Divine-Inspirer or the counter-inspirer. It is critical to distinguish the illuminations themselves, and the period of time *after* the illuminations—the period of afterglow. *Carefully, thoughtfully and cautiously examine your afterglow reflections and plans, before approving them or acting on them.*

This advice is especially important if you are transitioning from established habits and lifestyles. Those thoughts, words, and deeds, inauthentic expressions of your human nature, have deep roots and/or a long history. These long-established patterns of sin and dysfunction have created spiritual, mental and psychological grooves. The grooves are your *default narratives* for defining "normal" and "success." These *false-but-familiar* narratives are narcissism's anti-

268

story. They draw strength from your broken heart and wounded innocence.

We experience the spiritual and physical wreckage of the Original Fall in our wounded hearts. Our lost innocence is combined with the evolution of sin in our families, clans and social groups. The energy fueling our narcissistic anti-story shields us from pain and shame both real and perceived. As you gradually receive the grace and illumination to relinquish the anti-story, you will experience a void. Surrendering the false definitions of success, and the habits that support these false narratives, creates the void. You will feel a powerful compulsion to fill that void, a compulsion that is *easily exploited* by the counter-inspirer.

When you relinquish your anti-story, you will also have the desire to make up for lost time and to correct the mistakes of the past. These desires can also fill your heart with urgent and pressing agendas for change. These agendas may *feel* honorable and right. This is true especially in light of your past misdeeds and errors. One must exercise caution, however, because these urgent and pressing agendas for change can lead away from the truths, positive resolutions and commitments recently illumined by Divine grace.

If you experience strong inspirations to *change your life commitments*, test them and the *imagined* future plans they represent. Do the inspirations of this follow-up period (after the initial consolation) strike the heart gently? Do they create delight and peace? Is there a notable absence of electrical energy or nervous urgency towards immediate action?

Or do the inspirations and ideas of this follow-up period strike the heart violently? Do they disturb the heart with electrical excitement, and a compelling urgency to immediately enact the good ideas or plans being pondered? This latter effect is a clear sign that the inspirations and ideas will lead you away from life and love—fruit that endures to eternity—no matter how enlightened these ideas seem.

Be attentive! Be gentle as a dove and wise as a serpent. Honor the process of change. Wait for the signs of peace and humility, and test the decisions being pondered.

Conclusion

Spiritual discernment is an art that takes time to master. Its first phase involves knowing the objective rights and wrongs of thoughts, words and deeds as taught by the Commandments, Christ and the teaching Church. Spiritual discernment advances when you consciously attend to your affective/spiritual states and become aware of spiritual movements that are present in your life story. Next, you need to familiarize yourself with the language and signatures of the two different voices; that of the Divine-Inspirer and that of the counter-inspirer.

Finally, you need to learn to trust making decisions based on what you have learned from St. Ignatius' experience and wisdom. This means confronting fears that, in the past, incited cowardice on your part. It also means confronting narcissism's illusions that, in the past, incited self-satisfaction on your part. Confronting both these will feel difficult, but you must trust Ignatius' wisdom and act rightly. You will make mistakes. But learn from your mistakes, always trusting God's infinite mercy. God has infinite patience for those honestly struggling to live a new life in Christ.

In all of this, God will be your support and guide. Turn your attention and heart to God. God will give you the insight, wisdom and strength necessary to develop your spiritual self. Do not be fearful or discouraged as you gradually integrate the art of spiritual discernment into your life. The Divine-Inspirer will offer all of the graces and insights needed to lead you home. Be not afraid!

�☙

The Lord is king, in splendor robed;
robed is the Lord and girt about with strength.
And he has made the world firm,
not to be moved.
Your throne stands firm from of old;
from everlasting you are, O Lord.
Your decrees are worthy of trust indeed;
holiness befits your house,
O Lord, for length of days.
(Ps 93: 1-2; 5)

❧

Week Eternity

LIVING YOUR SACRED STORY DAILY

You have engaged all the spiritual disciplines for *Sacred Story*. Now is the time to ask God for help to be faithful to the relationship with Him that the prayer invites. Continue praying all the meditations in your 15-minute periods. Keep practicing all the other daily disciplines you have learned. You have all the necessary instruction. What follows are all the spiritual disciplines and insights of *Sacred Story* arranged at a single glance. If and when you have difficulties, temptations, stresses, fears, or anxieties associated with the daily consciousness exercise or *Sacred Story* prayer (when, not if!), read *Sacred Story Affirmations* and the *Guidelines for Health and Spiritual Growth*. Remember the anxieties Ignatius suffered as he began his journey. All spiritual and emotional crises soon pass. Christ Jesus will lead you home. Be not afraid!

THE DAILY DISCIPLINES AT A GLANCE

✠ Prayer Upon Waking—*Attune to the day ahead and invite God's help*

This should take about fifteen to thirty seconds. After you wake up, lay in bed and pre-vision the day ahead. What does it hold? Are you anxious or energized about the day ahead? What specific issues/persons/events are causing the anxiety and/or energy? Ask God to help you deal constructively with the anxieties or challenges, and give thanks for the events/persons that inspire energy. Ask God to keep you <u>aware</u> as the day progresses. Using the special name you identified, offer the day to God.

If you so desire, on Sunday morning you can do a brief pre-visioning of the week in the same way you do for a single day. You might consider looking ahead to any special feast days or saint's anniversaries that week. Ask for their intercession for your Sacred Story *at the beginning of the week and on their feast day.*

✠ Exercises During the Day—*Awakening to your life*

Each one of these should take no more than fifteen seconds. Consciously note the most significant events that inspire aggravation (anger, upset, fear, or temptation) or joy (gratitude, hope, faith). Every day holds many of these events. Consciously attend to the events that seem most notable by the strength of the reaction they incite in you. At the time these notable events transpire, take about ten seconds to: 1) turn to God in your heart and using your personal name for God, ask to understand why the event gripped you negatively or positively; 2) ask for graced insight to understand if the event is linked to something from the past that needs exploration/healing. Then go on with your day.

The more you engage this consciousness exercise in the day, the more readily you will remember these events at the time of your 15-minute prayer reflections on Creation, Presence, Memory, Mercy and Eternity. Every single event that happens in the day is in some way linked to one of these five meditations and your Sacred Story. But please note: do this exercise for notable events only (two or three times daily at most!). You will know which to attend to because they will grab you by the gut or the heart.

✠ *Sacred Story* **Prayer Mid-day—*Creation, Presence, Memory, Mercy, Eternity***

✠ Exercises During the Day—*Awakening to your life*

✠ *Sacred Story* **prayer Evening—*Creation, Presence, Memory, Mercy, Eternity***

✠ *Sacred Story* **Day Journal—*Briefly note two significant events of the day***

This should take no more than one minute. Before going to bed, jot down the two most notable events of the day—one negative (depleting hope) and one positive (increasing hope). All you need is to note two events. Write a short phrase to remember both what the event was and your reaction to it. Here are some examples:

"Depleting Faith, Hope & Love" examples
1) Office meeting—*very dispirited about things working out in the future*
2) Letter from Joyce—*very hurt that she excluded us from the event*
3) My moral indiscretion on Saturday—*how come I never seem to improve?*

"Increasing Faith, Hope & Love" examples
1) The incredible sunset Tuesday—*thank you God for your creation!*
2) Saturday's confession—*cried because of the priest's hopeful words*
3) Bob's medical news—*Thank you God for hearing our prayers!*

✠ **Prayer upon Retiring**—*Attune to your heart, invite God into your dreams*

✠ **Week's-end Journal**—*Listen for trends, patterns, and links*
  This should take about ten minutes. Read your journal comments from the week. Notice any patterns or trends. Did any persons appear more than once? Can you discern patterns in the events depleting hope or increasing hope? Does a certain type of failure occur at "predictable times"? Jot down any patterns you discover. Then write the two most significant "depleting hope" and "increasing hope" events from the week.

Here is a sample of this weekly journal:

"Patterns" examples with suggested insights/actions
1)   Fear of being criticized always precedes my gossiping about others (perhaps I need to ask God's help on why I fear being criticized and examine what in particular I fear. I will also pray to hold my tongue, to see what I can learn from this discipline)
2)   Every time I meet Carol or someone who reminds me of Carol I get angry (I need to ask God to help me to forgive Carol)
3)   I have constant anxiety around regular confession because I am afraid that the priest will think I am not a good person (I need to learn not to let fear control my decisions)
4)   Three times my boss appeared in my journal (do I need to make a decision?)
5)   I seem more negative than positive about God's love for me (I need to challenge this feeling and affirm God's love by focusing on gratitude)

Strongest "Depleting Hope" Example
"My moral indiscretion on Saturday—how come I never seem to improve?"
Strongest "Increasing Hope" Example
"Saturday's confession—cried because of the priest's hopeful words"

Sample note to myself: "My two examples above seem to be connected. I fear that I never seem to improve yet I also felt great hope when I went to confession. I will trust the feelings of hope and not the feelings based on fear."

✠ **Month's-end Journal**—*Listen for trends, patterns, links*
  This should take no more than 15-minutes. Read over your weekly summaries and do the same winnowing process with them as you did for the individual weeks.

✠ **Renew with Monthly Reconciliation**—*You will be powerfully graced*

This should take one hour total between preparation and confession. Spend thirty minutes reading over your journal summaries and writing a one page letter to Jesus. Use the same pattern as your Whole-Life Confession. Do not write more than one page! Discipline yourself to tell the Lord the <u>most</u> essential things for which you need His help and forgiveness, and no more. Take your letter to Reconciliation and make your confession. Keep your letters and use them for prayer. You will see your growth and begin to understand much better the outlines of your own Sacred Story and the SACRED STORY of Jesus as well.

✠ **Consult the *Affirmations* Frequently—*They are your thumbnail discernment aids***

✠ **Consult the Guidelines for Healing and Spiritual Growth—*You need them***

✠ **Live Your Faith—*Engage its spiritual disciplines, serving God and neighbor***

SACRED STORY AFFIRMATIONS

My *Sacred Story* takes a lifetime to write.

Be Not Afraid:
Fear comes from the enemy of my human nature.

The pathway to God's peace and healing runs through my heart's brokenness, sin, fear,
anger and grief.

God resolves all my problems with time and patience.

ℰℴ

I will have difficulties in this life.

There are just two ways to cope with my difficulties.
One leads to life, one to death. I will choose life.

ℰℴ

"Impossible" is not a word in God's vocabulary.

Sacred Story leads to my freedom and authenticity,
but does not always make me feel happy.

ℰℴ

My life's greatest tragedies can be transformed
into my life's major blessings.

Times of peace and hope always give way
to times of difficulty and stress.

Times of difficulty and stress always give way
to times of peace and hope.

ℰℴ

I will not tire of asking God for help

since God delights in my asking.

The urge to stop *Sacred Story* practice
always comes before my greatest breakthroughs.

જી

God gives me insights, not because I am better than others,
but because I am loved.

The insights and graces I need to move forward in life's journey
unfold at the right time.

જી

My personal engagement with *Sacred Story* accomplishes, through Christ, a work of
eternal significance.

Inspirations can have a divine or a demonic source. I pray for the grace to remember
how to discern one from the other.

જી

Christ, who has walked before me, shares my every burden.

Christ, who has walked before me, will help me resolve every crisis.

Christ, who has walked before me, knows my every hope.

Christ, who has walked before me, knows everything I suffer.

Christ, who walks before me, will always lead me home to safety.

જી

I will strive to curb temptations to react to people and events.

I will ask myself what causes my anger and irritation at people and events.

I will seek to identify the source of my anger and irritation.
I will give thanks for what angers and upsets me;

for identifying their source will help to set me free.

I will strive to listen, watch and pray; listen, watch and pray.
I will listen, watch and pray!

☙

Everyone has been mortally wounded spiritually, psychologically, and physically by
Original Sin and the loss of paradise.

Journeying with Christ to the roots of my sins and addictions
will help break their grip.

I will not waste time worrying about my sins and failures.
I will use my time wisely and ask God to help me
understand the source of my sins and failings .

I will trust that Christ came to heal all my wounds.

☙

I alone control Christ's ability to transform my life into a *Sacred Story*.
The process begins when I ask for the grace to
honestly name my sins and addictions.

The process continues when I invite Christ to illuminate my narcissism.

Only God's grace and mercy can write my *Sacred Story*.

☙

I will strive daily to pick up the cross, for it leads to my life.

The closer I get to holiness, the more I will see and feel sin's disorder in my life.

The more I experience sin's disorder, the more tempted I will be
to disbelieve my life as *Sacred Story*.
The way through the temptation is to surrender my powerlessness to God.

☙

It is never too late to open my heart to Christ
and live my life as *Sacred Story.*

Christ, who is close to the brokenhearted, restores my lost innocence.

The path to my *Sacred Story* is
Creation, Presence, Memory, Mercy, and Eternity.

જી

TWO BENCHMARK GUIDELINES
FOR SPIRITUAL DISCERNMENT

To help your awakening and initiation into spiritual discernment two benchmark guidelines will be helpful in many life situations. It is important to understand that Divine inspiration called consolation does not always *feel good*. It is equally important to realize that unholy inspiration called spiritual desolation does not always *feel bad*. Both benchmarks are intended to influence the direction of our life towards or away from God in every thought, word and deed.

Benchmark One—Consolation

These specific features characterize authentic Divine inspirations called consolations. They will:

1) Increase the heart's love for God and others.
2) Increase the virtues of docility, humility and self-generosity.
3) Not run contrary to the truths and teachings of Scripture, the Tradition and the teaching Church.

Consolation can be the consequence of the Divine Physician's Spirit working in you. This form of consolation helps strengthen your heart and soul, encouraging you to turn to God. Consolation helps you to understand and choose thoughts, words and deeds that express your authentic human nature made in the Divine image.

Consolation can also be the consequence of the body/spirit aspect of your Divinely-shaped human nature. God created your human nature as a gift in the Divine image and likeness. In spite of Original Sin's impact, cooperating with God's grace activates embedded life forces of your Divinely-shaped human nature, helping to heal biochemical, physiological and emotional imbalances; energizing you; and enabling thoughts, words and deeds that express your authentic human nature.

Benchmark Two—Desolation

These specific features characterize authentic counter-inspirations called desolations. They will:

1)   Increase narcissism, displacing God and others.
2)   Decrease docility and humility, and increase pride and self-satisfaction.
3)   Arouse hungers and desires that, although they feel good, will typically contradict the truths and teachings proposed by the Scripture, Tradition, and the teaching Church. This is because the author of counter inspirations is opposed to Christ and will lead you away from life and truth. Counter-inspirations will produce desires *that feel authentic* because they are linked to *fallen* human nature's physical lusts and spiritual pride. They are the familiar default drives of a broken heart and a broken human nature.

Desolation can be the consequence of the enemy of human nature working in you. This form of desolation helps weaken your heart and soul, encouraging you to turn from God. Desolation helps you choose thoughts, words and deeds that are opposed to your Divinely-shaped human nature.

Desolation can also be the consequence of your own fallen human nature. God created your human nature as a gift in the Divine image and likeness. Yet because of Original Sin's impact, not cooperating with God's grace erodes embedded life forces of your Divinely shaped human nature, helping to destroy biochemical, physiological and emotional balance; de-energizing you; and increasing thoughts, words and deeds that in opposition to your authentic human nature.

When struggling with these issues, the Guidelines for Integrated Healing and Spiritual Growth will be of help.

ATTENDING TO MY REACTION RESPONSES
ANGER, FEAR AND GRIEF

General Awareness Exercises During the Day

*When you experience your manifest
sins and addictions, practice:
Declare, Describe, Descend, Denounce, and Decide*

Using your own words speak personally to Christ:

✠ **Declare** the specific sin, addiction, narcissistic habit or destructive compulsion as a false lover.

✠ **Describe** the specific sin, addiction, narcissistic habit or destructive compulsion as coming from the enemy of your human nature.

✠ **Descend** with Christ into your memory, to see and feel your first experience of this specific sin, addiction, narcissistic habit or destructive compulsion, asking Him to compassionately reveal the stress fractures, loneliness and wounds in your heart it promised to satisfy.

✠ **Denounce** the sin, addiction, narcissistic habit or destructive compulsion for its ruinous effect in your life.

✠ **Decide** for Christ to heal this wound, diffuse the stress, anxiety and fear feeding it, and transform its damaging effects on your life into *Sacred Story*.

When you are struggling with these issues, the *Guidelines for Foundational Healing and Spiritual Growth* will be very helpful.

ᘒ

ATTENDING TO MY REACTION RESPONSES
ANGER, FEAR AND GRIEF

Particular Awareness Exercises During the Day

When You Have Identified Your Particular Sin of Narcissism and React with Anger, Anxiety, Fear or Grief:

Determine if Original Sin's principal manifestation in your life story is in the form of aggressive or passive narcissism. Take notice of the sudden anger, anxiety, fear or grief that creeps up during your day. Pay particular attention to how these emotions might be touching your narcissism, manifesting as sin and contributing to addictive tendencies. For those one or two stand-out events in a day that capture your attention, do this short exercise below.

Speak to Christ from your heart:

✠ **Ask to not react but instead** to be conscious of what you are reacting to

✠ **Ask to feel** the heart's fear, temptation, anxiety, anger and grief present in the reaction

✠ **Ask for knowledge—for graced insight—**to begin dismantling this immature, damaging, (aggressive-electrifying or passive-depressing) and self-glorifying process

✠ **Ask who or what** initiated this particular pattern of reaction—of overpowering or blaming others—and why?

✠ **Ask for courage** to face the negative story of being the aggressive winner or the passive victim. Facing this can cause panic when you are used to being its slave, but once confronted, facing it can bring you peace and freedom.

ᙦ

ORIGINAL SIN'S NARCISSISM IN MY LIFE STORY

THE PASSIVE NARCISSIST	THE AGGRESSIVE NARCISSIST
Self-identifies as a *victim*.	Self-identifies as a *winner*.
Is determined to have others notice how special he/she is by *pointing to his/her unfair suffering.*	Is determined to have others notice how special he/she is by *defeating all opponents.*
Is cynical and excuses bad behavior by insisting it is justified because of how much he/she *has suffered.*	Is cynical and excuses bad behavior by insisting it is justified because he/she *has earned it.*
Wallows in self-pity when hurt, whether the hurt is real or imagined.	*Is vindictive* when hurt, whether the hurt is real or imagined.
Blames anyone who criticizes or opposes him/her.	*Threatens* anyone who criticizes or opposes him/her.
Protects him/herself from being hurt again by *keeping wounds as fresh as possible.* If anything is too difficult or painful, he/she will *retreat into those painful memories* and turn *inward*, away from others.	Protects him/herself from being hurt again by *eradicating vulnerabilities.* If anything is too difficult or painful, he/she will act in a *conqueror role* and *dominate* others.
Wins by *emotional manipulation.*	Wins by *direct confrontation.*
Is secretly attached to his/her own woundedness.	Is secretly attached to the *power of defeating others.*
Is terrified of *taking control and personal responsibility*, and has difficulty admitting it to him/herself.	Is terrified of *surrendering control and being vulnerable*, and has difficulty admitting it to him/herself.

284

Sacred Story Integration & Awareness Template

The *Sacred Story* practices awaken you to patterns of sin and dysfunction, grace and healing. The Divine Physician helps you identify and unmask the diseases caused by Original Sin, so that you can continue integrated healing and grow in interior freedom. In this wholeness you are able to serve the great Work of Reconciliation.

No thought, word or deed is ever neutral. Everything one thinks, says, or does contributes to the work of the Divine-Inspirer or the counter-inspirer. This is not a reason to become obsessed about everything you think, say or do. It is a reminder to be attentive to the spiritual reality of life, and labor with God's grace to choose Christ.

As you listen to your life each day, keep the *Sacred Story* Template in mind. You are seeking a comprehensive view of the enemy of human nature's work to keep you asleep, ***and*** a comprehensive view of the Divine Physician's work to awaken you. Watch your life with compassionate, patient, and merciful attention. That is the way of the Divine Physician who is working for your redemption and complete, integrated healing. As your memory awakens and you become conscious of your life's issues, you will become sensitive and discerning of movements in both directions as shown by the arrows in the template following.

Manifest Sins
The Fruit or Ornamentation
Manifest Fear, Anger, and Grief, moral weaknesses, vices, addictions, and sinful habits that are the most visible to you.

↓   ↑

Core Sins
The Trunk or Superstructure
Disobedience and narcissism, along with its fear, anger, and grief, that forms the trunk or superstructure of your daily life, feeding on originating sins and events.

↓   ↑

Original Sins
The Roots or Foundation
Ancient, Originating Events that Rooted the Patterns of Disobedience and Narcissism Along with its Fear, Anger, Grief.

THE FOUR STAGES OF IGNATIUS' CONVERSION

STAGE ONE
THE AWAKENING

A graced experience of God's love opened Ignatius to: → ↓	**GIVE THANKS FOR FAVORS RECEIVED** ↓
A dissatisfaction with vain fantasies which led to surrendering to holy daydreams, characterized by consolation, which in turn: → ↓	**PRAY FOR GRACE TO SEE CLEARLY** ↓
Caused him to review his life and actions leading to: → ↓	**GIVE A DETAILED ACCOUNT OF CONSCIENCE: GENERAL AND PARTICULAR** ↓
Grief with yearning for penance and repentance for his past sins, culminating in: → ↓	**ASK PARDON FOR ONE'S FAULTS** ↓
Ignatius' passion to amend his life and a desire to love God wholeheartedly. →	**RESOLVE AND AMEND TO SERVE GOD** *and others*

STAGE TWO
FIRST CRISIS:
SPEAKING TRUTH TO POWER

A enemy voice evokes Ignatius' fear of a lifelong struggle with his sinful habits. → ↓	**CONSCIOUS FEAR AND ANXIETY OVER SURRENDERING SINFUL AND ADDICTIVE HABITS** ↓
Ignatius rejects the "enemy of human nature" and confronts his false promises. → ↓	**CONFRONTING THE THREATENING "VOICE" OF SIN AND ADDICTION WITH THE "TRUTH" THAT THEY BRING DEATH, NOT LIFE** ↓
Peace is restored after truthfully naming sin and addiction as death dealing. →	**PEACE RETURNS AND ANXIETY DISSOLVES**

STAGE THREE
SECOND CRISIS:
SURRENDERING CONTROL AND
ADMITTING POWERLESSNESS TO SAVE ONESELF

Ignatius' struggle with scruples hiding his vainglory ↓ →	The initial confrontation with one's root sin ↓
Ignatius' constant re-confessing to seek salvation by willpower alone → ↓	The effort to control one's root sin ONLY by personal effort or force of will ↓
Ignatius' suicidal impulses, disgust and the desire to walk away from his new found faith ↓ →	Despair and desire to give up faith when human effort alone fails ↓
Ignatius' tracing the spirit of disgust to a demonic source → ↓	Insight that desire to reject the spiritual journey is a temptation ↓
Ignatius abandoning his compulsive confessing of past sins →	Admitting powerlessness to save oneself and surrendering prideful actions

STAGE FOUR
LIFE-LONG PATIENCE
WHILE GOD WRITES OUR *SACRED STORY*

Ignatius justifying himself, anxiously recoils and focuses on his sinfulness → ↓	Panic over one's salvation due to weakness and sinfulness →	**PURGATION** ↓
Ignatius, no longer fearful, regrets not having responded sooner to God's graces → ↓	Sadness at slowness of one's response to God's love and invitation to intimacy →	**ILLUMINATION** ↓
Ignatius' intense joy at the thought of dying and being with God →	An ardent, all-embracing love of God and desire for complete union with the Trinity →	**UNION**

SACRED STORY PRAYER MEDITATIONS

Pray the whole 15-minute Sacred Story prayer once or twice daily and consciously repeat to Christ Jesus the five-word refrain whenever you are in the grip of fear, anxiety, grief or sins, addictions and destructive compulsions.

CREATION

*I believe God created everything in love and for love; I ask for **heart-felt** knowledge of God's love **for me**, and for **gratitude** for the **general** and **particular** graces of this day.*

PRESENCE

*I believe God is **present** in **each moment** and **event** of my life, and I ask for the grace to **awaken**, **see** and **feel** where and how, especially in this present moment.*

MEMORY

*I believe every violation of love committed by me and against me **is in my memory**, and I **ask God to reveal them to me**, especially those that have manifested themselves today, **so I can be healed**.*

MERCY

*I believe that **forgiveness** is the only **path to healing and illumination**. I beg for the **grace of forgiveness**, and the **grace to forgive**, especially for the general and particular failures of this day, and from my past.*

ETERNITY

*I believe the grace of **forgiveness opens my heart**, making my every thought, word and deed bear **fruit that endures to eternity**. I ask that everything in my life serve Christ's Great Work of Reconciliation.*

℆

Take Lord, receive, my liberty, my memory, my understanding, my entire will. Whatsoever I have or hold, You have given to me. I surrender it all back to you to be governed by your will. Give me only Your love and grace. This is enough for me, and I ask for nothing more. Amen.

Your ways, O Lord, make known to me; teach me your paths.
Guide me in your truth and teach me, for you are God my savior,
and for you I wait all the day.
Good and upright is the Lord; thus he shows sinners the way.
He guides the humble to justice, and teaches the humble his way.
All the paths of the Lord are kindness and constancy
toward those who keep his covenant and his decrees.
The friendship of the Lord is with those who fear him,
and his covenant, for their instruction.
(Ps 25: 4-5, 8-9, 10, 14)

Abide in Me

Abide in Me
A Daily Relationship with Christ as Savior,
Divine Physician and Lord of All

I invite you to pray with the first few verses of chapter fifteen from the Gospel of St. John. Take as many minutes, hours or days as you wish to pray with St. John. There is no hurry.

I am the true vine, and my Father is the vinedresser. Every branch of mine that bears no fruit, he takes away, and every branch that does bear fruit he prunes, that it may bear more fruit. You are already made clean by the word which I have spoken to you. Abide in me, and I in you. As the branch cannot bear fruit by itself, unless it abides in the vine, neither can you, unless you abide in me. I am the vine, you are the branches. He who abides in me, and I in him, he it is that bears much fruit, for apart from me you can do nothing. If a man does not abide in me, he is cast forth as a branch and withers; and the branches are gathered, thrown into the fire and burned. If you abide in me, and my words abide in you, ask whatever you will, and it shall be done for you. By this my Father is glorified, that you bear much fruit, and so prove to be my disciples. As the Father has loved me, so have I loved you; abide in my love. If you keep my commandments, you will abide in my love, just as I have kept my Father's commandments and abide in his love. These things I have spoken to you, that my joy may be in you, and that your joy may be full. (Jn 15: 4-11)

The Ignatian *Examen* that inspires *Sacred Story* prayer became an active part of my Jesuit life in 1994. Having entered the Society of Jesus in 1973, I had already lived for twenty years as a Jesuit—eight of those years as a priest. My practice of this prayer was inconstant for many years. By most measures, one could say that I *had* a Christian vocation. I mean this in much the same way that one looking at a Catholic married couple with children or a single person doing service work would agree that each of these persons *have* a Christian vocation.

A life of prayer and daily Mass, a yearly eight-day retreat, and a fair amount of *theological living* (faith-oriented reading plus lots of God/Church conversations) made me feel I *had* a real religious life. And I did. The question for me had become instead: was I fully *living* a Christian vocation? The answer to that is much more complex. For simplicity's sake, let me say that I have learned more clearly that a Christian vocation is not equivalent to simply belonging to a religious order. To use an analogy, a *Christian marriage* is different from *being Catholic and married with children.*

My Christian vocation requires that I daily open myself to Jesus and allow my actions, emotions, desires, loves, hurts, fears, and plans (especially my precious plans), to be shared with and shaped by Jesus' influence. Sharing means that I submit myself to Jesus and let Him have a say in what I am doing and who I am daily becoming, what I hold on to and what I relinquish. Acting in a Christian way means that I no longer belong to myself. Rather, I belong to Christ.

Some good friends of mine who have been married for several years recently shared with me one of the biggest adjustments they have had to make as a result of being married. They can no longer make plans in blissful isolation but have to consult with each other about practically every aspect of their lives. This consultative sharing can be both a joy and an annoyance. Each one is called out of the prison of their own ego and invited to love, sacrifice, and make adjustments so that the other can grow and flourish. We really grow when we are called out of ourselves. But there is joy in sharing intimately in the life of the Beloved. We are created for the joy of sharing intimately in the life of the other. We are made in the image and likeness of God who *is relationship*.

A Christian vocation requires an intimate relationship with Christ. It requires making this relationship a priority on a *daily* basis. *Sacred Story* prayer, more than any other spiritual discipline I have encountered in my forty years in religious life, brings me face-to-face with Christ in a relationship that calls me out of myself. It is the most effective path that has enabled me to be true to the man and priest that God desires me to be. It is not always easy and I do not want to minimize the challenge it has been in terms of my honesty and openness. It is a joy and an annoyance for exactly the same reasons as any serious relational commitment. I have had moments of aggravation and difficulty in praying *Sacred Story*. I have also experienced times when I did not want to pray because I knew I would be confronted with things I would prefer to ignore.

Here is a typical example. Some time ago, I was struggling internally with someone who, I judged, had wronged me. I was hurt, frustrated, and upset from what I perceived to be an injustice against myself. I discovered I was not at all upset when this person experienced misfortunes, for I felt this person *deserved* it. In prayer, I was not speaking with Jesus about this person. Instead I found myself rehearsing conversations in my head about how I had been wronged. My focus was on myself.

One day I was awakened to my lack of Christian charity. Instinctively I understood that I needed to bring my feelings about this person to Jesus and yet, I resisted. A part of my heart wanted to simply rehearse my justified hurts. It took several *Sacred Story* prayer periods for me to begin to speak *from my heart* to Christ about what I was feeling. The *insight* that I needed to reach out and forgive this person came in a split-second. I was also able to accept some of the fault lines in my own personality which may have contributed to the initial difficulties. It is amazing how that clarity comes with honesty. This was a *graced* experience!

However, upon leaving the time of *Sacred Story* prayer, a new inspiration took hold. Perhaps it is unwise to forgive? I could lose ground. The re-emerging frustration and darkened spirit—the counter-inspiration—accompanying this new inspiration was in *marked* contrast to the peacefulness I had experienced previously in the time of *Sacred Story* prayer. In testing the spiritual inspirations, it was clear which inspiration was from the Divine-Inspirer and which inspiration was from the counter-inspirer. Honestly, I was strongly tempted to *ignore* the truth of my spiritual discernment and go with the refusal to forgive. But I was being invited by God to *disarm*. I was invited to be vulnerable. It was an invitation to greater spiritual freedom, the freedom that Ignatius calls *detachment*. Freedom *sounds* good, but it is not something we always really want.

This event was a wake-up call because it clearly presented the difficult choice of forgiveness. It may sound odd but it gave me the conviction that Jesus is interested in *everything* I am doing. Every thought, word and deed I have is important to Christ. He wants to be part of everything I experience. *Sacred Story*, prayed faithfully, has made me aware of what *being in relationship* with Jesus means. I feel the effects of the surrender that is necessary for a real relationship with Jesus, and I feel it in a particularly powerful way twice a day. I have chosen to make spiritual surrender the center of my Jesuit life. And praying *Sacred Story* prayer has revealed how many areas of my daily life I keep off-limits from Christ.

A strong intellectual tradition is a characteristic of the Society of Jesus; it is a good in and of itself. But there is something that Ignatius wanted Jesuits to value above learning: virtue, the spiritual life, and the surrender of our will and our hearts to Christ. The human gifts we cultivate only reach their fruitfulness in light of a well-grounded spiritual life. In Section Ten of the Jesuit Constitutions, entitled "How the Whole Body of the Society is to be Preserved and Increased in its Well-being," Ignatius says:

Thus it appears that care should be taken in general that all the members of the Society devote themselves to the solid and perfect virtues and to spiritual

pursuits, and attach greater importance to them than to learning and other natural and human gifts. For these interior gifts are necessary to make those exterior means efficacious for the end which is being sought.
(Part X [813] 2.)

This advice is written for Jesuits, and for the care and growth of the Society of Jesus. Yet it offers good pragmatic Ignatian wisdom that is applicable to any vocation or situation in the Church. Human gifts and qualities reach their perfection and the height of their potency when the bearer of those gifts and/or qualities is grafted to the vine of Christ—when they surrender to Christ. This holds true for the talents of the athlete, the intellectual acumen of the college student, the artistic skills of the singer or architect, the healing gifts of the doctor or nurse, the ministry of religious and priests, the leadership skills of the politician and the professional business person, and the love of husband and wife for each other and their children.

The personal decision I face daily—twice daily—is how much of my life will I allow to be grafted onto the vine of Christ? How much will I allow myself to *abide* in His Love? Jesus must have been looking at grapevines when He spoke this passage from John's Gospel. The vine or stalk is the source of all nutrients. Only shoots which grow directly from it, or have been grafted onto it, bear fruit. As I look back over my life, I can see that I have produced all sorts of fruit by my *own* effort. What has become a much more important question at this point is: how much of what I produce is the fruit of my relationship with Jesus? In other words, have I allowed myself to become a "daily disciple" of Jesus by being in relationship with Him? Am I grafted onto the vine of Christ?

The bottom line of my experience of *Sacred Story* is that I am being challenged to open *all* of my heart and my life to God's grace. While the commitment to the Jesuits and the priesthood always felt full-time and lifelong, the *relationship* with Jesus seemed to have an on-again, off-again feel to it. Quite frankly, I was more in control than Christ. Now I feel that I have truly begun to commit to *Jesus*. Twice daily I need to come to Him with my ups and downs, my joys and angers, my loves and victories, my failures and grief, and my *constant* need.

My *constant* need: what does that mean? It means that *Sacred Story* prayer makes me more aware of my weakness, my failures, and my need for redemption. I have been graced with the eyes to see the reason for Christ's redeeming sacrifice, more clearly than ever before. It is a sacrifice and grace I cannot live without. Perhaps it is the same discovery of the alcoholic or drug addict. One day, the addict finally wakes up and realizes that the life they thought they controlled is actually out of control.

The only way to salvation is to surrender to love's sobriety and embrace. The alcoholic genuinely in touch with the truth of her/his life knows they are *always recovering* and are never *fully* recovered. One must live constantly with the knowledge of her/his vulnerability and turn to God for help and aid. It is a life of submission, humility, and holy dependence.

Is the invitation to submission, humility and holy dependence the best way for me to convince you to stay committed to *Sacred Story* prayer? Is this good marketing? Perhaps not, but I am convinced that while your issues may be different from mine, your experience will pull you into the same position of humility, submission, and dependency on God when confronted with the truth of your weakness and need.

What could possibly be attractive about living this way? Praying and living *Sacred Story* enables a person to be vulnerable, humbly submissive and dependent on God. I can rely on Jesus, who has promised to give me what I need: "If you remain in me and my words remain in you, ask for whatever you want and it will be done for you." (Jn 15: 7)

These words utterly change a person and their world view. Jesus offers this relationship so that my joy "may be full." How so? Because I experience that even in the weakest and most vulnerable condition of my life, Love does not walk away from me. Love has irrevocably committed Himself to me. He sacrificed for me so that I could be whole, and He wants the knowledge of this great love to be known by me on the most intimate level. He has also promised that this life of discipleship gives great glory to the Father in heaven. Allowing oneself to abide in His love will bear fruit that will give glory to the Father of Jesus Christ. What an awesome reality!

At the beginning of a retreat or in my daily *Sacred Story* prayer, I try to commit to this relationship. The renewal of my vocational commitment to Christ in the daily engagement with *Sacred Story* prayer is a means to deepen the knowledge of my radical dependence on God. It fosters the joy of a personal relationship with Christ Jesus that grounds me and opens me up to the deepest yearnings of my heart.

The more I open my heart to a serious relationship with Christ, the more I come to understand the joy for which I have been created. You also have been created for this joy. That is why I am confident you will remain in the embrace of *Sacred Story* and the Lord Jesus who loves you beyond all reckoning. The Love that grounds the universe holds you in His Heart.

ᘓ

Glorious Lord Christ,…
You who are the first and the last,
The living and the dead and the risen again;
You who gather into your exuberant unity
Every beauty, every affinity, every energy,
Every mode of existence;
It is you to whom my being cried out with a desire
As vast as the universe,
'In truth you are my Lord and my God.'[28]

ᘒ

NOTES

NOTES

NOTES

NOTES

NOTES

NOTES

NOTES

ENDNOTES

[1] Paul Doncoeur, SJ, *The Heart of Ignatius*, (Baltimore: Helicon, 1959), 34.

[2]   There is no need to read the Scripture passages during your 15-minute prayer periods. If your heart leads you to read these Scripture passages apart from the 15-minute prayer periods, you are encouraged to follow your heart!

[3]   A suggestion: Use this name to address God every time you naturally think of God throughout the day. For example, you may say in your heart before a meeting: "Lord Jesus, be with me now." Say it, and then just move on with your meeting. Do not make this a tedious exercise, but one that feels natural and relaxed. You do not have to think long and hard about God. The purpose of this spontaneous prayer is just a short, friendly reminder of God's presence. Use this name if you find yourself conversing with God during the day.

[4]   Ignatius is very specific that spiritual exercises should be kept to the exact time allotted for them. The only exception he makes is that an exercise may be extended by *one minute* if one is having difficulty, or is experiencing some upset or turmoil. Ignatius believed that this brief extension of an exercise in times of difficulty works positively to help us confront and not be cowed by spirits of darkness and the psychological and emotional anxieties they manipulate.

[5]   If you feel called, you can reflect on the entire Decalogue as enumerated in the *Catechism of the Catholic Church* (CCC, 561-672). You can either purchase an inexpensive paperback or you can access the text online: http://www.vatican.va/archive/ccc_css/archive/catechism/p3s2c1a1.htm

[6]   "Compulsion, impaired control, persistence, irritability, relapse, and craving—these are all the hallmarks of addiction—any addiction." Gabor Maté, *In the Realm of Hungry Ghosts: Close Encounters with Addiction* (Berkeley: North Atlantic Books, 2010), 136-7.

[7] Gabor Maté, *In the Realm of Hungry Ghosts: Close Encounters with Addiction* (Berkeley: North Atlantic Books, 2010), 136-7.

[8]   *Catechism of the Catholic Church (CCC) 1469--John Paul II, RP 31, 5.*

[9]   Our studies have shown that those who committed to two times a day for prayer were more faithful in cultivating a sustainable daily practice. Also, research revealed that those who practiced a simple logbook or journal exercise were also more faithful to the prayer disciplines.

¹⁰   See endnote #13.

¹¹   From the *Catechism of the Catholic Church* [CCC #1854-64] on THE GRAVITY OF SIN: MORTAL AND VENIAL SIN:

Sins are rightly evaluated according to their gravity. The distinction between mortal and venial sin, already evident in Scripture, became part of the tradition of the Church. It is corroborated by human experience.

Mortal sin destroys charity in the heart of man by a grave violation of God's law; it turns man away from God, who is his ultimate end and his beatitude, by preferring an inferior good to him. *Venial sin* allows charity to subsist, even though it offends and wounds it.

Mortal sin, by attacking the vital principle within us - that is, charity - necessitates a new initiative of God's mercy and a conversion of heart which is normally accomplished within the setting of the sacrament of reconciliation: When the will sets itself upon something that is of its nature incompatible with the charity that orients man toward his ultimate end, then the sin is mortal by its very object, whether it contradicts the love of God, such as blasphemy or perjury, or the love of neighbor, such as homicide or adultery. But when the sinner's will is set upon something that of its nature involves a disorder, but is not opposed to the love of God and neighbor, such as thoughtless chatter or immoderate laughter and the like, such sins are venial.

For a *sin* to be *mortal,* three conditions must together be met: "Mortal sin is sin whose object is grave matter and which is also committed with full knowledge and deliberate consent."

Grave matter is specified by the Ten Commandments, corresponding to the answer of Jesus to the rich young man: "Do not kill, Do not commit adultery, Do not steal, Do not bear false witness, Do not defraud, Honor your father and your mother." The gravity of sins is more or less great: murder is graver than theft. One must also take into account who is wronged: violence against parents is in itself graver than violence against a stranger.

Mortal sin requires *full knowledge* and *complete consent*. It presupposes knowledge of the sinful character of the act, of its opposition to God's law. It also implies a consent sufficiently deliberate to be a personal choice. Feigned ignorance and hardness of heart do not diminish, but rather increase, the voluntary character of a sin.

Unintentional ignorance can diminish or even remove the imputability of a grave offense. But no one is deemed to be ignorant of the principles of the moral law, which are written in the conscience of every man. The promptings of feelings and passions can also diminish the voluntary and free character of the offense, as can external pressures or pathological disorders. Sin committed through malice, by deliberate choice of evil, is the gravest.

Mortal sin is a radical possibility of human freedom, as is love itself. It results in the loss of charity and the privation of sanctifying grace, that is, of the state of grace. If it is not redeemed by repentance and God's forgiveness, it causes exclusion from Christ's kingdom and the eternal death of hell, for our freedom has the power to make choices for ever, with no turning back. However, although we can judge that an act is in itself a grave offense, we must entrust judgment of persons to the justice and mercy of God.

One commits *venial sin* when, in a less serious matter, he does not observe the standard prescribed by the moral law, or when he disobeys the moral law in a grave matter, but without full knowledge or without complete consent.

Venial sin weakens charity; it manifests a disordered affection for created goods; it impedes the soul's progress in the exercise of the virtues and the practice of the moral good; it merits temporal punishment. Deliberate and unrepented venial sin disposes us little by little to commit mortal sin. However venial sin does not break the covenant with God. With God's grace it is humanly reparable. "Venial sin does not deprive the sinner of sanctifying grace, friendship with God, charity, and consequently eternal happiness."

While he is in the flesh, man cannot help but have at least some light sins. But do not despise these sins which we call "light": if you take them for light when you weigh them, tremble when you count them. A number of light objects makes a great mass; a number of drops fills a river; a number of grains makes a heap. What then is our hope? Above all, confession.

"Therefore I tell you, every sin and blasphemy will be forgiven men, but the blasphemy against the Spirit will not be forgiven." There are no limits to the mercy of God, but anyone who deliberately refuses to accept his mercy by repenting, rejects the forgiveness of his sins and the salvation offered by the Holy Spirit. Such hardness of heart can lead to final impenitence and eternal loss.

[12] GOD WILLED HUMAN NATURE [CCC #362-8].

The human person, created in the image of God, is a being at once corporeal and spiritual. The biblical account expresses this reality in symbolic language when it affirms that "then the LORD God formed man of dust from the ground, and breathed into his nostrils the breath of life; and man became a living being." [*Gen* 2:7.] **Man, whole and entire, is therefore *willed* by God (emphasis supplied).** In Sacred Scripture the term "soul" often refers to human *life* or the entire human *person*. [Cf. *Mt* 16:25-26; *Jn* 15:13; *Acts* 2:41.] But "soul" also refers to the innermost aspect of man, that which is of greatest value in him, [Cf. *Mt* 10:28; 26:38; *Jn* 12:27; *2 Macc* 6:30.] that by which he is most especially in God's image: "soul" signifies the *spiritual principle* in man.

The human body shares in the dignity of "the image of God": it is a human body precisely because it is animated by a spiritual soul, and it is the whole human person that is intended to become, in the body of Christ, a temple of the Spirit: [Cf. *1 Cor* 6:19-20; 15:44-45.]

Man, though made of body and soul, is a unity. Through his very bodily condition he sums up in himself the elements of the material world. Through him they are thus brought to their highest perfection and can raise their voice in praise freely given to the Creator. For this reason man may not despise his bodily life. Rather he is obliged to regard his body as good and to hold it in honor since God has created it and will raise it up on the last day. [GS 14 § 1; cf. Dan 3:57-80.]
The unity of soul and body is so profound that one has to consider the soul to be the "form" of the body: [Cf. Council of Vienne (1312): DS 902.] i.e., it is because of its spiritual soul that the body made of matter becomes a living, human body; spirit and matter, in man, are not two natures united, but rather their union forms a single nature.

The Church teaches that every spiritual soul is created immediately by God - it is not "produced" by the parents - and also that it is immortal: it does not perish when it separates from the body at death, and it will be reunited with the body at the final Resurrection. [Cf. Pius XII, *Humani Generis*: DS 3896; Paul VI, *CPG* § 8; Lateran Council V (1513): DS 1440.]

Sometimes the soul is distinguished from the spirit: St. Paul for instance prays that God may sanctify his people "wholly", with "spirit and soul and body" kept sound and blameless at the Lord's coming. [*1 Thess* 5:23.] The Church teaches that this distinction does not introduce a duality into the soul. [Cf. Council of Constantinople IV (870): DS 657.] "Spirit" signifies that from creation man is ordered to a supernatural end and that his soul can gratuitously be raised beyond all it deserves to communion with God. [Cf. Vatican Council I, *Dei Filius*: DS 3005; *GS* 22 § 5; *Humani Generis*: DS 3891.]

The spiritual tradition of the Church also emphasizes the *heart*, in the biblical sense of the depths of one's being, where the person decides for or against God. [Cf. *Jer* 31:33; *Deut* 6:5;   29:3;   *Isa*   29:13;   *Ezek*   36:26;   *Mt*   6:21;   *Lk*   8:15;   *Rom*.5:5.]

13   MAN IN PARADISE [CCC #374-9]

The first man was not only created good, but was also established in friendship with his Creator and in harmony with himself and with the creation around him, in a state that would be surpassed only by the glory of the new creation in Christ.
The Church, interpreting the symbolism of biblical language in an authentic way, in the light of the New Testament and Tradition, teaches that our first parents, Adam and Eve, were constituted in an original "state of holiness and justice". [Cf. Council of Trent (1546): DS 1511.] This grace of original holiness was "to share in divine life". [Cf. *LG* 2.]

By the radiance of this grace all dimensions of man's life were confirmed. As long as he remained in the divine intimacy, man would not have to suffer or die. [Cf. *Gen* 2:17; 3:16,19.] The inner harmony of the human person, the harmony between man and woman, [Cf. *Gen* 2:25.] and finally the harmony between the first couple and all creation, comprised the state called "original justice."

The "mastery" over the world that God offered man from the beginning was realized above all within man himself: *mastery of self.* The first man was unimpaired and ordered in his whole being because he was free from the triple concupiscence [Cf. *1 Jn* 2:16.] that subjugates him to the pleasures of the senses, covetousness for earthly goods, and self-assertion, contrary to the dictates of reason.

The sign of man's familiarity with God is that God places him in the garden. [Cf. *Gen* 2:8.] There he lives "to till it and keep it." Work is not yet a burden [*Gen* 2:15; cf. 3:17-19] but rather the collaboration of man and woman with God in perfecting the visible creation. This entire harmony of original justice, foreseen for man in God's plan, will be lost by the sin of our first parents.

14   For Augustine, the problem was the will, not the body. He came to define Original Sin as narcissism, the turning of the will "to live according to oneself" (secundum se vivere). Here is his classic account from *On the City of God*, Book 14:

(13) Moreover, our first parents fell openly into the sin of disobedience only because, secretly, they had begun to be guilty. Actually, their bad deed of their bad will was nothing else than pride. For "pride is the beginning of all sin" (Sir 10:13). And what is pride but an appetite for inordinate exaltation? Now exaltation is inordinate when the souls cuts itself off from the very Source to which it should keep close and somehow

makes itself—and thus becomes—an end in itself. This takes place when the soul becomes inordinately pleased with itself, and such self-pleasing occurs when the soul falls away from the unchangeable Good which ought to please itself. Now this falling away is the soul's own doing, for If the will had merely remained firm in the love of that higher immutable Good which lighted its mind into knowledge and warmed its will into love, it would not have turned away in search of satisfaction in itself and, by so doing, have lost that light and warmth. And thus Eve would not have believed that the serpent's lie was true, nor would Adam have preferred the will of his wife to the will of God or have supposed this transgression of God's command was venial when he refused to abandon the partner of his life even if it meant a partnership of sin.

Our first parents, then, must have already fallen before they could do the evil deed, before they could commit the sin of eating the forbidden fruit. For such bad fruit could come only from a bad tree. That the tree became bad was contrary to its nature, because such a condition could come about only because of a defect of the will—and a defect is whatever goes against nature. Notice, however, that such worsening by reason of a defect is possible only in a nature that had been created out of nothing. In a word, a nature is a nature because it is something made by God, but a nature falls away from That Which Is because the nature was made out of nothing." William Harmless, SJ, *Augustine In His Own Words* (Washington, DC: The Catholic University of America Press, 2010),351-2.

¹⁵ Ignatius was a great admirer of St. Francis of Assisi and it was the Franciscans who managed the holy sites in Jerusalem. There he could be near the sons of St. Francis and walk in the footsteps of Jesus.

¹⁶ *Brothers and sisters: The Spirit scrutinizes everything, even the depths of God. Among men, who knows what pertains to the man except his spirit that is within? Similarly, no one knows what pertains to God except the Spirit of God. We have not received the spirit of the world but the Spirit who is from God, so that we may understand the things freely given us by God. And we speak about them not with words taught by human wisdom, but with words taught by the Spirit, describing spiritual realities in spiritual terms. Now the natural man does not accept what pertains to the Spirit of God, for to him it is foolishness, and he cannot understand it, because it is judged spiritually. The one who is spiritual, however, can judge everything but is not subject to judgment by anyone. For "who has known the mind of the Lord, so as to counsel him?" But we have the mind of Christ.* (I Corinthians 2: 10b-16)

A sermon by Pope St Leo the Great: *I SHALL PUT MY LAWS WITHIN THEM*

Dearly beloved, when our Lord Jesus Christ was preaching the Gospel of the kingdom and healing various illnesses throughout the whole of Galilee, the fame of his mighty works spread into all of Syria, and great crowds from all parts of Judea flocked to the heavenly physician.

Because human ignorance is slow to believe what it does not see, and equally slow to hope for what it does not know, those who were to be instructed in the divine teaching had first to be aroused by bodily benefits and visible miracles so that, once they had experienced his gracious power, they would no longer doubt the wholesome effect of his doctrine. In order, therefore, to transform outward healings into inward remedies, and to cure men's souls now that he had healed their bodies, our Lord separated himself from the surrounding crowds, climbed to the solitude of a neighboring mountain, and called the apostles to himself.

From the height of this mystical site he then instructed them in the most lofty doctrines, suggesting both by the very nature of the place and by what he was doing that it was he who long ago had honored Moses by speaking to him. At that time, his words showed a terrifying justice, but now they reveal a sacred compassion, in order to fulfill what was promised in the words of the prophet Jeremiah: Behold the days are coming, says the Lord, when I shall establish a new covenant with the house of Israel and with the house of Judah. After those days, says the Lord, I shall put my laws within them and write them on their hearts.

And so it was that he who had spoken to Moses spoke also to the apostles. Writing in the hearts of his disciples, the swift hand of the Word composed the ordinances of the new covenant. And this was not done as formerly, in the midst of dense clouds, amid terrifying sounds and lightning, so that the people were frightened away from approaching the mountain. Instead, there was a tranquil discourse which clearly reached the ears of all who stood nearby so that the harshness of the law might be softened by the gentleness of grace, and the spirit of adoption might dispel the terror of slavery.

Concerning the content of Christ's teaching, his own sacred words bear witness; thus whoever longs to attain eternal blessedness can now recognize the steps that lead to that high happiness. Blessed, he says, are the poor in spirit, for theirs is the kingdom of heaven. It might have been unclear to which poor he was referring, if after the words Blessed are the poor, he had not added anything about the kind of poor he had in mind. For then the poverty that many suffer because of grave and harsh necessity might seem sufficient to merit the kingdom of heaven.

But when he says: Blessed are the poor in spirit, he shows that the kingdom of heaven is to be given to those who are distinguished by their humility of soul rather than by their lack of worldly goods. (Taken from *Roman Catholic Office of Readings, Book III, Weeks of the year 6-34*).

17   People today often form judgments about human nature based on the experience of human nature in its fallen state. We forget that at one point human nature, as a unity of body and spirit, was undivided: Our hearts were undivided. With the Fall, our hearts are divided and we can no longer easily determine right and wrong: "Ignorance of the fact that man has a wounded nature, inclined to the evil, gives rise to serious errors in the areas of education, politics, social action and morals." [CCC #407].

18   THE PRIMACY OF THE SPIRITUAL OVER THE MATERIAL:
Every year science grounded in a *materialist only* view of the universe confronts inexplicable phenomena, indicating the primacy of the spiritual realm as the main animator of the physical world. Mario Beauregard's *The Spiritual Brian* is a work on this topic and the source of some of the ideas below. See also the classic work, *The Healing Light* by Agnes Sanford. Sanford's Christian healing ministry helped launch the Catholic Charismatic Renewal movement.

✠   Why does the placebo effect work where the mind creates curative processes reducing or eliminating ill and diseased states in the human organism?

✠   Why do repeated studies show that some persons are able to mentally affect physical objects outside themselves with odds of this being mere chance at a trillion to one?

✠   Why are the neurological brain maps of individuals in deep prayer states (*feeling connected* to a reality outside themselves) identical to individuals *actually* in direct contact to other persons—both maps display the radically complex neural brain states of *real* experiences involving human emotion, body representation, visual, motor imagery and spiritual perception?

✠ Why do deep spiritual experiences rewire the neural networks of the brain and lead to deep, long-lasting, attitudinal and behavioral changes such as growth in compassion, love for others, willingness to forgive and awareness of the unity of creation?

✠ Why, when persons are revived after clinical death (zero heart or brainwave activity), do they frequently possess vivid recall of all the events that took place while they were "dead"?

✠ Why, since the discovery of quantum theory, do some physicists affirm that the universe is more *mental than physical* in the way it behaves? (Richard Conn Henry "The Mental Universe," *Nature* 436, no. 29, July 7, 2005).

✠ Why can people with certain mental disorders be trained to rewire their neural networks using *attentive consciousness* (demonstrating that the mind creates the brain and not the other way around)?

[19]   From a sermon by St Bernard of Clairvaux, "On the Stages of Contemplation:"

Let us take our stand on the tower, leaning with all our strength on Christ, the most solid rock, as it is written: He has set my feet on a rock, he has guided my steps. Thus firmly established, let us begin to contemplate, to see what he is saying to us and what reply we ought to make to him. The first stage of contemplation, my dear brothers, is to consider constantly what God wants, what is pleasing to him, and what is acceptable in his eyes. We all offend in many things; our strength cannot match the rightness of God's will and cannot be joined to it or made to fit with it. So let us humble ourselves under the powerful hand of the most high God and make an effort to show ourselves unworthy before his merciful gaze, saying, "Heal me, Lord, and I shall be healed; save me and I shall be saved." And again, "Lord, have mercy on me; heal my soul because I have sinned against you."

Once the eye of the soul has been purified by such considerations, we no longer abide within our spirit in a sense of sorrow, but abide rather in the Spirit of God with great delight. No longer do we consider what is the will of God for us, but rather what it is in itself.

For our life is in his will. Thus we are convinced that what is according to his will is in every way better for us, and more fitting. And so, if we are concerned to preserve the life of our soul, we must be equally concerned to deviate as little as possible from his will.

Thus having made some progress in our spiritual exercise under the guidance of the Spirit who gazes into the deep things of God, let us reflect how gracious the Lord is and how good he is in himself. Let us join the Prophet in praying that we may see the Lord's will and frequent not our own hearts but the Lord's temple; and let us also say, My soul is humbled within me, therefore I shall be mindful of you.

These two stages sum up the whole of the spiritual life: when we contemplate ourselves we are troubled, and our sadness saves us and brings us to contemplate God; that contemplation in turn gives us the consolation of the joy of the Holy Spirit. Contemplating ourselves brings fear and humility; contemplating God brings us hope and love. (Sermo 5 de diversis, 4-5: : Opera omnia, Edit. Cisterc. 6, 1 [1970], 103-4) Used in the *Roman Catholic Office of Readings for Wednesday of the 23rd week in Ordinary Time* with the accompanying biblical reading taken from Habakkuk 2:5-20).

From Gaudium et Spes

Although *he was made by God in a state of holiness, from the very onset of his history man abused his liberty, at the urging of the Evil One. Man set himself against God and sought to attain his goal apart from God. Therefore man is split within himself.* As a result, all of human life, whether individual or collective, shows itself to be a dramatic *struggle between good and evil, between light and darkness.* Indeed, man finds that by himself he is incapable of battling the assaults of evil successfully, *so that everyone feels as though he is bound by chains.* But the Lord Himself came to free and strengthen man, renewing him inwardly and casting out that "prince of this world" (John 12:31) who held him in the bondage of sin. *For sin has diminished man, blocking his path to fulfillment.* The call to *grandeur and the depths of misery, both of which are a part of human experience, find their ultimate and simultaneous explanation in the light of this revelation.*

Though made of body and soul, *man is one.* Through his bodily composition he gathers to himself the elements of the material world; thus they reach their crown through him, and through him raise their voice in free praise of the Creator. For this reason man is not allowed to despise his bodily life, rather he is obliged to regard his body as good and honorable since God has created it and will raise it up on the last day. Nevertheless, wounded by sin, man experiences rebellious stirrings in his body. But the very dignity of man postulates that man glorify God in his body and forbid it to serve the evil inclinations of his heart.

Now, man is not wrong when he regards himself as superior to bodily concerns, and as more than a speck of nature or a nameless constituent of the city of man. For by his interior qualities he outstrips the whole sum of mere things. He plunges into the depths of reality whenever he enters into his own heart; God, Who probes the heart, awaits him there; there he discerns his proper destiny beneath the eyes of God. Thus, when he recognizes in himself a spiritual and immortal soul, he is not being mocked by a fantasy born only of physical or social influences, but is rather laying hold of the proper truth of the matter.

Man judges rightly that by his intellect he surpasses the material universe, for he shares in the light of the divine mind. By relentlessly employing his talents through the ages he has indeed made progress in the practical sciences and in technology and the liberal arts. In our times he has won superlative victories, especially in his probing of the material world and in subjecting it to himself. Still he has always searched for more penetrating truths, and finds them. For his intelligence is not confined to observable data alone, but can with genuine certitude attain to reality itself as knowable, though in consequence of sin that certitude is partly obscured and weakened.

The intellectual nature of the human person is perfected by wisdom and needs to be, for wisdom gently attracts the mind of man to a quest and a love for what is true and good. Steeped in wisdom, man passes through visible realities to those which are unseen.

Our era needs such wisdom more than bygone ages if the discoveries made by man are to be further humanized. For the future of the world stands in peril unless wiser men are forthcoming. It should also be pointed out that many nations, poorer in economic goods, are quite rich in wisdom and can offer noteworthy advantages to others.

It is, finally, through the gift of the Holy Spirit that man comes by faith to the contemplation and appreciation of the divine plan. (Vatican II—Gaudium et Spes: The Dignity of the Human Person (13-15).

[20] The following section from the Church's *Code of Canon Law* describes the *types* of beliefs that are non-negotiable for faithful Catholics. This is not intended as a list of all those things one *must* adhere to in order to be considered a "faithful Catholic." The most important aspect is the ***docility of spirit*** granted by God that *enables* one to approach the teachings and the authority of the Church with trust, instead of a spirit of

obstinacy. The spirit of docility, trust, humility and obedience characterize God's presence in one's soul.

A person must believe with divine and Catholic faith all those things contained in the word of God, written or handed on, that is, in the one deposit of faith entrusted to the Church, and at the same time proposed as divinely revealed either by the solemn magisterium of the Church or by its ordinary and universal magisterium which is manifested by the common adherence of the Christian faithful under the leadership of the sacred magisterium; therefore all are bound to avoid any doctrines whatsoever contrary to them. Each and every thing which is proposed definitively by the magisterium of the Church concerning the doctrine of faith and morals, that is, each and every thing which is required to safeguard reverently and to expound faithfully the same deposit of faith, is also to be firmly embraced and retained; therefore, one who rejects those propositions which are to be held definitively is opposed to the doctrine of the Catholic Church. [Can. 750 §1, §2].

21   Ignatius provides wise counsel for those tempted by evil thoughts and feelings and helps us know how to conduct ourselves during such times. He writes this advice to Sister Theresa Rejadell:

"I insist that you think of God as loving you, as I have no doubt He does, and that you correspond with this love and pay no attention whatever to the evil thoughts, even if they are obscene or sensual (when they are not deliberate), nor of your cowardice or tepidity. For even St. Peter and St. Paul did not succeed in escaping all or some of these thoughts. Even when we do not succeed fully, we gain much by paying no attention to them. I am not going to save myself by the good works of the good angels, and I am not going to be condemned because of the evil thoughts and weaknesses which bad angels, the flesh, and the world bring before my mind. God asks only one thing of me, that my soul seek to be conformed with His Divine Majesty. And the soul so conformed makes the body conformed, whether it wish it or not, to the divine will. In this is our greatest battle, and here the good pleasure of the eternal and sovereign Goodness. May our Lord by His infinite kindness and grace hold us always in His hand." Ignatius of Loyola: Letters and Instructions (St. Louis: The Institute of Jesuit Sources, 2006), 25.

22   Such panic attacks and terrors are similar to aspects of what psychologists refer to as "catastrophic thinking," often suffered by those with serious anxiety disorders. The "racing thoughts" of catastrophic thinking may lead to ideas of self-wounding or other types of bodily harm, similar to what Ignatius experienced at Manresa when, in the grip of severe scruples, he had an urge to throw himself off a cliff.

23   Those suffering from bio-chemical addictions would be wise to seek professional guidance on extracting oneself from their grip. It is notable however that because of our mind-body connection, people who are withdrawing from spiritual darkness and spiritual addictions often "feel" a dread that is similar to the feelings experienced during bio-chemical withdrawals. It is obvious that eliminating physical addictions will be a tremendous benefit to one's overall health, but despite this knowledge, the bio-chemical addict still "feels" afraid of letting go of the addiction. It is clear that the fear and dread we experience when withdrawing from sinful addictions is very similar. Despite the painful emotions, we know that withdrawal from spiritual and physical addiction only leads to life.

24   Review the Definition of Counter Inspirations.

[25]   See Week 37 Encouragement and Wisdom.

[26]   See endnote # 16.

[27]   For a modern example of these types of temptations, see Week 38 Encouragement and Wisdom.

[28]   Thomas M. King, SJ, *Teilhard's Mass: Approaches to The Mass on the World* (Mahwah: Paulist Press, 2005) 120.

About the Author

Fr. William Watson, S.J., D. Min., has spent over thirty years developing Ignatian programs and retreats He has collaborated extensively with Fr. Robert Spitzer in the last fifteen years on Ignatian retreats for corporate CEO's. In the spring of 2011 he launched a non-profit institute to bring Ignatian Spirituality to Catholics of all ages and walks of life. The Sacred Story Institute is promoting third millennium evangelization for the Society of Jesus and the Church by using the time-tested *Examination of Conscience* of St. Ignatius.

Fr. Watson has served as: Director of Retreat Programs at Georgetown University; Vice President for Mission at Gonzaga University; and Provincial Assistant for International Ministries for the Oregon Province of the Society of Jesus. He holds Masters Degrees in Divinity and Pastoral Studies, respectively (1986; Weston Jesuit School of Theology, Cambridge Massachusetts). He received his Doctor of Ministry degree in 2009 from The Catholic University of America (Washington D.C.).

A Note to
Parish Pastors, Adult Faith Formation Directors,
RCIA Directors, Campus Ministers and
Vocation Directors

The Sacred Story Institute is working toward a full complement of pastoral resources for the Forty Weeks program. If you would like to help make this happen, please contact us at the email address on the following page. Also, please let us know what type of materials you would find helpful to make this resource more flexible for your use.

In the meantime, you will find very basic resources you need to use *Forty Weeks* for parish renewal, RCIA and prayer groups. Please access these resources at the members site for 40 Week Parish Course at sacredstory.net When you register as a member, you can access the program materials. Membership is free.

Sacred Story Press
Seattle, USA
sacredstoryrpress.com

Sacred Story Press explores dynamic new dimensions of classic Ignatian spirituality, based on St. Ignatius' Conscience Examen in the *Sacred Story* prayer method pioneered by Fr. Bill Watson, S.J. We are creating a new class of spiritual resources. Our publications are research-based, authentic to the Catholic Tradition and designed to help individuals achieve integrated, spiritual growth and holiness of life.

We Request Your Feedback

The Sacred Story Institute welcomes feedback on *Forty Weeks*. Contact us via email or letter. Give us ideas, suggestions and inspirations for how to make this a better resource for Catholics and Christians of all ages and walks of life.

For bulk orders and group discounts, contact us:
admin-team@sacredstory.net

Sacred Story Institute & Sacred Story Press
1401 E. Jefferson Suite 405
Seattle, Washington, 98122

So what do you do when people
get on your nerves –
People are selfish, self centered
Egotistical, arrogant –
Love them where they are.
What is the root of that?
We want people to be different
    They aren't
We want them to be saints
    They aren't.
Kindness – help me to be kind
Arrogance. Total arrogance.
Think of their brokenness